To

Nessa,

With my best

regards,

Monia Mazigh

june 26. 2015

HOPE
& DESPAIR

HOPE & DESPAIR

MY STRUGGLE TO FREE MY HUSBAND, MAHER ARAR

MONIA MAZIGH

translated by
PATRICIA CLAXTON
& FRED A. REED

McCLELLAND & STEWART

Library and Archives Canada Cataloguing in Publication

Mazigh, Monia
Hope and despair / Monia Mazigh.

ISBN 978-0-7710-5758-8

1. Mazigh, Monia. 2. Arar, Maher. 3. Human rights. 4. Detention of persons.
5. Deportation. 6. False imprisonment. 7. Prisoners' spouses – Canada –
Biography. 8. Prisoners – Syria – Biography. 9. Torture victims – Syria – Biography.
I. Title.

FC641.M39A3 2008   971.07092   C2008-901759-5

We acknowledge the financial support of the Government of Canada through the Book Publishing Industry Development Program and that of the Government of Ontario through the Ontario Media Development Corporation's Ontario Book Initiative. We further acknowledge the support of the Canada Council for the Arts and the Ontario Arts Council for our publishing program.

Typeset in Garamond by M&S, Toronto
Printed and bound in Canada

McClelland & Stewart Ltd.
75 Sherbourne Street
Toronto, Ontario
M5A 2P9
www.mcclelland.com

1 2 3 4 5   12 11 10 09 08

For my children, Barâa and Houd

Verily, along with every hardship is relief.

THE QUR'AN, CHAPTER 94 — AL-SHARH [SOLACE], VERSE 6

CONTENTS

FOREWORD

My decision to write a book has not been easy. First, while my life has become public and people recognize me in the street, I'm still a shy person who deeply values her privacy. To speak about oneself, for me, means in a way revealing oneself to others, means something like standing naked in the town square, and I have always before refused to get involved in this dangerous exercise.

Another thing that has held me back until now is my children. I have always thought that writing a book would mean putting not only my own life on view but also my children's lives. Later on, would they agree with the choice I had made? They might be critical, asking: Why didn't you simply turn this painful page? Why write a book and lay out our lives for the world to see? These possible questions always worried me.

But, pondering all this, I came to the conclusion that writing a book would in a way be assembling a family album, like making a collection of photographs of a certain stage of our lives. It's important for my children to know how we lived together while their father was in prison. When they grow up, they will understand better what happened. I hope that this book will help answer their questions, and even if they don't agree with my choice, at least they'll be able to read about this distressing period of their lives and know that their mother wrote the story, not someone else.

I have continued to work since the beginning of the Maher Arar affair. I have divided my life between work and my family for the last five years, with practically no respite in which to relive the facts and digest all that has happened to us. Now, in order to devote more time to writing, of my own volition I have left my job as assistant professor at Thompson Rivers University.

Writing is helping me to accept my new life. It's a remedy for the speed and strength of the change that has affected our lives. When there's a new birth in a family, it takes months for all the family's members to adapt to the new routine. When one of the parents loses his or her job, it takes months, sometimes years, for the whole family to recover from the psychological and financial pressures of such a loss. In my own case, in the last five years I have seen my husband disappear in circumstances akin to a thriller novel, then reappear, but changed forever. I have seen myself become a single mother living on welfare, then, very recently since the compensation, considered by people around me to be an exceedingly rich woman. I have seen myself change status from victim and wife of a presumed terrorist to modern-day heroine of the likes even of Laura Secord. All these fast and volatile changes have affected not only me personally but also my husband and my children; none of us have escaped untouched. By writing, I hope to give myself an opportunity to "taste" the flavours of these changes, reflect on them, and finally come to accept them. Although I'm not suffering from any illness, this will be a process of healing and recovery.

One day I was appearing as a witness regarding my husband's case before the House of Commons Standing Committee on Foreign Affairs. I had prepared a page that I was to deliver before the parliamentarians. I was nervous and there were a lot of journalists there that day. I knew certain of the Members of Parliament present, like Alexa McDonough, Marlene Catterall, and Irwin Cotler, but most of the others were strangers. I was telling myself that I must deliver that page from memory. I didn't know that even the most seasoned bureaucrats habitually read their notes prepared in advance. I wanted to do my best. For me, it was an opportunity to plead my husband's case before these MPs, and I did not in any way want to blow this chance.

When the time came, I began to speak slowly; I was no longer nervous, I had become calm, but suddenly, halfway through, my tears began to fall. I couldn't stop them. I wanted to impress the MPs with my courage, and my body betrayed me. I remember Marlene Catterall (the Member of Parliament for my riding) telling me later that day that this was the first time she had ever seen me cry, and it was true, because I had never cried in public, or wept to draw sympathy. It was as if my tears had been dried up or imprisoned, and there, suddenly, in front of all the Members of Parliament, journalists, and parliamentary clerks, they came out as though set free, to show everyone that above all I was a human being.

This book is by no means a glorification of what I accomplished in the space of a year, or a dry recitation of facts. It's just a story, but a true story for which I have done my best to remember dates, names, and words spoken. My notebook has helped me throughout to recall certain occasions and certain incidents. Sometimes it has been enough to see someone's name scribbled in tiny letters in some out-of-the-way corner of that notebook to remind me of the meeting that followed or the telephone call I placed. When my memory failed me, I would run to the newspaper clippings I had kept or the letters and emails I had written or received. Then, uncannily, my scattered or tangled memories would come together and I could continue writing my story.

I was lonely through all of this year, not only with the obvious loneliness of being without my husband, but most of all feeling alone in this battle against gigantean foes. I would very often feel despair winning the upper hand. But then, softly at first, a glimmer of hope would shine through, grow, then almost force itself upon me, making me more determined than ever to win the battle. This is why I have given this book the title *Hope and Despair*.

In these pages I have named individuals and organizations who have helped me in my struggle, and to them I shall be eternally, infinitely grateful. They are not alone, however. Other individuals and organizations, some of whom I know and many I don't, have also helped me in their own ways: with their prayers, their presence, their letters and emails, the kindness or encouragement in their eyes; they will be in my heart and my thoughts forever.

TUNISIA

the end of the dream . . .

SEPTEMBER 25, 2002. It was a hot, humid, heavy September day. I woke up that morning with Houd beside me. I had taken him from his little bed just before dawn and nursed him; he had gone straight back to sleep. Now he was snoring gently, content to be close to me. I looked at this plump, healthy eight-month-old boy and felt both happy and tired. Houd had been a colicky baby since he was born in Ottawa. He would cry almost constantly for no apparent reason. Things were better now, but he had become very attached to me, maybe too attached. I couldn't leave him for long with his father; he would soon start to cry and want me there with him. Barâa, our five-and-a-half-year-old daughter, was sleeping peacefully in the bed on the other side of the room. There was a faint smile on her lips, and her long hair framed her round face like a halo. The sounds of me moving around were sure to waken her.

Our family's sleeping quarters, which had been my parents' bedroom, reminded me of a hotel room with its three beds. Maher was already up and about, packing in the next bedroom, which had been mine from the age of nine until I was twenty-one. I loved the little white room. As a teenager and then a young woman, I had never dreamed that my own children and my husband would one day be sleeping within the same walls that had seen me grow up.

After almost ten years away, I'd arrived last June to spend my summer vacation in Tunisia. I found a country that had changed, far different from the one I'd left to emigrate to Canada. Now the urban landscape seemed overwhelmed by freeways, interchanges, and overpasses. Small cars, which everyone called "the people's car," filled the main streets and the narrow lanes. Tunis "the green," as it once was known, looked like a metropolis, with its endless traffic jams and the stifling summer-long heat that would often leave me cloistered behind the walls of my little room. But most of all, the people had changed. I couldn't recognize anyone: ten years is a long time. My schoolmates and university friends were working now. Some had emigrated to France or the United States; others were simply caught up in their family or professional lives. When I took my children out on short expeditions or for a stroll, I would look into people's eyes in the hope of recognizing an old friend, an acquaintance, a familiar face. But I found no one but strangers. As people rarely pushed their babies in strollers on the narrow sidewalks of Tunis, I was an object of curiosity. All around me cars sped by, horns blaring. It didn't take me long to realize this was not the best thing to do.

Today, Maher was returning to Canada. Philippe, his former colleague at The MathWorks, had called him a few weeks earlier to tell him there was a real possibility of a contract. Maher was delighted; he didn't want to miss the opportunity to get back into his business. The last two years had been rough for the high-tech sector: the euphoria of the 1990s was over. The astronomical profits evaporated and jobs vanished. The wave of recruitment had carried us along to Ottawa; we had moved there from Montreal in late 1997. Maher had just completed his master's degree in communications and had found a job as an engineer in his field. We settled in Bayshore, like so many other

Indian, Chinese, and Arab immigrant families. At the time, Bayshore was a modest middle-class suburban neighbourhood in Ottawa's west end. Rents were still low. I had always lived close to downtown, so for me our move was one of the worst things that could have happened. In Montreal, I had lived in Côte-des-Neiges, I was close to the university, there were shops nearby, I could go to my classes by bus. I loved going into shops that sold exotic products and discovering other people, other cultures, other smells. In Bayshore, all the houses around us were the same. The husbands left in the morning to go to work for Nortel, NewBridge, and other trendy companies, while the women stayed home or formed little groups according to their race and language, a segregation they often seemed unaware of. However, I gradually adopted Bayshore; slowly I adapted to the new suburban lifestyle. My own studies kept me busy, and the multitude of activities available to young families like ours helped me change my mind.

Maher worked hard. He loved what he was doing. Sometimes he would work on weekends. His dream was to develop a high-tech product of his own, to become a successful businessman. We were almost the same age, we were both immigrants, and we had both come to Canada to build a better future. But each of us had an ideal. I was born in Tunisia; Maher in Syria. Tunisia is part of the Maghreb, the west of the Arab world, while Syria is at the very heart of the Machrek, the "east." Two Arab, Muslim, and Mediterranean countries so different politically and economically. My homeland is open to the world. Its pro-Western policies and liberal economic outlook have won the recognition and appreciation of the World Bank and the International Monetary Fund. I never experienced bread or sugar shortages, or midsummer blackouts. I grew up watching Italian TV, which all households could receive, and sometimes also French TV. The Tunisian intellectual elite was influenced by French universities; French was spoken almost everywhere. The women enjoyed rights of which their sisters in other Arab countries couldn't even dream. Maher had known nothing of such openness. Syria was a country at war with Israel. Its economy, cut off from international loans, was primitive by comparison. Hafez al-Assad, the Syrian president-for-life, had rejected almost all attempts at peace negotiations in the region. Sometimes when we were feeling homesick, Maher would tell me about the years of food rationing, blackouts, and the patriotic and nationalistic songs and slogans at school. Syria's intellectual elite looked to other Arab countries such as Egypt and Iraq. At the universities, in business, and in social settings, people spoke Arabic.

But for all the differences, both of us had lived under repressive political regimes. Before coming to Canada, we had both, in our own ways, dreamed of freedom and emancipation. Maher had arrived in Canada with his parents at age seventeen and had never been back. His whole family had settled in Montreal; he was the youngest in a family of six boys and one girl. None of his brothers or sister had gone on to more advanced studies. But Maher had other plans: he wanted to study, to go far in life. He didn't want to go back to Syria for his compulsory two-year military service; he didn't want to live in a country where one's religious practices could be a cause for suspicion and where intelligence agencies spied on everything people did, particularly the younger generation.

On that September day, Maher, at age thirty-two, was keen to seize the opportunity to restart the consulting firm that had been unsuccessfully seeking contracts for months. My own feelings were mixed. On the one hand, I wanted Maher to regain his confidence in his chosen field; on the other, I didn't want to remain alone in Tunisia with Barâa and Houd. And as Houd's temporary passport had expired, we couldn't all travel together. We had decided that Maher would take Houd's passport with him. He put it in one of his suitcases, along with his personal effects, saying, "I'll renew his passport in Ottawa, it will be faster." The three of us would then be able to leave for Ottawa a month later. We were already looking forward to our new future. Our vacation in Tunisia had become rather long and monotonous; I wanted Barâa to start school in Canada.

Two days before, we had gone to the supermarket that had recently opened in my parents' neighbourhood. Maher wanted to buy some small gifts for his mother and our friends in Canada. We bought some beautiful tea glasses, decorated with gold oriental motifs. Tunisians love to drink mint tea with their meals, the kind served in decorative glasses such as these. Because they were fragile, he now put them in his small black American Tourister carry-on bag, into which he also put a light jacket, his shoes, and some underwear. I helped him finish packing his other things in the blue suitcase. Barâa was now awake; she seemed sad to see her father's luggage almost packed, but she soon slipped away to play in the garden. Houd looked on with his mischievous eyes, not understanding what was going on around him.

Maher's flight was scheduled for the afternoon. In the course of his many trips to the United States as a MathWorks engineer, he had accumulated thousands of Air Miles with American Airlines. This trip he intended to cash them in. But there were no American Airlines flights from Tunisia, a former French colony. He would have to fly to Europe and from there to the United States before continuing on to Montreal, where we had left our car. From Montreal, it was a short drive to Ottawa. So he had a long journey ahead of him. Never, even for a minute, as I stood there with him that September morning, surrounded by suitcases and personal belongings, did I dream that I was not going to see him again for more than a year. Houd was sometimes in my arms, sometimes trying to crawl on the floor; Barâa had gone outside into the garden again to pick some bitingly sour grapes, which she deposited in an old basket and pretended to sell at the weekly street market.

It was almost 11:00 a.m. The sun was now high in the sky. I was in the old kitchen of our family house, getting lunch ready. But my heart was not in it; I wanted to finish as fast as I could, then go and lie down in the bedroom in hopes of finding a little coolness behind the closed blue shutters. I could feel the sweat trickling down my back. Houd was beginning to whimper and I knew he would soon start to cry; then I would have to drop everything and take him in my arms to soothe him. Maher was checking his messages on the computer one last time. He was ready. His flight would take him from Tunis to Zurich, where he would stay overnight. The next morning, he would board American Airlines Flight AA65 to JFK, and then on to Montreal.

"I'll call you tomorrow from my mother's, from Montreal. I should be there around seven o'clock in the evening, one o'clock in the morning Tunis time. You'll be awake, won't you?"

"All right," I replied, "I'll be expecting your call."

Maher went to the small bedroom, picked up his two suitcases, and took them as far as the garden door. I watched as he checked his Canadian passport. All his identification papers were in his black wallet. I stepped out into the garden with Barâa beside me and Houd in my arms.

"I'm going to get a taxi," Maher called as he closed the wrought-iron gate that led to the street. In Tunisia, people generally went outside to hail a cab. Hardly anyone used the telephone. I waited a few minutes. I was pensive. I wanted Maher to succeed, I wanted him to get the contract, but I felt a bit nervous. Suddenly, through the trees in the garden, I saw the yellow taxi pull up to the gate. Maher opened the gate, which gave a squeal that made me grimace; it was old and could use a drop of oil. He stowed his two suitcases in the trunk of the taxi. I was trembling a little and, stupidly, felt tears welling up. That's odd, I told myself. Maher had gone off on trips dozens of times before and I'd never felt like crying; after all, travelling was part of his job, it had become normal in our life together. I wanted to be strong in Maher's eyes, and in front of the children, so I fought back my tears. Maher kissed us all quickly and left without turning back. I heard the taxi's engine start up and went back inside, almost running with the children to get us all out of the sun.

The day was ending softly, a light breeze was blowing, which refreshed us after the suffocating midday heat. I spread a small kilim on the veranda at the back of the garden and sat there with the children, watching the magnificent colours of the sky. Houd was crawling after a toy, trying to grasp it. Barâa was playing with a collection of little plastic dinosaurs. Their names were a mystery to me, but she knew every one of them by their shape. When I was her age, dinosaurs didn't even have a place in my imagination. Instead, my brother and I played with paper airplanes or balls, or spent hours playing "school." My brother, Mourad, was now living in Hammamet, a small tourist town sixty kilometres from Tunis. He was a mathematics professor at a preparatory school for engineers. He had just called me to catch up on my news. He would be visiting us on the weekend. I thought of Maher; he must be in Zurich now. Tomorrow morning he will be leaving for New York; he will call me as soon as he gets to Montreal. I was impatient to hear from him. By now it was almost dark; time to get the children to bed. As usual, we were all going to sleep in my parents' old bedroom, but tonight Maher would not be with us.

We had been in Tunisia for three months now. I had come with the children in June, Maher had joined us a month later. It was our first vacation in years. Although my parents were living in Canada and I saw them often, I never saw my brother or my uncles and cousins any more. For Maher, business in Canada had been rocky. I was still on maternity leave; it was as though we had come to a crossroads. So we had decided to take a little step back and think about our plans for the future. Our vacation in Tunisia would give us an opportunity to reflect on our eight years together and what we hoped to do in the years to come – 2001 had not been a good year. The high-tech bubble of the late 1990s had burst, the whole sector was beginning to suffer. It was as though investors were waking up from their long, sweet dream to find reality staring them in the face. In Ottawa, each day seemed to bring new layoffs. Maher's friends or former colleagues were being let go, the list of the qualified unemployed was growing longer. Like most people, we expected the high-tech boom to go on forever; the boomerang didn't hit us at first. In early 2001, after two years of shuttling between Boston and Ottawa, Maher had left The MathWorks, the American company for which he had been working as an engineer, but the vice-president suggested that he work on contract from Ottawa. We were in seventh heaven. Life was good in Ottawa. The cost of living was reasonable and Maher was earning a good salary in American dollars; we couldn't have hoped for anything better.

But the events of September 11, 2001, turned everything upside down. I'll never forget that day. I was finishing my breakfast in the kitchen of our Bayshore house. Barâa was playing beside me. I was listening to the radio when the announcer said that a plane had hit one of the World Trade Center towers in New York. He talked about it as an event merely of note; no one realized its gravity at that point. I switched off the radio, not knowing that in the minutes to come the eyes of the whole world would be riveted on New York. That day I had intended to go to the University of Ottawa library. I was working as a research assistant for a professor in the Department of Management and needed to consult certain books. Maher was on yet another trip to the United States with a fellow MathWorks employee, presenting one of the company's software packages to a San Diego firm. Minutes later, the telephone rang. It was Maher calling from his hotel room. His colleague had just awakened him and told him to switch on the TV. A devastating attack had just occurred in New York. We were in shock. As more information became available, the name of al-Qaeda surfaced as the terrorist organization responsible for the attack. By midday, all the television and radio commentators were talking about Muslim terrorists. Maher called me again, warning me not to go alone to the library: "Your head scarf will be like a red flag; right now, there's a lot of anger against Muslims. . . ." I didn't change my plans and went to the library that day. But, behind the wheel, I was tense: Maher's words were ringing in my ears. I kept the car doors locked, worried that someone was going to jump me. But nothing happened. Yet the days and months that followed the attacks introduced a new atmosphere into our lives, one of suspicion and fear. Both of us had fled a repressive regime to settle in Canada. Many times, with our own eyes, we had seen the spectre of fear hovering over our family, and over the Arab-Muslim community.

Still, we didn't change our way of life. Maher continued with his work, I continued with my research project. But outside our home, we sensed a feeling of creeping distrust. It was as if we had to take every opportunity to show our loyalty to Canada and its democratic values. It was not enough to have chosen to live here, speak the language, send our children to school, pay our taxes, get along with the neighbours, respect the laws, vote in elections, do no harm to others: more was expected of us. Relations between Muslims and non-Muslims were increasingly tinged by a kind of awkwardness that was hard to dispel. Schoolchildren named Osama and Mohammed were often singled out, and racist remarks were frequent; it was no longer rare to hear it said that all Muslims were terrorists. But for the most part, Canadians' reactions were polite and more discreet. In the United States, things were worse:

"The American administration has required 80,000 non-citizens to be fingerprinted, photographed and registered, simply because they come from Arab or Muslim countries. A further 8,000 young men from the same countries have been summoned by the FBI for interviews and another 5,000 other non-citizens have been placed in preventive detention," wrote David Cole and Jules Lobel in *Less Safe Less Free: Why America Is Losing the War on Terror* (2007).

However, two incidents occurred in our lives that had a direct impact. The first took place on December 20, 2001. Maher was returning from a business trip to Boston. As usual, he had taken his MathWorks laptop computer and his PalmPilot. When he arrived at

Canadian customs, the customs officer began to rummage through Maher's belongings. Then she questioned him about his religion and his trips to the United States. She seized his computer and PalmPilot, telling him that he would have to pay customs duties on them. The computer was not his, he explained; he had bought the PalmPilot more than a year earlier when he was living in Boston. She would hear none of it, then took both away and asked him to wait until an evaluation had been done. Maher could not believe it. He called me from the waiting room and told me not to worry. He had no idea what was going on. When, later that day, he was finally authorized to leave the airport, he was not given back the two devices. Instead, he was given a receipt and told to come back and get them the next day.

That incident upset us deeply as a case of racial profiling. We didn't know at the time that intelligence agencies in both countries had begun to watch Maher closely. We attributed it to the multiple repercussions of 9/11 on the Arab-Muslim community. Canada was not the United States, of course, yet we could feel the vise tightening around us. We continued to live normally, but I became more and more aware that people were looking at me. I had worn a head scarf since my student days at the Institut des hautes études commerciales in Carthage, before immigrating to Canada. I had never explicitly felt racism against my person before, but now the way people were looking at me had changed from curiosity or ignorance to mistrust and suspicion. For us, the airport incident was the end of the honeymoon. Our marriage with Canada had been consummated; but now, hard reality was looming ahead of us. We could see it coming, but to maintain an appearance of normalcy, we tried to put it out of our minds. After the incident, Maher had made up his mind to seek advice from a lawyer. Michael Edelson's name was suggested to him, but – as always happens after a few days have passed – our anger began to fade and we put it out of our minds. Maher didn't go to see the lawyer.

The second incident was something else again. I was pregnant with Houd at the time; the baby was due in a few weeks. Maher had gone to Tunisia to attend to my father, who had returned to Tunisia for several months and had fallen quite sick. My brother, Mourad, could not stay with my father constantly on account of his work, and for me to travel this late in my pregnancy was out of the question. We decided that Maher would stay with my father until his health improved. Maher was scheduled to return to Canada in a few days. I was suffering from insomnia and spent most nights sleepless. Early one morning I began to doze off at dawn. Around seven o'clock, just as I was enjoying a little rest, I heard knocking at our door. I couldn't believe my ears. I thought I was dreaming and tried to go back to sleep. But the knocking resumed, more insistently, so finally I decided to get up. Eyes still bleary with sleep, I put on my housecoat, went downstairs, and opened the door. Before me stood two men. One faced me directly, while the other was a pace behind. The first was tall, wore a trench coat, and had piercing, icy-blue eyes. The other was slightly plump and seemed pleasant enough. The blue-eyed man showed me his federal police officer's ID. I took a step forward, trying to figure out what was going on. I thought I was sitting in front of the television watching an American detective movie. He asked me where my husband was. In Tunisia, I explained. The man wanted to know why he had gone there and when he intended to return. His questions came in rapid succession. He was obviously well prepared. His small eyes stared at me haughtily; again and again I felt ill at ease. There I stood with my bulging belly, my head scarf thrown over my head, my sleep-laden eyes, in a green housecoat with a bright red motif, answering questions from a plainclothes police officer. The scene was tragicomic. Finally, the second officer stepped forward to tell me there was nothing urgent; they only wanted to ask my husband some questions. They handed me a card with a telephone number, which I promised I would give to Maher and he would contact them. I closed the door and went back inside.

What was happening to us? Why was the RCMP interested in my husband? We had never had any problems with the police. To my way of thinking, we were a law-abiding family, an educated immigrant couple seeking our path in life. Never had I doubted my husband's honesty. I believed in him and wanted to help him so that we might succeed together. The early-morning arrival of these two police officers, with their suspicious, probing manner, had shaken me. I phoned Maher immediately and recounted the incident, gave him the police officer's name and number, and asked him to follow up. He called him and left a message.

A few days later, Maher returned from Tunisia. This time, he had made up his mind to speak to Michael Edelson. At their meeting, Edelson informed Maher of his rights; he would speak to the officer himself and find out what he wanted. The officer, he learned, wanted to ask Maher some questions in connection with an RCMP investigation. Edelson said he would accompany Maher to the interview. Since that day, we heard nothing more about the investigation, or from the police officers. The case was closed, or so we thought. Little did we realize that, in fact, our troubles were only beginning. In the first months after the officers' visit, we wanted to put aside what had happened by blaming it on the current climate of fear. Still, I would hear stories of people losing their jobs because of their religion, and visits by intelligence agents to certain people's workplaces were increasingly frequent. But as always, I felt sheltered from these dangers, as if they only happened to others.

Maher's business was not doing well. I had just given birth to Houd and would not be looking for work for the coming months. We decided to give up the house we were renting in Bayshore, move into the small apartment Maher had been renting for years for my mother and that he used as an office when he needed peace and quiet, and go to Tunisia for a two- or three-month holiday. It would not be a luxury vacation, but it would give me a chance to visit the country I had not seen for ten years, and allow us both to reflect calmly on what lay ahead.

SEPTEMBER 26, 2002. The day after Maher's departure from Tunisia, I did almost nothing worth mentioning. In the afternoon, I took the children to the shopping centre near the family home. Across from it, the city had transformed a large vacant lot into a park. It was not like parks in Canada, with lots of greenery and trees. But it did have a big pool with fountains in the middle. The ground was covered with paving stones, dotted here and there with beds of little plants or patches of grass. There were also small concrete benches. I liked this place because there were usually other children about. Barâa could ride her bicycle and I could push Houd in his stroller without worrying about cars. I would sit and watch people around me, lost in my thoughts. Before, the area had been empty land. I had walked across it many times to take the bus or go to the shopping centre. The hardest was in winter when drenching rains would descend on Tunis and turn the field, and others like it, into a morass of sticky brown mud that clung to our shoes and spattered our clothing. There was none of that now; the place was clean and well maintained. After spending part of the afternoon in the park, I went home with the children. They were cheerful and happy.

That evening I planned to wait up until around one o'clock in the morning to speak to Maher. The children were already in bed. I stayed with them a while, then when I felt they were well asleep I went into my old bedroom to lie on the bed and read. I kept many of the novels I used to love in a small bookcase. I picked up *The Citadel* by A. J. Cronin, in a French translation. I had discovered this Scottish author when I was sixteen and had read many of his books, translated into French. I felt like immersing myself once more in a universe that brought me back to those marvellous years when, heedless of the world around me, I would spend hours reading.

The hours flew by, but the telephone didn't ring; it was now two o'clock. I couldn't sleep. I put down my book and went into the other bedroom. The children were slumbering peacefully. I lay down on the bed and closed my eyes. Why had Maher not called? Had he missed his flight? Which flight could it have been? The one for Zurich, for New York, or perhaps for Montreal? I wanted to telephone my mother-in-law in Montreal, but I didn't want to create a panic. I decided to wait. There was no question of sleep. I tossed and turned on the bed, longing for the sun to rise then and there. I was tired, thoughts whirled in my head like a merry-go-round; I wanted to stop them, but as soon as I grasped them they would escape. Suddenly I saw Maher before me, angry and unsmiling. I asked why, but he didn't reply. I wanted to go to him, but he vanished.

I opened my eyes; the room was bathed in daylight. My head was heavy. I had slept only two or three hours. I went into the living room. The telephone was still there. I picked up the receiver to make sure there was nothing wrong with the line. I heard the buzzing of the dial tone; everything was normal. Maher had not called me. Why, why? I kept asking myself.

Had something happened to him? Was he sick? In hospital somewhere? Impossible. He was in good health; he hadn't complained of anything before leaving. Had someone hurt him, tried to rob him? In that case, I would have known; he would have called here in Tunis. Could he have been arrested in the United States? After all, the Americans had just introduced new security measures for non-citizens entering the country. All day long I stared at the telephone. There were times I thought I heard it ringing; I would run to pick up the receiver. It was only my imagination. I wanted to call my mother-in-law, but I decided to wait. I didn't want her to worry. Her health was fragile and she was especially fond of Maher, the youngest of her six sons. After all, what could I say to her? Did Maher arrive yet? She knew he was coming back to Ottawa, but he had not told her when; he wanted to surprise her. My own mother was in Ottawa. She knew that Maher was due soon, she was waiting for him to telephone, but I didn't want to call her either. It was as if I was ashamed to tell her that I hadn't heard a word from him.

Around midday I made up my mind to call my brother. I couldn't keep it to myself any longer. I was almost going out of my mind. His first words were:

"So, did Maher call?"

My voice was trembling, I felt like crying but couldn't.

"No," I replied.

"What? Where is he? What happened?" Mourad asked.

"I don't know. Maybe he missed his plane. He'll certainly call me tonight, don't you think?" I said as if to reassure myself. I had the feeling that Mourad was trying not to alarm me; he tried cracking jokes:

"Well, maybe he decided to stay in Switzerland, it's so beautiful there." Mourad had lived in Switzerland and really liked the country.

I tried to smile but couldn't. My heart was heavy; never since we were married had I felt as alone as at that moment. Maher travelled constantly and I often stayed home. But this time was different; there was silence and uncertainty. I had no idea where he was. Barâa was in the living room. She was pretending to play, but I knew she had been listening to my conversation with Mourad, she understood everything. She was very mature for five and a half. When I hung up, she said:

"Baba must be in a hotel. Maybe he doesn't have enough money to call us."

"Yes, maybe," I replied evasively, "but I'm sure he'll call us this evening."

I didn't know why, but it was as if I had set an imaginary deadline in my head. If Maher didn't call this evening, it would mean that something serious had happened. I didn't want to think too much about what "something serious" might be: arrest, death, kidnapping . . . all kinds of horror-movie scenarios unfolded before my eyes. Each time, though, I would shake my head to blot out those images and remind myself that soon the telephone would ring and I would hear the music of his voice.

I had trouble falling asleep that night. I would sleep a little, then wake with a start. I got up, sat on the edge of the bed, listening for the sound of the ringing telephone. Nothing. It was the noise of passing cars fading quickly into the night. Tired as I was, I no longer felt like sleeping. I wanted to wake up and talk to someone. I wanted to share my fear, my pain, and above all my feeling of helplessness. Was my husband dead? Was I to be a widow with two young children? What should I do, who should I contact, talk to? With a heavy head I fell asleep again and dreamed dreams I couldn't understand. Was I slowly, surely slipping into hell? I saw myself ill, gaunt, walking straight ahead, alone. I got to my feet, got ready for prayer, and prayed. At first not a word came to my lips; it was as if I'd suddenly been struck dumb. Then I felt release, and my tongue loosened. Now the words flowed like an endless monologue. Sitting upright, kneeling, resting on my heels, I groped toward the light.

SEPTEMBER 27, 2002. When I rose that morning I had made two decisions: I would call the Canadian Embassy in Tunis and Michael Edelson, Maher's lawyer, in Ottawa. I began with the embassy. I located the telephone number on the Internet. It was still too early to call Canada. I would have to wait until three o'clock that afternoon, when it would be nine o'clock in the morning in Ottawa. I counted the hours almost by the minute. I wanted the time to pass quickly, to make Ottawa and Montreal time my own. The voice at the Canadian Embassy had an accent that sounded a bit Québécois, a bit French, and a bit Arabic. The lady's name was Thérèse Laatar. She asked me some questions: Where do you live in Canada? What is your telephone number and your address in Tunis? I explained that my husband, a Canadian citizen, had not contacted me since leaving Tunisia two days earlier.

"He was scheduled to arrive in Montreal last night and was to call me right away, but he didn't," I told her. There was a long silence, as if Madame Laatar was taking notes or did not really understand the matter. She didn't seem convinced but promised to contact the Consular Section in Ottawa. She would call me on Monday.

I hung up. I was discouraged; waiting till Monday seemed like an eternity. Time seemed to have frozen, the minutes passed like hours. I stared at the big clock in the living room and had a sudden urge to grab the hands to change the time. I tried to get a hold of myself. Thousands of thoughts were racing, jostling in my head, but I didn't know what to do. I waited for offices to open in Ottawa; I had to tell Mr. Edelson about my husband's disappearance. I wanted to make sure it was not connected with the visit by the police in January.

I picked up the telephone and called Michael Edelson's office. I got straight through to him. I explained the situation. He remembered Maher's story. I felt like a drowning woman, flailing about in desperation. The lawyer, the embassy official, and my family were the hands that I would cling to with all my strength to keep from being swept away. Edelson promised to call the Crown Prosecutor's office to see if they knew anything about Maher's disappearance. Once again, I would have to wait; things were not going as I had hoped. The message was the same: patience was a virtue. I called my mother the same day and told her that there had been no word from Maher. She recounted that she had dreamed of me, that in her dream I was as pale as death, gesticulating that things were not going well. My mother's heart sensed evil looming. A fit of sobbing overcame me. I could no longer hold it back. At last someone was sharing my pain.

The next two days dragged by. I went out each afternoon, once the worst heat of the sun had passed, for a walk with the children. Across from the house there was a big parking lot surrounded by a fence. It belonged to the residents of two large buildings next door and was used more as a playground than as a parking lot. When I was a child, I used to spend hours on end riding my bicycle in this space. Neighbourhood children would come and bicycle or play ball, hide and seek, and even tennis. Now I was bringing my own children to the places I had played as a child, walking about, lost in thought, with Houd in his stroller and Barâa on her bicycle. The local children came and went, playing for a while, then running off; sometimes a mother would put her head out a window high up in one of the buildings and call her children to come in. I wouldn't stay outside for long, afraid that I might miss a call from Canada, any kind of call. Let it be a comforting voice or good news telling me that Maher was safe and sound and back in Ottawa, I thought. But the call never came. When I returned to the house, the same silence haunted the rooms and filled my heart with grief. During these two days, I spoke to my mother-in-law and one of my brothers-in-law. Maher's entire family was living in Canada since they had all emigrated from Syria. My brother-in-law, Taoufik, told me they were trying to contact American Airlines, but the agent refused to give any personal information. Taoufik was trying to find out if Maher had arrived in New York or was still in Zurich. But it was fruitless, nobody knew anything, or nobody wanted to say anything. Taoufik went to report Maher's disappearance to the Montreal police, but everything was at a standstill. Again and again, our requests were met with silence.

Monday finally came. I was dying to know if the Canadian Embassy official would call or if I was going to get some news from Michael Edelson. Since the previous Wednesday I had been completely in the dark about my husband. I didn't know where he was or if he was even still alive. I was living each moment in the hope of learning that everything was back to normal, that life would go on as before. I attempted to convince myself that soon everything would be fine. I had never been fond of change, and I was not about to accept it now. I wanted nothing more than to get back my quiet, normal life, divided between my family and my career. There had been a balance; now this incident had changed that and I was feeling the impact day and night. In fact, I was in a state of denial of this drama, as I tried to assure myself that everything would soon work out for the best.

OCTOBER 2, 2002. The idea of returning to Canada alone with the children had never occurred to me. I had expected Maher to come back to Tunis and that we would return home together. On Tuesday, my mother called from Ottawa. She had been living with me in Canada for years and was helping me to raise the children.

"Maher just called," she said. My heart was pounding, I waited for what was coming. "He's being held in the United States. I'll spell the name of the prison for you. Federal Bureau Prison, Brooklyn," she repeated slowly.

The words echoed in my head. Now I understood why Maher had not called. He was in prison. He was behind bars. I was expecting anything except prison. That had never crossed my mind. "What did he say?" I asked.

"He wants a lawyer. He's afraid he'll be sent back to Syria, that's all he told me," she said.

"Didn't he tell you why he's in prison, what he's charged with?"

"No," she replied with a long sigh. "No, he hung up right after that."

I kept talking to her. My throat was constricting. I didn't know how to handle the news. Part of me was relieved to know that he was alive, but a great sadness swept over me. I tried to imagine Maher in prison; I couldn't. Before he married me, he was his mother's baby, her youngest child, the only one to have graduated from university, her pride and joy, "a gift from heaven to light my final days," she would say. Now her beloved, cherished, coddled child was in prison. Barâa's papa, who often took her to the park to play, run, and swing was now a prisoner. Houd's patient papa, who would hold him in his arms and rock him, trying to calm him, was now behind bars. My whole life seemed to be crumbling, my dreams collapsing. I sat at the living-room table with my head in my hands and cried.

The same day, I telephoned Michael Edelson to tell him the news. He explained that because Maher was in the United States I would have to find an American lawyer. He promised to give me names of lawyers who could help. The questions tumbled through my mind. Should I go to the United States to see my husband? What lawyer would accept this case? Apart from a few trips I had made as a tourist,

I knew nothing about the United States. I had no idea how the American judicial system worked. Try as I might, I could not imagine how Maher was spending his days in prison. Not knowing what he was charged with, I kept wondering how to help set him free. Maher's family, my own, and Michael Edelson now knew that Maher was in prison, but no one else. I didn't want to tell anyone else; I felt embarrassed, ashamed, ill at ease. People might make fun of us. Everything would soon be all right, I tried to convince myself.

I was startled when Maher's friend Ahmed called me in Tunis. Ahmed lived in Ottawa with his wife, Racha, and their two children. We were good family friends, often going on picnics together and exchanging invitations to the evening fast-breaking meal during the month of Ramadan. Ahmed was also an engineer. He and Maher had met at McGill and had both found high-tech work in Ottawa. My mother had told Ahmed about Maher's arrest. He was deeply concerned; I could sense it over the phone. He promised to call Riad Saloojee, the head of the Canadian Council on American-Islamic Relations (CAIR-CAN), to see what could be done to have Maher released. I had heard of Riad Saloojee and his organization but had never met him.

Ahmed's telephone call was like a gift from heaven. In my depressed state, I needed information like this to help me forget how low my spirits were. Day by day, I was becoming more aware of the new turn my life had taken. I felt so tiny before the immensity of the task ahead. With each passing day, I saw my hopes being crushed, but gradually now I felt a strength growing in me, a strength I had not expected to find. My despair was great, but greater still was my determination to find my way out of the labyrinth I had barely entered. My inborn naivety and optimism would help see me through.

OCTOBER 3, 2002. I was no longer in contact with Thérèse Laatar; it was now Maureen Girvan, consul at the Canadian Consulate in New

York, who was giving me news of Maher. The first time she called me was to describe her visit to Maher at the Metropolitan Detention Center (MDC) in Brooklyn.[*]

"He was disoriented, he cried a lot and wanted to know how you all were," she told me. It tore my heart to hear those words. It was as if I could see Maher, downcast, alone and in shock, with no one to talk to, and here I was, thousands of kilometres away and unable to help him.

"Have the Americans given a reason for his arrest?" I asked.

Maher had showed her a sheet of paper explaining the Americans' refusal to allow him entry to the United States on account of his belonging to the terrorist group al-Qaeda. The news hit me like an icy blast. I had not yet overcome the first shock of knowing that Maher was in prison; now I was hearing that he was a suspected terrorist. This was the worst accusation they could throw at him. Practically all chances of my seeing him again seemed to vanish once more.

"But he's innocent. Maher doesn't belong to al-Qaeda or any terrorist group!" I declared.

There was a long silence, then Ms. Girvan explained that the Americans had made that decision. A lawyer must see Maher as soon as possible and start to work on his case. And as if to change the subject, she said, "You can write him a letter. Here's the address." I took the address and promised to write.

"Can he talk to me on the telephone?" I continued.

"He can telephone you if you send the money to his account in prison."

"I'll arrange to send him the money," I said, fighting back the tears.

I needed to talk to Maher on the telephone, to ask him how he was, to hear his voice, to know how he was being treated. That evening,

---

[*] I found out later that, in the United States, all federal prisons are named Federal Bureau Prison. The institution where Maher was incarcerated was called the Metropolitan Detention Center.

my brother-in-law Bassam and Maher's friend Ahmed called me. CAIR-CAN had suggested an American woman lawyer by the name of Amal Oummih. Ahmed also promised to send a $200 money order in Maher's name to the detention centre. Things were happening so fast that my head was spinning, but I also felt useless where I was. I couldn't send money or talk constantly on the telephone. Never had physical distance weighed so heavily as during those days. I longed to cross the ocean to be close to Maher, to let him know I would not fail him.

OCTOBER 5, 2002. Amal Oummih's voice surprised me. I had expected a female voice with an Arabic accent, but the voice I heard over the telephone was a firm, almost masculine voice with a New York accent. Oummih was an immigration lawyer of Moroccan origin. I didn't meet her in person, but I placed my husband's fate in her hands. She had visited Maher in prison; he had told her the Americans wanted him to sign a document authorizing his deportation to Syria, which he refused to do. He had received the money for telephone calls, she said, but the guards would not give him the code to make a call. I felt my blood run cold. Why would they do that to him? Why was he being held in prison? Oummih told me that he cried all through their conversation, that he was very confused and disoriented. I held back my tears and let her talk; I didn't want to miss a word. At the end of our conversation, she said she would find another, more specialized lawyer and would keep me informed of developments in the coming days.

Maher still didn't call me in the days that followed, although I had received confirmation that Ahmed had transferred $200 to his prison account for long-distance calls. I couldn't understand why, and told Maureen Girvan about my worries. She told me that prisoners' accounts took time to be activated; I should wait.

"Wait, wait! I've been waiting for weeks and haven't got anything!"

I burst out. Everyone wanted me to be the exemplary patient woman, the subservient woman who takes her knocks and doesn't react. It was less upsetting if I waited and kept my mouth shut than if I spoke up and made noise. "I've been waiting long enough, I want things to happen!" I said.

"I'll go to the prison tomorrow to see how he is," she promised.

I kept hoping that in a few days I would hear my husband's voice. I counted the days, but no call from Maher broke the silence of our house in Tunis. Time dragged on, monotonous and gloomy. Barâa kept asking me questions. She wanted to know where her father was, why he was in prison, and what he had done to get arrested. Each time I answered her, I found words of hope. I didn't want her to share my distress; things were going to change, her father would be back soon, I told her. But she wasn't convinced; looking into her eyes, I could see her innocence shadowed by a veil of sadness, and I felt a burning inside me because there was nothing I could do.

OCTOBER 8, 2002. Maureen Girvan called me to tell me that she had gone to visit Maher in prison; the guard had told her he was no longer there.

"It could be good news. The MDC is the worst prison for people suspected of terrorism. If he has been transferred to another, it's because things are not so serious any more."

"But where is he then?" I said.

"In some cases, it takes us six months to find out where a Canadian prisoner is being held, the Americans can transfer him from one prison to another as much as they want, but we'll find out in the end."

I felt like telling her it sounded like a good thing she didn't know, but I held my tongue. I wanted to believe what she was saying, because her words rang nicely in my head.

Suddenly a dreadful thought popped into my mind: "What if they've deported him to Syria!"

"Oh no, I don't think the Americans would deport him to Syria. For two reasons: first, it's less expensive for them to send him to Canada than to Syria, and even if they do decide to deport him, they would send him to Zurich, where his flight originated; and second, Maher was travelling with a Canadian passport and therefore they should send him back to Canada."

I liked the sound of her words. They had the power to soothe me, to reassure me that all was well. They calmed all the horrible thoughts that were tormenting me. Even if I was feeling worried, I told myself that Ms. Girvan was surely right. The discussion showed how completely both of us, living outside the post–9/11 mindset, still continued to believe in the same old "outdated" rules and principles while the American administration had cast aside international law and was operating according to its own rules.

From that day on, the thought that Maher might have been sent to Syria began to haunt me. I had never set foot there, but from the stories Maher had told me and things I had read about Arab countries, I knew that Syria was a police state that made life hard for its citizens. Many communist, Islamist, and liberal opponents of Hafez al-Assad were rotting in prison. The Muslim Brotherhood, a political movement founded in Egypt but with a wide following throughout the region, had mounted a serious threat to al-Assad's government; they might well threaten his son Bashar's rule. Maher did not belong to the Muslim Brothers, I knew that, but as a practising Muslim, he would be seen as a sympathizer by the Damascus regime. Besides, someone who leaves the country of his birth and does not return is often considered a kind of political defector or even a traitor. But what worried me most was that if the Americans had sent him to Syria on charges of terrorism, the Syrians would have only one option: to show the world they did not trifle with terrorism. Maher would be a political gift, allowing them to demonstrate, to the Americans in particular, how sincere they were in the fight against terrorism.

Again and again I asked myself: Why would he be sent to Syria?

Why wouldn't the Americans send him back to Canada? Wasn't Syria a "rogue state" according to the American administration; hadn't the U.S. State Department called Syria a "state sponsor of terrorism"? Why would Maher be sent there? Was it for the simple reason that he was Syrian and could be treated like all Syrians? And what if they threw him into prison there? No, that was something I didn't even want to think about. Maher was in the United States; it would only be a matter of days before he would be returned to Canada and the whole nightmare would be over and forgotten. Why was I pessimistic? I was more than determined to forget the thought that Maher might have been deported. Each time the idea crossed my mind, I tried not to think about it. But deep down, I was afraid.

OCTOBER 10, 2002. I was changing Houd's clothes when the telephone rang. I put Houd gently in his playpen and then ran to the living room to pick up the phone. It was Maureen Girvan calling from the Canadian Consulate in New York. I was panting, trying to catch my breath. From her tone, I knew something serious had happened. Yesterday, she had been bright and almost jovial. Today, I could hear the tension in her voice.

"Is there something new?" I asked.

"There is," she said. "I don't know if your brother-in-law Taoufik has spoken to you, but we've learned that Maher has been deported to Syria." I thought my heart was going to stop beating. My foreboding had been right all along; they had sent him to Syria. I would never see him again.

"But I told you, I warned you, you didn't believe me!" I lashed out. For the first time I was overwhelmed by anger. Anger at my own naivety, but also at the consul, at her assurances and the flawed reasoning she had fed me the day before. Ms. Girvan was embarrassed. She told me that never had she witnessed such a thing while working for Foreign Affairs. She swore she had sincerely believed Maher would be deported to Canada. But I was infuriated. Nothing she could say would stop me. When I had finished my tirade, she told me she would call me back and give me news. I put down the telephone slowly; all my dreams were going up in smoke. I had let myself be deceived by her arguments. I had convinced myself Maher would be deported to Canada because that was what I wanted to believe. Now, everything was destroyed. I would have to begin again, build a whole new imaginary structure. The next day, Ms. Girvan called, her tone optimistic again. Rumours were circulating that Maher was in Jordan, not Syria.

"If that turns out to be true, it's good news," she said.

Jordan was indeed more open to the West than Syria; the country maintained good relations with Canada. If Maher were in Jordan, there would be a greater chance of obtaining his release than if he were in Syria. But were we sure he was being held in Jordan, was this nothing but rumour, or was it true? Both she and I were building up new hopes to cling to, while up there, the people who knew where Maher was must have been chuckling at our foolishness. Ms. Girvan promised me that the Canadian ambassador in Washington, Michael Kergin, would speak to well-placed people in the American administration to find out where Maher had been sent.

The days that followed reminded me of the first days after Maher's disappearance. The minutes passed slowly, the telephone didn't ring, and I felt disoriented, torn between hope and despair. Every time I called the consul, she told me that her inquiries had produced no results, and the only reply from American officials was: "You won't find him in the United States." It was a clever manipulation of words to say that they didn't have him any more but weren't going to reveal where he is, leaving me to twist in the wind. It was as if I didn't deserve to know my husband's location.

The same day, Riad Saloojee from CAIR-CAN phoned. I detected a mixture of optimism and discomfort in his voice. I sensed that, deep down, he understood the seriousness of the matter. After all, Maher was a practising Muslim arrested in the United States after the events of September 11, 2001. Everything was against him. The secrecy surrounding his arrest combined with the almost tragic circumstances had given the case a whiff of mystery, but at the same time made it as critical as it was sensitive. Riad was in direct contact with the press. It was his job to communicate with journalists on matters relating to Islam and Muslims. We agreed that we would let things cool down. Our strategy was to allow diplomacy to do its work before talking to the press. We didn't want to hurt Maher's chances of being freed in any way, because we thought it only reasonable that he would soon be released. Even without any promise or concrete action, our conversation buoyed my hopes. One word was enough to plunge me into despair, another was enough to give me an almost joyful air, a lightness of heart that surprised me and allowed me to go about my day-to-day tasks.

Barâa kept asking me questions: "Do you think Baba will come home? Are we going to go to Canada soon?"

My answers were always the same: "Yes, of course he'll come back, of course we'll all go to Canada together." Then, as if correcting myself, I would murmur, "Inshallah . . . God willing."

The day after our talk, Riad called to tell me that the *New York Times* had published a small article on Maher's arrest. I was caught off-guard. I didn't know if it was a good or a bad thing, but I knew there would be consequences and the news would soon be spread in Canada. It didn't take long. Riad phoned me back later in the day to ask if I was ready to give my contact information in Tunis to Canadian journalists. Without a moment's hesitation I replied, "Certainly!" I could not have known that my decision to speak to the media that day would broadcast my husband's story to the whole world, and that my life would be changed forever.

Reporters began to call me in Tunis. Their growing interest was like having friends to talk to. I spoke to them about my fears of never seeing my husband again and my disappointment with the Canadian government for not doing enough for one of its own. Never before had I talked to the media, but every time I hung up the telephone I felt better. These sessions were like therapy: I talked, got things off my chest, and felt relieved. When the news broke in Ottawa, my mother phoned to say that she was attending her regular English class that day and by chance noticed a copy of the *Ottawa Citizen*. On page one she saw our wedding picture, Maher and me smiling. She almost fainted, she told me.

"I wanted to hide all the copies of the paper so no one would see them," she said. "I didn't want people to know that my son-in-law was arrested and was in prison."

But for me, the media was my only hope of ever seeing Maher again. I had been robbed of my husband, and he had been robbed of his rights. I was not even allowed to talk to him or find out where he was. My response was simple: I chose to speak to the world, to be open and to denounce the way we were being treated.

A few days later, Ms. Girvan called to inform me that she would no longer be in charge of the case. Was this the result of those damned little words, that Maher was no longer in the United States, or was it an indication that the case was getting serious and that more experienced diplomats were called for? I couldn't be sure. There was probably some truth in both possibilities, but Ms. Girvan quietly dropped out of the picture.

"Thanksgiving is coming in a few days and I'm leaving for the West Coast to visit my family," she told me. "Mr. Gar Pardy will be your new contact. He's the director of Consular Affairs in Ottawa. Here's his number . . ." I jotted it down in my address book, sensing in my heart that a new page had just been turned.

I decided to call the Member of Parliament for my riding. I knew Marlene Catterall by name, from brochures she had sent us, which showed her greeting senior citizens or attending community events, but I had never approached her in person. I wanted politicians to get involved in Maher's case not only because he was my husband, but also because it was a case of flagrant injustice and the government's reaction had been weak and timid. It was as if it were looking on from afar, waiting to see which way the wind would blow before taking action. I found myself talking to Kathy, Mrs. Catterall's assistant; I explained the whole story and she promised me a reply. Several weeks went by before I was to speak directly to Mrs. Catterall. It was around ten at night in Tunis; the children had already been in bed for an hour when the telephone rang.

"It's Marlene," she said, "your Member of Parliament."

My heart began to beat furiously, I was expecting the worst. She told me that the Canadian government was looking into Maher's case and that the minister of Foreign Affairs, Bill Graham, had made inquiries. She would try to give me some news as soon as possible. The first thing that came to my mind was to thank her; I liked the fact that she had taken a personal interest and was calling to tell me where things stood. Gradually, I was learning to be patient, learning to live with misfortune while hoping for better days.

OCTOBER 15, 2002. I wanted to speak to politicians. I wanted to speak directly to Prime Minister Jean Chrétien. I didn't realize that this is not as easy as one might think. First of all, I was in Tunisia, and the highest-ranking government figure I could meet was the ambassador. Besides, I had no idea that even in Canada, ordinary people rarely get to meet the prime minister. But I was determined to deliver a message. I called Madame Laatar and told her that I had a message to present to the Canadian government. She set up an appointment. The day before, I asked my brother, Mourad, to mind the children. In my notebook I jotted down some notes:

> *Message I am sending to the Canadian government, to its head, Mr. Jean Chrétien.*
>
> *My husband, a Canadian citizen, is a good family man. He has worked in Canada, paid his taxes and has always behaved like a good*

citizen. He was arrested by the American government, then deported to Syria, the country of his birth. As his wife and mother of his two children, as a Canadian, I ask the Canadian government to give me in writing the reasons for this unjust and brutal deportation. I ask that my husband be returned to Canada and that his documents be returned to him. I think that what has happened is very serious and could lead to undesirable consequences for ethnic communities living in Canada. Henceforth, any citizen of other than Canadian origin is under threat of deportation to the place of his or her birth.

I have confidence in our government and expect an explanation from it regarding the hitherto unknown fate of my husband.

I intended to deliver this message verbally when I met with the embassy staff. I attempted to learn the words by heart, repeated them over and over in my mind. It was no use.

My children had become accustomed to seeing their uncle. He would visit us as often as he could. The school year was just beginning and Mourad was busy again teaching courses. But he would find the time to make the trip between Hammamet and Tunis. Maher's arrest and imprisonment had drawn us even closer. I felt him beside me, supporting me with his thoughts, his attitude, and his words. When I had telephone interviews at the children's dinner hour, he would take Houd in his arms and amuse him so that I could talk uninterrupted by an infant's cries. Mourad was more than a brother to me; he was a friend who was always there when I needed him.

I set out for the embassy, passport in hand to be sure they would let me in. The building was much different from the one where, at age twenty, I had had my first interview before I emigrated to Canada. Twelve years had passed and the place had become bigger and more modern; now it had the look of a fortress. Guards with walkie-talkies searched visitors with metal detectors, airport-style. I was admitted and spent a few minutes in a waiting room, which I barely recognized.

Madame Laatar came to fetch me and together we took a small elevator to the next floor. There, in a huge office, I met the first secretary of
the embassy, Luce Doré; Madame Laatar stayed with us. In a corner of
the room I noticed a television set tuned to the CNN worldwide news,
and I wondered if Maher's case had been reported. Madame Doré was
civil and polite. She said practically nothing; it was mostly Madame
Laatar who responded to my comments and tried to keep the conversation going as a dialogue instead of a long monologue on my part.
Effortlessly, the words I had prepared the day before came out; I could
no longer hold back. The two faces across from me remained almost
impassive; it was as if each of my comments brought only silence. I
was deeply disappointed by their coldness. I was being naive; this was
my introduction to diplomacy. Yet I was not angry, I was not insulting;
I spoke calmly, attempting to explain the troubles that had beset my
family, I was calling out for help. But I couldn't help feeling that the
Canadian government was not taking me seriously or sharing my
concern. Indifference and bureaucracy seemed to be the rule. In order
to survive and overcome the problems I faced, I would have to learn
this new language. I returned home; the children were happy to see
me, but I felt like shutting myself in my bedroom and wailing my distress at the top of my voice. I didn't do anything like that; I choked
back my tears, swallowed a glass of water as if to wash down a knot in
my throat, opened the refrigerator, stood there for a moment looking
in, then took out a package of meat and began to prepare the children's evening meal.

OCTOBER 16, 2002. "Why don't you call Amnesty International?"
said Mourad. "Perhaps they could help you."

I liked the idea. My first contacts with the Canadian government
had been discouraging; it was like banging my head against a stone
wall. I wanted a human approach. I found Amnesty International's

Ottawa telephone number, hoping to talk to Alex Neve, its secretary general. I had expected that I might get through to his assistant or his voice mail; instead, I found myself speaking to him directly. His voice was warm and reassuring; he listened as I explained the whole story. Amnesty had decided to launch an emergency campaign calling on its members around the world to write to the American, Canadian, and Syrian governments, he told me. Mr. Neve could not free Maher with the wave of a magic wand, but I felt certain that he was taking the matter seriously. He promised that his organization would continue to monitor the case actively. After you've taken a nasty fall, sometimes all you need is a helping hand to get you back on your feet. My phone conversation with Mr. Neve had that effect. No promises were made, but now I felt I existed, that my story was having an impact, and that together we could make things happen.

I had the same feeling a few days later when Alexa McDonough, the leader of the New Democratic Party, called me from her parliamentary office in Ottawa. I knew only her name and her party, and I was pleasantly surprised when she said she was watching the case closely and would do her very best to prod the government to do more. I knew nothing about what was going on in Parliament, or that the NDP was asking Minister of Foreign Affairs Bill Graham questions about my husband. I thanked God for this unexpected help. For me, it was like a gift from heaven that each day brought new indications that Maher's case was not a simple one, and the fight was just beginning.

OCTOBER 21, 2002. Gar Pardy called to tell me he had just spoken to the Canadian ambassador to Syria; according to Syrian authorities, Maher had only just arrived in Syria.

"So where has he been all this time, then, sightseeing in some other country?" I replied with a touch of sarcasm.

Mr. Pardy went on, his voice showing no reaction: "You know, it's very rare that the Syrians admit to holding prisoners in their country, but in Maher's case they have shown a great deal of openness and co-operation."

Since the day Maureen Girvan informed me that Maher had probably been deported to Syria, it was hard for me to imagine where he was being held. At first I thought he was still in New York, then Syria. But perhaps he had stopped in Jordan. In the end, there was total silence, shrouded in mystery. With every passing day, with every new rumour, I would tell myself that soon the nightmare would be over. But then the speculation would start up again and I would be overcome with a deluge of information, not knowing who to believe. Syria's admission that Maher was now there was perplexing. When we had learned that he might be in Jordan, the Jordanian ambassador to Canada denied it; I then concluded that Maher must be in Syria. But the news that he had only just arrived in Syria made me think that he had been in Jordan all along. Who was lying and who was telling the truth? It was a preposterous story; I didn't know who to believe. But one thing was certain: more than one party was hiding the truth. For a year, I was convinced that Maher had spent ten days in Jordan, while in fact he had stayed only a few hours in that country.

On the day I heard the news from Syria, Amnesty International launched its promised emergency campaign. Even though I was certain Maher was being held in Syria, I took comfort in the Amnesty appeal. I no longer felt alone. How fervently I hoped that Amnesty's members would begin to write letters asking for Maher to be returned to Canada! These were the small things that kept my hopes alive.

The next day, Mr. Pardy emailed to inform me that the Canadian consul in Damascus had been granted permission by the Syrian authorities to visit Maher; I would hear from him again as soon as he had a report. This he presented to me as good news. As for me, I was at a loss to know how to react. Of course I had been worried sick about my husband, not knowing where he was, not knowing even if he was still alive. And here was Mr. Pardy, informing me that not only was Maher alive but that the Canadian consul was going to visit him.

"Never have the Syrians allowed us to visit a prisoner. Usually they don't even recognize that they're holding a prisoner," he said, his enthusiastic tone verging on pride. He was doing his job and was pleased with the progress made on Arar's file. But where was I supposed to fit into all this? Was I supposed to laugh or cry at the news that my husband was being held prisoner in Syria, a country I didn't know, on charges that were never spelled out but were probably in some way connected with terrorism? Should I show gratitude, express my thanks, laugh with peals of joy that my husband would receive a visit and some day, perhaps, might be released? My heart was not overflowing with joy; it was as if my feelings had vanished. How I wanted to believe that none of this was true, how I longed to escape.

On October 23, I received a brief email from Mr. Pardy recounting this vaunted first visit:

> Dr. Mazigh, I have tried to call and will keep trying . . . In any
> event, the Canadian Consul met with Maher this morning. He is
> well and asked that his concern for you and the children be sent.
> We provided him with information on your concerns and he was
> most appreciative that you and the children are well and still in
> Tunis. He stated that his needs are all being looked after. The
> Syrian authorities indicated that he will remain at the present
> location in Damascus for some time yet.

So, according to the Canadian consul in Syria, Leo Martel, Maher was in good health and the Syrians were looking after him very well. I would not believe a word of what I was reading. I reread this message dozens of times; the aim could be to placate me, keep me in Tunisia, to make me think everything was for the best in this best of all possible worlds. Alas, I saw in it exactly the opposite of what these people were trying to put over on me. What my heart was telling me was that Maher was in a bad way. Reading between the lines, I saw only resignation, fatalism, humiliation. This was not the Maher I knew. He had always been a man with a will to overcome obstacles; the man I knew was ambitious, determined to become a top engineer in his field, never satisfied with mediocrity, and always working to improve himself. Yes, I knew him as a religious man, but he didn't let himself be led. "We must seek the way, and God will guide us," he would always tell me when he prepared business presentations to financial backers. He dreamed of developing and then selling software of his own design. He dreamed of becoming the head of a company; he was a man who never gave up. I didn't want to hear anything more of that message. Could those words have come from Maher? Was this the same Maher I had married eight years ago? How could he have changed? In what circumstances? Why? Only later would I learn the truth.

Since the day Mr. Pardy told me that Maher was really, truly in Syria, I didn't want to stay in Tunisia one day longer. During those last weeks, I had been comforting myself with the illusion that all the rumours would turn out to be false and Maher would miraculously reappear. Now there was no longer any doubt in my mind. I had to get back to Canada. Things were getting more complicated; it was becoming clear to me that Maher would not be back soon. Here, my hands were tied. Canadian journalists were interested in Maher's case, but contact was limited by the six-hour time difference between the two countries. Six weeks had gone by since Maher's arrest, and yet very little had changed. For people around me, the shock of his arrest and deportation to Syria had begun to wear off. Lives were getting back to normal. Except for mine. My life was shattered forever. I felt it every moment, while feeding Houd or while brushing Barâa's long, silky hair. Everything I did reminded me of my life before; every day the look in my children's eyes reminded me of my husband's eyes. The month of Ramadan had begun several days earlier. As usual I was fasting, but this time Maher was not with us. At sunset I would hurriedly finish my plate, alone, and go to look after Houd, who would be getting bored in his playpen. Normally, our whole pattern of life would change with Ramadan, the house filling with the fragrances of the small dishes and special recipes that we would try only at this blessed time. This year it had a very different connotation for me: I was alone, my soul ached, and I was thinking every minute of Maher.

> *Tunis, November 1, 2002.*
> *Dear Maher,*
>   *Our vacation is ending on a dramatic note. In a few days I'm going home to Canada with Barâa and Houd. I would have so loved you to be with us as was planned in the beginning but destiny has willed it otherwise. Don't worry, the Canadian government will assure our safety during the trip. I hope it will not be too long before you rejoin us. From there, I will be able to do all in my power to bring you the necessary support and see you finally back with us. Barâa will go to "Senior Kindergarten," she is already very happy at the thought of seeing her little friends again. Houd has four little teeth and can already shake his head for "no." He's a caution, you won't recognize him. These children are a gift from heaven. Just one word for you: COURAGE, and I know it's something you have. I will support you till my last breath.*
>   *We all love you.*
>   *Monia, Barâa and Houd.*

FIRST WEEK OF NOVEMBER 2002. To return to Canada, I had to have a passport for Houd. Because of a long public sector strike in Ontario, we had been unable to obtain a birth certificate for him. After several attempts, we had succeeded in having a three-month temporary passport issued, which would enable him to travel to Tunisia. He was about four months old at the time. When Maher decided to return to Ottawa in late September, we had thought it was a good idea for him to take this temporary, now-expired passport with him and renew it in Ottawa so that we could all return together. He had put it in his luggage. But our carefully laid plans had gone awry, Maher never arrived in Ottawa, and I had no idea what had happened to the passport. I was stuck in Tunis without a passport for my son. I called Mr. Pardy and explained the situation. He said he would talk to Madame Laatar at the Canadian Embassy in Tunis and a travel document would be issued to allow Houd to travel from Tunis to Montreal.

That same day, I took the children to the shopping centre to get Houd's passport photos. The early November weather in Tunis was more pleasant. The sun's rays had lost their bite. In the evening I was careful to close the windows, and brought out the woollen blankets. My excursions with the children had become few and far between. I went out only for shopping; my life was spent in the house, ruled by the telephone calls I was making to, or receiving from, Canada. Once Houd's photo session was over, I took the children to the amusement area to ride on the merry-go-round. Cotton candy, lollipops, and all kinds of goodies for children were sold. Parents watched their children climb aboard little cars, helicopters, or motorcycles and have their turn, which would end almost as soon as it began. I bought a few tickets for Barâa and kept Houd in his stroller because he was too young to ride alone. Standing there under that sort of miniature circus tent, I watched Barâa come by and then disappear behind the other toy cars and planes. Each time she saw me she would smile and I would make myself smile in return. With each passing day, I was coming to realize that life had not stopped with Maher's arrest, that although Barâa was sad, she wanted to keep playing and growing and doing the things that other children her age loved to do. I marvelled at the joy that radiated from Barâa, at her enthusiasm. Gently, softly, she was giving me back my hope. When I smiled at Barâa as she rode round and round, it was almost as if I had forgotten my troubles.

NOVEMBER 11 OR 12, 2002. Houd's travel document was now ready. I could pick it up at the Canadian Embassy. But, Madame Laatar explained, it was not enough to enable Houd to leave Tunisia. I would need authorization from the Tunisian Interior Ministry. Houd was a Canadian national, but since his passport was not in my possession, the Tunisian authorities would have to verify that he had really entered the country, and only they could grant him the right to depart. Leaving Barâa with our neighbour, an old friend of my mother, I took Houd in my arms in a taxi first to the Canadian Embassy. I didn't wait long. Madame Laatar gave me Houd's travel document and told me that all I needed now was the authorization from the Tunisian Interior Ministry. I left the embassy, Houd still in my arms, and took another taxi. The Interior Ministry was not far away. I arrived before this immense grey building, more like a concrete fortress. I had never set foot in it before. I entered by a small door, the one designated for the general public. There was a waiting room with some chairs and a reception desk. I explained to the official on duty that I wanted an authorization for my son to leave the country. I gave him my name. He told me to take a seat and wait. I sat down with Houd on my knee. He was happy and not complaining. People were coming and going, inquiring about their passport applications. I soon realized that these people were having trouble getting their Tunisian passports. The minutes ticked by, but the official didn't call me to give me the document. Each time I went to ask him how much time it was going to take, he told me to wait. Finally, after about an hour, another official came into the room and called my name. I stood up and went over to him.

"What is your husband's name?" he asked.

"Maher Arar," I said slowly. "My husband is not Tunisian. He is a Canadian of Syrian origin."

Not waiting for me to finish what I was saying, the official turned on his heel and left the room. I stood there, looking a bit foolish, not understanding what had just happened. I went back to my chair and waited some more. Houd was beginning to get hungry. I had nothing to give him, so instead I stood up and walked about, rocking him in my arms. There was another person waiting along with me, a man of a certain age, polite in manner and well dressed. I didn't speak to him, but from the look on his face I could see that he was sympathizing with me. I approached the desk officer again and explained that I had to go home, my daughter was waiting with a friend. But his only answer was to be patient. He took a candy out of his pocket and told me to give it to the baby. This act of kindness surprised me. I sensed in his voice that he was almost imploring me not to leave the building. What did all this runaround mean? I had no idea what was going on. Then the same official as before came back into the room.

"When did your husband leave Tunisia?"

"On September 25."

I had not finished speaking before he left, almost at a run. I saw him climbing a flight of stairs. Things were taking a new turn, and I began to suspect that I was not going to get the authorization for Houd. A sudden fear took hold of me: what was I going to do? I knew just how complex my situation was. My two children were Canadians, but I was trapped in Tunisia, with my husband imprisoned somewhere in Syria. I knew no one in the Interior Ministry who might be able to help me. Then my thoughts turned to my daughter; Barâa must be worried, I said to myself. When I had left that morning I expected to be back by about noon. Now it was almost one o'clock in the afternoon and no document had been issued.

Suddenly another official, a rather short man who smelled strongly of sweat, appeared and called my name. He had come in by the same door through which I had first entered the waiting room. He said, "Follow me." I was relieved. I followed him, with Houd now dozing fitfully in my arms. He led me down a small lane in the same complex, opened a door, and motioned me in. I asked no questions, believing I would soon have my authorization. We were in a vestibule that gave onto a flight of poorly lit stairs. As I followed him up the stairs, the stench of damp concrete and urine invaded my nostrils. I shuddered with disgust. I wanted to hold my nose, but my hands were carrying Houd. The official was walking fast and I was doing my best to keep pace. We were moving through a labyrinth of stairs, long corridors, and closed office doors. Finally he came to a stop in front of a door, pushed it open, and left.

I was now in a small office with two tables. Two officials were sitting behind the tables. There was a tiny window letting in a few rays of sunshine. Most likely these two men were waiting for me; I understood that I was there for an interrogation. My fear dissipated, I became calm, but I was curious and a little offended. The two officials didn't look threatening. One had an old typewriter in front of him, along with some files and sheets of paper; to me, he looked thick-headed and browbeaten. The other was holding a pen and kept turning it over and over. I stood there, in the middle of this room, Houd still clinging to me, my arms almost dropping. I had been holding him for three hours now.

"Where is your husband?" asked the official behind the typewriter.

"In Syria," I replied.

What is the purpose of this interrogation? I wondered. Who had ordered it? The Americans? The Canadians? Or did the Tunisians want their own file on Maher and me in order to look good in the espionage and information-gathering community? I knew none of this and continued to answer their questions. The official asked me what we were doing in Tunis and I explained that we were visiting, and that my husband had wanted to return to Canada on account of his work. Suddenly he sprang the name of a Tunisian.

"Does your husband know a Mr. Lotfi?"

The name didn't ring any immediate bells, but as he continued to question me I recalled vaguely that Maher had in fact met someone of that name. Our neighbour, a friend of my father, had referred him to this person who, he said, could put Maher in touch with the local business community and help him obtain contracts in Tunis. Things were really serious, I realized. Were the Tunisians watching us too? Why? Was it on their own initiative or at the request of the American or Canadian intelligence agencies? Still, it was not surprising that we would be watched; Tunisia was a police state where most people spied and reported to the police on what they knew about their employees, their neighbours, even their own families. But as always, I had felt insulated from this surveillance, I felt different. Never had I felt I should not see such-and-such a person or refrain from saying something for fear of being arrested. I lived normally and naturally, unaware of what the police were doing to intimidate or frighten people.

The official then questioned me about Canada: where I lived, what I had studied, at what university. In short, what he wanted was a detailed copy of my resumé. I kept my replies to a minimum, but the situation was beginning to exasperate me. Finally I exploded.

"Aren't you ashamed of what you're doing?" I told them. "Do you realize I've been in this ministry for three hours with my baby and I must have my authorization so I can leave for Canada?"

There was an awkward silence and I sensed that they were embarrassed. As if they were surprised to see me react, as if finally they were realizing how stupid they were. But I could understand that if you spend years doing this kind of work, your feelings and your sensitivities dry up; even if you are moved occasionally to react, you end up losing whatever compassion you might have had. My two interrogators were this kind. They were men incapable of reaction, they submitted and made others submit. But I, with my cheeky attitude, a baby in my arms, and a scarf on my head that contradicted my Tunisian accent and revealed my middle-class roots, had touched off a small revolution in the heads of these men who were used to seeing everything in black and white.

"You will have your authorization, I promise you, but first you will have to stay with us a little longer."

"Would you like a yogurt for the baby?" added the second official.

"No thank you. My son doesn't eat yogurt. I want my documents and I want to go home," I shot back.

They wanted me to take them for nice guys now. But as if to contradict them, two or three more men burst into the office. I don't know if this was a tactic used by the intelligence agencies, but the office was now full of men. They looked like small-time thugs, staring at me with a mixture of curiosity and threat. I didn't move, and stared right back at them with a mock submissive look that enraged and infuriated them. For certain, they expected me to start crying. I did not do them that favour. One of them was dressed in a suit and tie. I could see the hatred glistening in his eyes. He wanted to break me down, I could feel it.

"This isn't a daycare. You shouldn't bring your kid along." This was the way he talked to his wife, I thought.

"Who do you want me to leave my child with anyway?"

I was surrounded by a pack of wolves doing everything they could to make me look weak, to intimidate me. But I was standing my ground, proud of who I was, reminding them of the baseness of their work and insisting on what I wanted. I was surprising myself, I was not letting go. They were losing the battle.

The session was over. The official who'd been typing asked me to follow him, the others left by way of the stairs. It was two o'clock in the afternoon. My heart was aching; Houd had eaten nothing, Barâa must be very frightened to see that I hadn't come back. Once again I was led to the same waiting room. It was now deserted. I waited another forty minutes, then the same official who had asked the name of my husband brought me the document I had been waiting for since that morning. It had cost me four hours, a failed intimidation session, and most of all sore arms from carrying Houd. But at last I felt free. I tried to forget the whole episode. Soon we would all be leaving for Canada.

NOVEMBER 14, 2002. As planned, Mourad came to our house early in the morning. The sky was overcast. A mixture of cloud and pollution hung low on the horizon.

The day before, I had spent four hours at the pediatrician's office. Houd had had a high fever, so I decided to take him to see a doctor. Our flight was the following day and we had a long journey in front of us. I was worried about him, I wanted to be sure he was not in danger. The doctor's waiting room was full to bursting. Anxious-looking parents glanced often at their watches. A secretary with dyed-blonde hair stepped into the room to tell us the doctor had been delayed by an emergency operation and we would have to wait. A deathly silence reigned, sometimes broken by a baby crying. Houd, limp with fever, would start each time a child cried and begin to cry too. I would rock him in my arms and whisper softly that everything was all right and Mama was with him. My words soothed him, and he would fall back into a troubled sleep. Our turn finally came. The pediatrician examined Houd. "I see nothing to worry about," he said. "Give him aspirin." I explained that we were leaving the next day for Canada. If the fever persisted, he advised me, have a urinalysis done as soon as we got there.

Back home, I gave Houd his medicine, but his fever continued to rise and fall. I went to fetch Barâa from our neighbour and began to pack for the journey. I stuffed clothes, toys, and books higgledy-piggledy into big duffle bags. I wanted to pack the essentials and get this journey over with as quickly as possible. As every night, I read Barâa a story, then we said our prayers together. This night, before closing her eyes, she whispered, "Mama, I'm happy. I feel Baba will soon be back." I smiled at her, kissed her on the forehead, and left the room after turning off the light.

The next morning, we were having our breakfast in the old kitchen for the last time. I looked at our house lovingly – but with a sense of hurt. I liked our family home. It was a modest place with nothing extravagant about it. An unpretentious house in a fast-changing neighbourhood facing invasion by the nouveaux riches of Tunis, a symbol of resistance against the tidal wave of hideous, cumbersome new buildings. It was where I had spent much of my childhood and the years of my youth. But to my dying day this same house would remind me of that morning in September when my life turned upside down. It was as though the house was telling me, in a mocking voice, that I would never forget it even though I had emigrated to Canada, even though I had chosen other houses and other places to live in.

Mourad loaded the duffle bags and Houd's stroller into the trunk of his car. We all got inside. Even Houd seemed calm this morning. I didn't know if it was still the effect of the fever or if he understood what was happening. Our house was not far from the airport. The trip was silent. I looked at the tall palm trees planted along the highway to the airport and thought about Maher. What was he doing? Did he know that we were going back to Canada? When would I be able to see him again?

"Here we are," said Mourad. I jumped, I had been lost in thought. We got out of the car and started toward the terminal building. In the departure hall I saw two people waiting for me: Thérèse Laatar and another embassy official. I knew they were going to be there. I needed them to be on hand because I was not sure the Tunisian authorities would let me leave without causing problems. After the incident at the Interior Ministry building, I no longer wanted to leave anything to chance. I had learned my lesson; never again would I play with fire. Thérèse seemed pleasant enough that morning. Perhaps the sight of the children made her change her attitude. She was usually too businesslike for my tastes. She gave me her card and told me to call her as soon as we cleared Tunisian customs to let her know if everything had gone all right. She came with me to the Tunis Air counter for the luggage weigh-in. I felt reassured; at last I had help. My Canadian passport and Barâa's were in order; for Houd I had only a travel document, just a sheet of paper indicating his place and date of birth with his photograph above. I also had that wretched document authorizing him to leave the country, the one I'd obtained two days earlier at the Interior Ministry. At last I was ready to go through Tunisian customs and on to begin a new stage of my life in Canada. Mourad kissed us all and asked me to call him as soon as we arrived in Montreal. The customs officer who examined our papers barely glanced at me. I gave him all the documents; he entered the names on his computer, and I waited there in front of him, wondering what the verdict would be. Houd was swinging his little feet, he looked happy in his stroller, and Barâa waited too, impatient to get onto the plane. She had begged me to order a children's menu for her and was as anxious as I was to get through customs. Slowly, the officer checked all the papers, then gave them back to me, scratched his chin, played a bit with his big black moustache, and said, "Bon voyage, madame."

Sudden relief. My fears evaporated and, as if to avoid the possibility that he might change his mind, I hurried off with the children to the tax-free zone, found a public telephone, and called Thérèse Laatar.

"Everything went fine, there was no problem. We're going now to the departure gate," I told her. She seemed pleased too, wished me bon voyage, and hung up. I checked the number of our departure gate. We finally reached a large hall where I sat down with the children. The walls were decorated with beautiful Roman mosaics. As I sat thinking about the new life waiting for us, I admired the beauty of these works. Curiously, in the thousands of tiny pieces of stone glued one beside another to form everyday scenes of Roman life, I found a feast for the eyes that took my mind away from my sadness.

BACK IN CANADA

the storm begins . . .

NOVEMBER 15, 2002. The Air France plane touched down gently on the Dorval airport runway. From my seat in the centre of the aircraft, I tried to see through the window. I could see nothing. It was dark, perhaps eight or nine o'clock at night. Barâa had not slept at all during the flight; she was a little tired but delighted that she would soon be back in Ottawa. Houd had gone to sleep but was now awake. I offered him his pacifier and a small rattle, but he turned his head away. He was looking around and smiling at the other passengers instead. My heart was racing. What was in store for us? I was returning to Canada, but I felt as though I had lost all my happiness, as though a heavy weight was pressing down on me. It was all I could do to stand up. The flight attendant invited passengers with small children to leave the plane; I hurried on ahead. Houd's stroller was waiting at the beginning of the exit ramp. I put Houd in it, took Barâa by the hand, and prepared to make my way to the customs desk. A young black lady dressed in uniform had come to meet us. In planning our return journey, I had insisted to Mr. Pardy that I needed someone to help me, that I was worried about my children. Everything about my life now seemed to be uncertainty. I was looking hard for "official assurances," for some sense of security. I understood that the lady worked for the Montreal airport authority, but I was in another world and didn't even catch her name. We went to pick up our luggage, which I hefted onto a baggage cart, with the lady's help. The children were quiet, not knowing what was going on. At last we came to customs. A customs agent beckoned me forward. She wanted to search my belongings. She asked for my Canadian passport, I handed it to her, then she opened my bags. Where was I coming from? she asked. She wanted to see the children's travel documents too. I handed her Barâa's passport and Houd's travel document. She took them and went into a small office. I couldn't see anything. A minute passed, two, almost ten minutes, then she reappeared. Her stony expression unchanged, she searched again through my two duffle bags. Suddenly she happened upon a file box full of my favorite recipes. In an instant her eyes lit up, as if she had found what she was looking for, then she opened it, realized her stupid mistake, and put it back with a visible touch of disappointment. Then she asked to see my health insurance card, my credit cards, and even the cash I had on me. She counted out the American dollar bills one at a time and put them back in my wallet, asked for my Tunisian passport, and took it with all my other documents into the small office. The airport employee was still with us.

"I've never seen anything like this!" she said, rolling her eyes.

⁓

We waited. Still the agent didn't come back. The children were as if in a state of suspended animation. I was feeling more and more intimidated and uncomfortable. What should I do? On the one hand, I wanted to get it over with and leave, but on the other, I wanted to know why I was being treated this way. It was becoming increasingly clear to me that the agent was going into her small office to get orders from someone else, then coming back to carry them out. My stomach was churning. Was this a foretaste of the new life that awaited me outside the high, cold walls of the airport? Time passed, my patience was running out. I looked at the children; they were exhausted. We had left our house in Tunis early that morning and now it was almost ten o'clock at night, Montreal time. I saw the customs agent come back; she handed me my documents, then asked, "You're travelling alone? Where is your husband?"

That was the last straw. I couldn't restrain myself.

"Really! You go through this whole song and dance as if you don't know where my husband is? You wouldn't have done it if you didn't know where he was, isn't that so?" The agent defended herself. She didn't know anything about what was going on. She didn't follow the news, she said.

"You must follow the news because you work every day with people coming from abroad," I snapped back.

It was clear that she didn't like my replies. She ignored what I was saying. Now she wanted to be done with me, made a last cursory search through my belongings, then gave me permission to go. But I still had to hand Houd's travel document over to Immigration. I pushed the heavy baggage cart with the duffle bags almost dragging on the floor. Finally I found the right place. A smiling lady was waiting behind a window. She took the document, asked me a few questions, and was about to let me leave when the customs agent walked up with what seemed like a smirk on her face, called the immigration official, and the two left together to another office. Through a small window I could see them talking. Again I felt ill at ease. Was it humiliation, fear, or sadness that took hold of me? But I did nothing. I was too tired to react. Ten minutes later, the immigration officer came back, asked me a few questions, then let me leave. I was both relieved and despondent. My head was spinning, I had to get out of this place at all costs.

We were finally moving toward the exit when, out of the blue, I remembered that I had to stop off at the Lost and Found. My mother had reminded me to recover Maher's suitcase. It was a small room filled with travel bags of every size, shape, and colour – black, brown, white, damaged, crushed. Suitcases were everywhere, some leaning against the walls, some on shelves, others on the floor. Suddenly, my heart stopped beating. I spotted the blue suitcase and raised my head as if expecting to see Maher standing with a smile in front of his things. But it was only his suitcase. The lock had been broken. Gently I opened it: on top, I saw Houd's expired passport. It was among Maher's clothes. I closed the suitcase and put it on top of the duffle bags. The baggage cart could barely move. Pulling the stroller along behind me, we headed for the exit. Bassam and Taoufik, my brothers-in-law, were waiting for us. It was eleven o'clock at night. There was worry on their faces. They thought we had missed our flight. I felt the blood pounding in my temples. I clutched Barâa's little hand in mine. I could only think of one thing: to rest.

Bassam drove us through the dark, nearly deserted streets of Montreal. The children were asleep in the car, their heads drooping to one side. In silence, I watched the bleak buildings parading by. I was trying to focus on the new life, which was promising to be fraught with hardship and strain. This silent, gloomy trip taking me from the airport to my in-laws' house was very different from the one I had taken with Mourad from Mirabel airport to the Côte-des-Neiges district eleven years before. It had been my first visit to Canada. Mourad, who had been living here for years, had sponsored me to come and live and finish my studies in Canada. It was the first time I had set foot in a country other than Tunisia.

I had grown up reading books by French authors, speaking French at school, and watching European or American films on television. I dreamed of seeing cities such as Paris, Rome, and London, visiting their museums, walking their streets, and seeing the people I'd often read about. Emigrating to Canada meant an opportunity to step out of the world of books, to experience for myself what I had lived vicariously through reading. Canada would give me something my birth country had denied me, I thought: the opportunity to fulfill my intellectual capacities independently of my political or religious affiliations. In Tunisia, I belonged to no political movement or party; I had always protected my independence of thought.

At age twenty, after several years of reflection and meditation, I decided to cover my head and adopt a modest style of dress. I became a veiled young woman, in other words. It was my personal choice; by making it, I sought to deepen my spiritual life, to free myself from all the social pressures experienced by young women of my age. I felt that the girls I knew cared too much about their appearance and bodies and neglected their inner beauty, their natural and mystical attributes. Since my childhood, I had been fascinated by prayer, by the dialogue between human beings and their creator. Although they were practising Muslims, my parents never forced religion on us; they guided us, but let us choose our own way.

My choice drew several reactions: my close friends expected it, but others who didn't know me well were surprised and some were shocked. How can you be educated, middle-class, and wear a head scarf? How can you give up your freedom and cover your head with a symbol of women's submission or religious fundamentalism? But I had enjoyed a great deal of freedom in my parents' house; I didn't associate with religiously oriented political groups; I was not under anyone's influence. But the society I grew up in did not respect my personal choices nor my self-determination. In that society, success had a single face and a single name. When I received my Quebec selection certificate, then my Canadian landed immigrant status, I was jumping for joy. At last, a country where I could continue my studies, become the university professor I'd dreamed of becoming, without worrying about my appearance or my religious beliefs.

I shall never forget my fascination with Montreal's streets, so broad and impressive compared with the tortuous lanes of Tunis. Mourad drove us to his little apartment on Rue Decelles. I was happy, chattering non-stop, badgering him with question after question: "And what is this neighbourhood? And that cathedral, what's it called?" On and on I went, like a country kid discovering the lights of the city for the first time. I was enchanted, dazzled. Mourad laughed; it was culture shock, he told me. I didn't know what my brother was saying. I was feasting my eyes on all the space that was opening before me, I wanted to take in the smell of freedom in deep breaths; to make the new life that lay before me mine.

But on this day of return, I was far from dazzled; I was sad, pensive, and downcast. Silent, I waited for us to arrive at my in-laws' house, longing for the trip to be over so I could rest at last. Finally the car pulled up in front of the house; the lights were still lit; my mother-in-law was waiting at the door. Bassam carried Houd in his arms and I wakened Barâa gently so she could walk to the house. Quickly I undressed the children and got them into their pyjamas and into the big bed. My mother-in-law had laid a narrow mattress beside the big bed; this was where I would spend the night. I closed the door and went to the living room; it was almost midnight. My brothers-in-law had left, each to his own home. My mother-in-law was sitting in a rocking chair, her eyes were red. How she seemed to have aged!

"Good Lord, what is happening to us? Do you think we'll ever see Maher again?" she said, almost moaning.

"Yes, when God wills it," I replied.

"Try to get some sleep, Monia. You look exhausted. I'm going to stay up a while and go to bed a little later."

As if I had been waiting only to hear those words, I left at once and went to the bedroom. The children were sleeping peacefully; I kissed them, then slipped into bed on the mattress and quickly fell into a deep sleep.

The next day, Bassam drove me to pick up my car. Before leaving for Tunis the previous summer, we had left our car in the garage of some Montreal friends. I took Houd with us, leaving Barâa with her grandmother.

Houd would burst into tears every time he saw a new face. He didn't know where he was, what was happening to us. He had to see me, to feel my presence before he would calm down. All my efforts over the past months to have him get over his colicky period seemed to have been for nothing: he was like a baby only a few weeks old all over again. I was at my wits' end. People would ask me why Houd was afraid, why he was crying all the time. They had already forgotten that Houd was experiencing the tragedy of his father's disappearance in silence, that he didn't have words to express his grief and distress. He was the most fragile of us, but also the one least expected to show a reaction. We tend to think that babies can't understand, that they can't grasp the seriousness of situations. But I'm convinced that they need to feel safe and are constantly alert to signals in our voices, our eyes, our touch. If the signals don't give them assurance of safety, they will cry out for it. The sudden change in our lives had not been lost on Houd. He was living it every day and only a return to normal could bring him what he was asking for. I wanted to get back to Ottawa as quickly as possible. There I would feel at home; there I could give Barâa and Houd the semblance of stability they would need to deal with this new stage in their lives.

With my car retrieved, we drove back to my mother-in-law's to pick up Barâa, loaded our luggage into the car, and left for Ottawa, where my mother had been waiting for us since the day before. It was getting late; time for me to leave, get back among my own things, to my old routine. Maybe I could pick up pieces of my life as it was before . . .

Night had fallen when we finally reached Ottawa. The trip had gone well, the children had been good. I parked the car in front of the big white-and-brown building where we had moved before leaving for Tunis the previous summer. We had been renting the apartment for years for my mother. When she had come to live in our house to help with the children, Maher kept the apartment as an office for his consulting company. It was not far from Bayshore; last summer we had left our things there, not wanting to pay a high rent while we were away in Tunisia. Our plans were to rent a house when we came back. Maher's arrest had turned our plans upside down. From now on, this was where I would be living, with my mother and my two children.

Curiously, I felt relieved to be back in Ottawa. Was it nostalgia for the five years Maher and I had spent together in this city, or was I really feeling at home again? I didn't know for sure. I climbed the stairs with Houd in my arms and Barâa beside me to our second-floor apartment. I knocked at the door, then turned the keys and entered. My mother was sitting in front of the TV; she'd been expecting us. Barâa ran to her grandmother's arms and Houd began to cry, frightened as always. I was glad to see my mother again too. She was always there, always ready to help me without a word of complaint. She had always been at my side during my pregnancies and when I was preparing my thesis defence. Whenever I needed her, I could count on her. As I embraced my mother, I felt I had recovered a piece of my life before, with Maher. But unfortunately, deep down I knew that I had become a single parent, that I must accept the role and get used to it.

Before giving birth to Houd, I had had a research contract with a professor at the University of Ottawa. When Houd was a year old, I had planned to look for work again, teaching at a university, I hoped. A year before, I had completed a doctorate in finance at the McGill University Faculty of Management. I had had two job interviews, one with the École des hautes études commerciales de Montréal and the other with the University of Ottawa. I had been certain that I would be accepted and I would be offered the job, but both times I was turned down. Budgetary restrictions, they told me. Yet I was perfectly bilingual with a fresh degree from one of the most prestigious business schools in Canada. I'd suspected that my head scarf may have bothered certain members of the selection committee, but I had no proof and had to accept the verdict with bitter disappointment. One day I would succeed, I reassured myself. I would be teaching in a management department.

But on this, my first day back in Ottawa, everything had changed. There I was, sitting in our small apartment with my mother and my children, eating in silence. My struggle would be a different one now. It was going to be a near-impossible task, and I knew it. With my husband suspected of terrorism, thrown into a Syrian prison thousands of kilometres away, two children to look after, and a political and social climate of fear and paranoia, how could I possibly win my wager? Questions spun in my head, questions I didn't want to answer. The best I could do was let them keep spinning. Hope and doubt clashed in my mind; I amused myself keeping both alive. I wanted the battle to be ongoing, for it never to end. Whenever I felt doubt gaining the upper hand, I would give myself thousands of reasons for believing that Maher would be back, that everything would be over, and I would suddenly come alive again and gain strength. Then slowly but surely, doubt would creep in and the questions would return to haunt me; where there had been hope, now doubt would reign.

The next day, I went to see the principal of the nearby school and registered Barâa for first grade. She had already missed two months of school and I was anxious for her to return to a semblance of normalcy. She was pleased finally to have friends, to play with children her own age, and to be learning to read. Since her father's arrest, she had grown more mature. Was it her natural sense of responsibility coming to the fore in order to help me, was she trying to understand the meaning of things, or was it the burden she must have felt she was bearing that made her seem wise beyond her years? Or robbed her of part of her innocence? The two of us went off to buy a school bag, a lunch box, and some new clothes.

Houd's constant crying was breaking my heart; he would not recognize my mother and calmed down only when I was with him. Luckily, I remembered leaving a little swing in the basement of the building. I went to get it and put Houd in it. It had a little crank that would swing Houd gently back and forth. He liked the floating feeling and began to smile and doze off. I looked at this scene: Houd nodding in his swing, my mother in the kitchen, and Barâa stretched out on the sofa smoothing her new clothes. Our lives were slowly getting back to normal; slowly, painfully; each of us searching for a new meaning.

But thousands of kilometres away, behind bars, Maher was living a tragedy far beyond what we could ever have imagined. What was he doing? Where exactly was he? What was he eating? I knew nothing whatsoever. True enough, following his first consular visit, Mr. Pardy had informed me Maher was well, but how could a few lines of email possibly heal my soul and calm my beating heart? I read those words dozens of times and found nothing: they were cold and futile. I wanted more, I wanted details, but I was wasting my breath. Mr. Pardy kept assuring me that it was fortunate that Mr. Martel could visit Maher at all. As if he was trying to convince me that justice was too much to ask for, that I should accept fate and be quiet.

NOVEMBER 18, 2002. My arrival in Ottawa had not gone unnoticed by the press. While still in Tunis, I had told several journalists who were asking for news of Maher that I would be coming home soon, but I didn't tell them the exact date. I didn't want to have a crowd waiting at Dorval airport. Once back in Ottawa, I wanted to continue what I had begun in Tunis: to share my story and my husband's with the Canadian people and to demand response and action from the Canadian government. Lee Greenberg of the *Ottawa Citizen* called me for an interview. He had found the number in the phone book. I had no idea what strategies were best to follow in dealing with the media, I was only following my heart. I felt the injustice done to Maher so deeply that I was willing to try anything to set it right.

The apartment was a mess, full of duffle bags still stuffed with books, clothes, and toys, not to mention boxes of this and that from our move the previous summer. But I had no time to put the place in order.

I agreed to meet Lee at a nearby Tim Hortons. It was dark by now, so I drove there. I found Lee at a table with a photographer. The interview began with Lee asking how I had met Maher and when we had married. I particularly liked this question as it took me back eight years to when I was twenty-four. I was finishing my master's degree in finance at the École des hautes études commerciales de Montréal. Maher and I met through a friend of my brother. I had been living with my brother, Mourad, since arriving as an immigrant in Montreal; he and I were both students. My days were devoted to my studies: this was my new life in Canada. Mourad was working toward his doctorate in applied mathematics at the École polytechnique. To cover our expenses, he always managed to land an academic excellence scholarship or part-time jobs as research assistant or lecturer. At twenty-four, I wanted to meet someone special, to get married and start a family. When Maher came to visit us one day at our Decelles Avenue apartment, I immediately liked his bright smile and his sense of humour. We continued to see each other and talk; it was not long before we had made up our minds to get married. Maher was completing his B.A. in computer engineering and was assembling and selling computers on the side. Our lives at the time were full of academic work and challenges; we were not rich, but I had been awarded a scholarship to begin my doctorate at McGill and that was enough for us. We were happy and never lost hope.

As I talked to Lee about this phase of our lives, I repeated that Maher was innocent and didn't deserve to be in prison. I also talked to Lee about the message Maher had sent through Mr. Pardy, in which he told us he loved us very much and that he was blameless.

"It's true that this message comforts me. At least I know he's still alive. But I didn't ask the Canadian government to visit him. I asked them to bring him back home to his family."

As I spoke, Lee was taking notes fast and furiously for fear of losing a word or expression, and the photographer was snapping dozens of pictures. I had never intended to have my picture published in the papers because I am a reserved, private person – particularly in circumstances like these. But now, I felt my back was to the wall; speaking out was the only strategy I had left.

I went home, exhausted by the interview. I didn't realize how taxing it could be. The children were still awake; Barâa was colouring and Houd was still in his swing. The three of us retired to the bedroom with its big bed and cot, while my mother slept on the sofa-bed in the living room. Things were cramped, but being close to one another helped us cope with the sadness that seemed to hover in the apartment. As usual, I read Barâa a story while Houd listened in silence, sitting contentedly on my lap. Then, softly, we said a prayer, and I put out the light. My mother was watching the news on television; she would nod off, then open her eyes and pretend to be watching, but I knew she was tired. There was nothing of interest on the news, and besides, I'd been reading it all day long on the Internet. I turned off the set, said good night to my mother, and went back to the bedroom to lie down beside the children.

NOVEMBER 19, 2002. I had an appointment with Gar Pardy. I had yet to meet him in person, even though I had spoken to him many times from Tunisia and had found him polite and courteous. He was adept at beating around the bush and repeating the same thing; although I often tried to put words in his mouth, it was a waste of time, particularly with a career diplomat like him. But today, I was in an optimistic mood, and once again my mind was full of questions. Perhaps there would be some new development; perhaps there would be some good news for me. I was always hopeful.

It was my first visit to Foreign Affairs, on Sussex Drive; it would not be my last. The huge building reminded me of an ocean liner docked at a wharf. I parked my car behind the building and went in, feeling tiny and fragile. At the reception desk I gave my name, mentioning that I had an appointment with Mr. Pardy. Someone came to escort me to his office. Gar Pardy was a tall man with a salt-and-pepper beard. He must have been about fifty. His spacious office was lined with pictures meant to attest to his competence and years of government service. He had twinkling, mischievous eyes; there was nothing condescending in his manner. He introduced me to his assistant, a tall, slender lady named Myra Pastyr-Lupul.

This meeting got off to a curious start: I wanted Mr. Pardy to tell me when Maher was going to return to Canada, and Mr. Pardy wanted to convince me that the Canadian government was doing everything in its power to free Maher. But he did not want to give me any guarantee or any promise. Every time I tried to pin him down, he would become evasive and promise only that Maher would be back one day. I found his words refreshing, encouraging, and in contrast to the worrisome silence of the politicians. Was it possible that Mr. Pardy knew something the politicians did not, or was it a tactic to lead me on? I spent almost two hours with Mr. Pardy and his assistant. I asked the questions, Mr. Pardy did the talking, and Myra took notes in silence. Sometimes the expression on her face changed, but that was all.

When I left the meeting, I felt I was walking on air. I went home imagining that things would soon work out for Maher. I'd felt the same way in the beginning, after Maher's arrest, when I believed that it was only a matter of time before he would be back. Mr. Pardy's words comforted me; they told me that the Department of Foreign Affairs was not aware of any proof of terrorism against my husband. Why, then, weren't the politicians raising a hue and cry? Why weren't they demanding Maher's return? I couldn't understand. When the journalists began to phone and ask what had happened at the meeting, I told them the thrust of my questions.

"I would like to see Jean Chrétien, John Manley, or other high officials say that my husband is innocent, and take action to bring him back to Canada. I want the Canadian government to clarify its position concerning my husband. Why is he still surrounded by this cloud of mystery?"

Without realizing and without any ulterior motive, I was making certain people in Ottawa uncomfortable and putting the government on the defensive.

The next day I went to see Michael Edelson. I was curious to hear about the legal side of this case from him. I had never paid Mr. Edelson any money; a friend of Maher, who was himself a lawyer, had raised $2,000 and turned the sum over to him. I wanted to know what he intended to do, and what he could do. He received me in a conference room at his office on Elgin Street. I told him everything that had happened, my ordeal at the Ministry of the Interior in Tunisia, how I had been treated at customs on my arrival in Canada. He took notes and asked some questions. He talked to me about the strategy he intended to follow.

"I think the best way to proceed in this case is to obtain a letter from the RCMP attesting that Maher has no link with terrorism. With such a letter, we can meet with the Americans and the Syrians and request that he be released. I have already tried this strategy for Liban Hussain, and I am quite confident it will work for Maher. I'll coordinate my efforts with Gar Pardy."

He told me he would soon request a meeting with senior police officers to inform them of his strategy and ask for their co-operation. I couldn't hope for better. I thought he was right, that we absolutely needed such a letter to free Maher. In my eyes, my whole future and the future of my entire family depended on a letter, or a few words at least, to remove any doubt and confirm that Maher was not a terrorist. How naive I was, how carried away by my optimism.

Meetings, television, press and radio interviews: this was the new life that awaited me in Ottawa. Every morning I rose and prepared Barâa's lunch, gave her breakfast, then drove her to school. Then I returned home to look after Houd, who was now crawling around on his bottom and prying into every corner of the apartment. The little swing was my saviour: it rocked him gently and continuously and he went to sleep there when he was tired. My mother was not attending adult English classes any more; now she stayed at home, looking after Houd when I went out to appointments, and doing the cooking. She had become such a great help to me I couldn't imagine life without her. But I couldn't let her do any heavy work. Any time I stayed at home, I was the one who did the cleaning and the laundry.

For now, we were getting by on the savings that Maher had left. But I knew that I would soon need money to pay the rent, car expenses, and food. I needed a job. My hope was to sign a contract for research or as a lecturer at the University of Ottawa. I called on the professor for whom I had done research work before taking maternity leave. I felt a bit uncomfortable, as if I was asking for charity. Could he help me find a position as lecturer? I asked; I spoke fluent French, had a doctorate in finance, and could teach a variety of courses in either language. However, throughout the conversation, I felt I had no chance; the professor was cautious, cordial, and extremely vague. Not wanting to embarrass him, I picked up my bag and left but not in anger. I knew it was going to be difficult to get back into the job market. When people met me, they were mistrustful, unwilling to take a risk. It was up to me to be more flexible, to look for work below my qualifications. Every day, I spent hours in front of the computer screen looking for job openings, ready to send off my resumé whenever I thought I could do the work. No one even answered. Was it bad luck, or the fact that people recognized my name? I couldn't know and will never know. From then on, I would have to get used to the consequences of my husband's arrest and the suspicion surrounding him. But being prepared to adapt to this new life didn't mean accepting the injustice, didn't mean bowing my head and leaving the field open to others to do whatever they pleased. No, I was determined to accept my difficult living conditions and to learn to cope with them just as I was learning to fight the prejudice and injustice that was afflicting all of us.

I did everything I could to give the children a semblance of tranquility; they should not have to share the doubt that would sweep over me. Every day I made an effort to show them that they were normal children who loved to play and laugh and dream, not the children of that strange character whose pictures were being shown on TV. It was not shame that upset me, but the fear that my children would grow up under a cloud. I registered Barâa for swimming lessons, the same ones she had been taking before Maher's arrest. I took the children and my mother with me to do routine shopping. We also went to visit our old friends, Racha and Ahmed. We talked about Maher, of course, but we also talked about children, school, and life. I took Houd out in his stroller for short walks in the little park beside our building. He would come back with rosy cheeks, looking refreshed and happy. Come evening, once the children were in bed I would sit down at my computer and read and answer my emails, draft letters, and read everything I could find on the Internet about Maher.

Sometimes I would reminisce, in the hope of briefly retrieving some long-lost moments of happiness. I remember Maher at a Baskin-Robbins in Montreal, asking the waitress in French for a cone with two scoops of ice cream. I laughed till I cried to hear him pronounce the word *boules* (scoops); he could not for the life of him get his tongue around the "oo" sound. Maher had learned French in Montreal. In Syria, most of his classes had been in Arabic. He had some classes in English but never any French; the only word of French he knew before coming to Montreal was *merci*. Syria was an exceedingly nationalistic country that had always insisted on the use of Arabic, and cultivated feelings of Arab identity and Arab unity. Only a social and intellectual élite spoke French, and Maher's family was not part of it. But when he immigrated to Quebec, Maher had made up his mind to learn French. He didn't want to go to Ontario to escape Bill 101, as many other families did. He stayed in Montreal and became familiar with the French culture. Sometimes when he was in a bad mood, he would say, "Oh, I'm always the oldest in my class because of those two years I spent learning French. At my age I should have finished my B.A. by now." Then immediately he would think again and say, "But at least I speak both English and French, don't I? You know what? Two years is nothing in a person's life!" But he just couldn't pronounce the "oo" sound. Now and then, just for fun, he would repeat the word *boules* several times in front of me; it was all I could do to stifle my laughter each time he muffed it. Those moments from the past would rush back into my mind every time I wrote him a letter.

Since my return, I had wanted to visit Alexa McDonough. I made an appointment and went to see her at her office in the Central Block of the Parliament Buildings. She was busy when I arrived and I waited in her office, looking at all the books and art works on the shelves. I smiled; I had never visited a political personality before. In Tunisia, such a thing was out of the question. It was a police state; politicians were seen as being above the common herd, a race seen only on TV. When I immigrated to Canada, I kept up with political issues by reading the papers and listening to the radio, but I had never had an opportunity to meet a politician. When Marlene Catterall and Alexa McDonough both phoned me in Tunisia and showed me so much sympathy and interest, I was impressed: first by their integrity and courage, but also by seeing a concrete example of how a democratic system works for the first time in my life. The very people who were responsible for making laws and regulations had called me, had approached me, without my asking. It was clear that I must work, do whatever it took to keep up my confidence in the system, fight to keep myself from falling prey to skepticism.

When Alexa McDonough entered the office, she found me lost in thought. She was warm and there was compassion in her eyes. She put me at ease at once and listened with close attention. I told her about my efforts to get the government to move, and how disappointed I was to see so little action taken to bring Maher home. She understood what I was telling her, and promised that this was a case she was not about to let drop. That sentence alone meant a great deal to me. It told me that in my solitude, in the isolation I was experiencing, there were people who were with me, supporting me, that they would not let me sink into bitterness or, worse, give up my fight. I told her about my idea of sending a letter to Prime Minister Chrétien and she promised to help me deliver it. She radiated optimism in her smile and her bearing. I felt a surge of hope well up in me; things were becoming clearer. As long as I had people like her to rely on, I wouldn't stop. Before I left, Alexa asked me if I knew Nazira Tareen.

"Nazira," I repeated. "No, I don't know the name."

"She's an extraordinary woman, you must meet her. I met her when I went to visit the main Ottawa mosque with Prime Minister Chrétien just after the events of 9/11. I've talked to her about you and she's anxious to meet you. We'll certainly talk some more about it. Someone in my office will get in touch with you and we'll arrange something."

"Yes, we'll keep in touch," I told her.

It was dark outside as I walked down the majestic white marble staircase and left the imposing walls of Parliament. An icy wind was blowing off the Ottawa River; I buttoned up my coat and quickened my pace to get to the parking lot.

Michael Edelson had promised to call me back with the results of his meeting with the senior RCMP officers. All my hopes were riding on the letter he had requested; my anxiety was high. The month of Ramadan was almost over; perhaps with the celebration of Eid-al-Fitr, which ends the holy month, Maher and I would be reunited. Secretly, to protect myself against discouragement, I dreamed that the Syrians would release him as a goodwill gesture, that everything would return to the way it was before. Maher had been in prison for two months now, and I could see no end to the ordeal short of a miracle. Though I was fighting tooth and nail, doing everything in my power, there were no concrete results. At night I would go to bed tired, full of despair, but every morning I would wake up filled with hope and energy. It was as if the night erased my pain and revived my courage. Journalists would call to ask if anything was happening. For me, every hour and every day brought something new. But the journalists cared little about the challenges of my everyday life; my husband's case was what interested them.

"Have charges been laid against him?"

How often had I heard the question? Yet I knew nothing more than they did: my husband was in a Syrian prison, suspected of terrorism, of belonging to the al-Qaeda network. That was what Gar Pardy kept telling me on the telephone. Were those words that came from Maher's mouth? I asked.

"No, the Syrians are telling us that Maher is a terrorist," he replied.

"But why would the Syrians know anything about Maher when he hasn't lived in the country for seventeen years? What is Canada's role in this? Why isn't it doing anything? Don't you think Canada should have information about Maher; shouldn't it be up to Canada to bring him to justice? Why are we leaving Maher to the Syrians?"

In a way, this was the same dialogue of the deaf I had been having with Mr. Pardy from the start: me trying to get him to talk and he trying to convince me that Canada was working diligently on Maher's case. But when this particular discussion with him had ended, I had a strange feeling. I had the impression I had convinced him – but I was not sure he was going to be heard by others in his department. It had begun to occur to me that decisions were being taken at other levels, in other departments.

Ottawa, November 22, 2002.

Dear Maher,

It is now nine days since I returned to Ottawa with our two children. I cannot describe to you my sadness to see our home and know this time that you are not with us. But don't worry, I am confident that, with the grace of God, we will be reunited and will be able to resume our lives with our two children. Barâa is well and keeps asking for news of you. She says she loves you and sends you a very big kiss.

Houd was a little upset by all the changes, but has been calmer the last few days. I am doing everything I possibly can to see you back here in Ottawa and am confident that you will be soon. Keep up your spirits, I'm proud of you, and I will never let you down. All our love and all our prayers are with you. Your parents and brothers send their greetings. Monia, Barâa and Houd.

NOVEMBER 26, 2002. This morning I spoke to Myra, Mr. Pardy's assistant. She told me earlier that the Canadian consul to Syria, Leo Martel, was scheduled to visit Maher again, and I was anxious to know what had happened. She had not yet received the report of the meeting, she told me, but promised to send it to me as soon as she did. Where exactly were those visits being held, I wanted to know. Myra told me the consul himself didn't know where he was being taken. He would arrive at a meeting point, where he would driven by the Syrian secret service in a car with curtained windows so he could not determine the route. Was the place a prison or a house or a detention centre? I wondered. Everything was shrouded in mystery.

When I turned on my computer the next morning, an email from Myra was waiting in my box. She wrote:

Monia,

We received the report of the meeting this morning. Maher was very grateful for the visit from the consul. Your letter was delivered to him. He dictated the following response for you:

"I would like to thank you again for keeping me up to date on your situation of the kids. I see hope in the words you write me. One thing I would like to say. I miss you and the kids and I miss the good time together. You are the most wonderful wife in the world. Lastly, I would like to teach Barâa the story from Joseph. Even though he was innocent, he was put in prison. I want Barâa to stay proud of her father. Last issue, I wish to know about the health of my mother. I love you all."

But the message had a new element. Now Maher was asking me to send him money; he wanted $300 American for his personal needs. I was shocked. Not only had he been thrown into prison, but I had to send him money too. I smiled, remembering a story I had heard about a dissident killed by a repressive regime: to add to the family's woes, the government had demanded that they pay for the bullet that had killed him. I didn't know whether this was a true story, but I saw a similarity with what was happening to me. What was Maher going to do with the money? Pay *baksheesh* to the guards, perhaps? Buy his prison uniform and soap? All these questions remained unanswered. But I couldn't refuse his request, knowing that Maher was in need and that whatever money I could send him would certainly help him in prison. Myra explained the procedure for transferring money. With a mixture of resignation and despair, I made the transfer.

Michael Edelson had still not called. I called his office and made an appointment. He met me in the same conference room as our first meeting. He did all the talking. He told me he had met a Mr. Michel Cabana of the RCMP, and asked him for a letter stating that Maher was not linked to terrorist activities in Canada. Mr. Edelson did not seem very happy; I sensed that things were not moving in the right direction.

"Here is what I received," he said, handing me a letter. I opened it and read:

> *Mr. Edelson, your letter dated October 31, 2002, to Me Ann Alder in the matter of Maher Arar refers. While I sympathize with the present situation of Mr. Arar's family and your plight in securing his release and return to Canada, I am not in a position to acquiesce your request at this time. As you can understand, the RCMP, as a matter of course, does not involve itself in subjects of foreign policies. Furthermore, it would be improper for me to comment on Mr. Arar's present situation relative to our ongoing investigation. At this juncture, I can only confirm that the RCMP did not play any role relative to Mr. Arar's present*

situation. The RCMP was only advised of Mr. Arar's transfer to Syria after the fact. I can also confirm that Mr. Arar does not have a criminal record in Canada. I apologize for not being of more assistance and recommend that you pursue diplomatic channels. . . .

I didn't want to read the letter to the end. I couldn't believe my eyes; I almost wanted to burst out laughing. I smiled, but I felt like crumpling the letter in my hands. I restrained myself.

"Why have they refused to give us the letter we wanted?" I asked.

"Because, according to them, they never write such letters."

"Even if my husband was kidnapped by the Americans and is languishing in a Syrian prison?" I said without looking up.

"That is their position and I couldn't convince them otherwise."

At that moment I realized that Mr. Edelson could do no more; he had done what he could do and, like me, he felt he had come up against a stone wall. I muttered some almost inaudible words to thank him for his help and his effort. Inside, I knew I had lost another battle.

By the end of November, I could feel that the journalists' interest in our case was dwindling. There was no fresh information; they couldn't keep reporting on me repeating the same story. For years I had been reserved, attached to my quiet, peaceful life; but now I was praying for something, anything, to happen. Something had to give, something new had to turn up: a letter, a comment, a politician with something to say. But wherever I turned, there was only silence. Was it the calm before the storm or was it the perpetual silence I must henceforth live with, having learned to master my anxiety? I wrote letters to the prime minister that I didn't send. I read them and reread them; they weren't right. My writing in English struck me as awful. I had written plenty of technical articles in English but had zero experience writing to politicians. Sometimes I would turn on my computer and read the different versions I had saved. But I could never make up my mind to send one. In Tunisia I was convinced that, once back in Canada, I would be able to work miracles; I could meet people, mobilize public opinion, make demands, and get results. But I was living in the clouds, caught up in a case that was too complex for me.

Since my return to Ottawa I had realized that life didn't revolve around Maher alone, that life went on – even without him. I understood more clearly now that over the past months I had been in shock, attempting to deny my new reality. In the last few days, I came to recognize the obvious: that Maher would not be coming home right away, that his case was going to take months, or years, or perhaps an eternity. Gradually, I was accepting my lot with a sense of resignation and serenity that I had not felt before. Admitting as much enabled me to continue my life in peace. I no longer strained to have it back exactly as it had been; I understood that it would never again be as it once was. But I promised myself to fight to have Maher treated with dignity and fairness. Ever since his arrest, I had been convinced of his innocence; what had upset me most was the way he was being treated, that he had been denied any form of justice. He had been robbed of his right to any form of trial or defence. And I, who had always believed in the rule of law and a just system founded on respect for the law, not on arbitrary decisions, was seeing my dreams being shattered. Doubt was gnawing at me; there was no way to know if Maher's case was an isolated one or whether it was the beginning of collapse of the presumption of innocence, the principle of "innocent until proven guilty." It was becoming vital for me to keep helping Maher, not only because he was my husband, the father of my children, my life partner, but also because I felt that our collective silence would be interpreted by those responsible for this tragedy as implicit consent to continue behaving as they were doing.

EARLY DECEMBER 2002. Ramadan had come to an end; I was dreading the thought of spending the first day of the Eid holiday with Maher far away from us. Pretending that our life was normal, I bought gifts for the children and new clothes, and the day before Eid, my mother and I made some little cakes. On the morning of Eid, we all went to prayers. People had thronged into a large hall rented for the occasion. We sat in the section reserved for women; the noise was deafening, exacerbated by a sputtering sound system and the constant wailing of babies. I found a place near the door where we could all sit together. The children didn't say a word. My mother scanned the faces of the women in the hope of finding an old acquaintance, but there was only a mass of well-dressed women practically scintillating beneath their jewels, greeting one another and talking and ignoring the male voice speaking and preaching at the microphone. The prayers were over quickly; I was eager to hear the sermon, looking for words of comfort, spiritual words to help me rise above the silence and fill the void in my heart. I held Houd on my knees, making efforts to hear through the noise of the women's laughter and greetings. The words reached me fragmented, piecemeal, but I understood that, on this day of Eid, the imam was speaking of love and compassion: "Today is a day for joy, put aside your troubles and thank God for . . ." But this was not the message I wanted to hear. Hope was what I wanted, words about justice and patience. Many women were standing and continuing to talk together while others knelt, resting on their heels, trying to capture a few intelligible words in this chaos of noise. I was disappointed, not finding peace in the words I had come to hear; I waited patiently for the imam to finish, my thoughts elsewhere. I was thinking of Maher. Did he know this was the day of Eid? What was he doing?

When it was over, I rose, kissed my mother, and wished her a happy Eid. We went home, but the atmosphere was gloomy and for some reason I was yearning to be alone. The children were happy with their gifts. We all played together and I didn't realize how fast the time was passing. That night as I lay down to sleep, I felt my tears begin to flow and I silently prayed to God to help me find the joy the imam had spoken of that morning.

Ottawa, December 6, 2002.

Dear Maher,

Today is Eid. A different kind of Eid this time, the first one since we were married that you are not with us. The children were beautiful in their new clothes. Barâa wore a mauve dress with a little lace vest sewn with satin flowers, and Houd a dark brown velvet jumper with a checkered shirt. I bought them some gifts. We miss you a lot, you know. All our prayers are for you, to see you back with us at last. Barâa has sent you a greeting card, I hope you will be able to read it. I have sent you $200 American, I presume that the Canadian consul will give it to you. I wish you much courage, and keep well. Your mother is in good health. She is praying for you. Monia, Barâa and Houd.

The telephone rang. It was Anthony, Alexa McDonough's assistant. He was passing on an invitation from Nazira Tareen. On the occasion of Eid, she was giving a little party at her house and inviting a large number of women, including Alexa and me.

"Don't forget, next Monday around noon or one o'clock. Alexa will be there and is looking forward to seeing you."

"Yes, I'll be there," I replied.

It would be a great opportunity for me to win support and tell Maher's story to more people and ask them to take action. Ever since the first days after Maher's arrest, I had made up my mind not to ask for help from private individuals unless they wished to give it. I knew that some people were afraid to be associated with me or with my husband; I didn't want to embarrass them or make them feel obliged to help me. But when someone held out a hand, I never refused it. The hand that Nazira was extending meant a lot to me. I didn't know this woman; I had heard from Alexa that she was president of a Muslim women's organization in Ottawa and that she was active in the community. She didn't know me but wanted to help. I was very happy to go to the party and promised myself to make good use of the opportunity.

DECEMBER 9, 2002. Monday finally came. Barâa was at school, I left Houd with my mother, took my car, and left for Nazira's. She lived not far from me in a fine residential neighbourhood with big, beautiful houses. I knocked at the door shyly. A middle-aged lady with sparkling eyes, dressed in an Indian sari, opened the door with a big smile.

"Oh, it's you, Monia, I recognize you from TV. Come in, come in, I'm Nazira. Alexa's not here yet, but she'll be here soon."

And so, as if we had known each other for years, as naturally and easily as could be, I stepped inside Nazira's house. The other guests had already gathered in small groups. I was ill at ease, not knowing anyone. In the dining room, tables against the wall were laden with food: meatballs, morsels of grilled chicken, sauces of every colour, different kinds of rice, dishes I had never seen before but that looked appetizing; fruits, exotic pastries – a feast, in short. I sat down on a sofa and looked at the women around me. They were of diverse origins: South Asian, Arab, Western . . . Many knew one another and were talking together. Nazira was very busy in the kitchen, bringing some last dishes out to the dining room. Then she came to invite all the guests to take plates and cutlery and go and serve themselves. It was like a buffet, each waiting her turn and, with her plate filled, going to sit in a chair or on the sofa in the living room. I did as all the others and went to the living room to sit and enjoy this food. Alexa arrived with her press secretary. She came to greet me and ask about my news. Nazira would come from time to time to ask if everything was going all right; she introduced me to several women.

"This is Monia Mazigh, the wife of Maher Arar, the Canadian in prison in Syria. We have to do something to help her," she would say.

Sometimes the woman knew about the affair, expressed her indignation, and I stayed with her to talk a while, but other times she knew nothing about it or showed little interest and the conversation would end abruptly. When all the women were seated in the living room, Nazira stood up and gave a little speech. After wishing everyone a joyous Eid, she introduced all the distinguished persons present; there were doctors, diplomats' wives, and of course Alexa McDonough. Near the end, she turned toward me and said, loud enough for everyone to hear:

"I'd like to present a courageous woman who is fighting to see her husband again. We have to help her today and I want you to hear her story. Meet Monia Mazigh, the wife of Maher Arar."

I was caught off guard; Nazira was asking me to speak before all these women. There was a lump in my throat, but I remembered that this was my chance and I must make good use of it. Suddenly the words came to my rescue and I spoke of my life since Maher's arrest. The disappearance, the anxiety, the imprisonment, the deportation, the appalling silence and the government's foot-dragging, the way my family's life had been turned upside down, the uncertainty. I spoke looking straight ahead of me, staring at an invisible point the better to concentrate, though once in a while I would look at the women around me and see some who, minutes before, had been carefree, happy, and laughing now blowing their noses and wiping away tears. What had I done? Was it my words, my story, or my expression that had moved them? I remained standing a minute, then sat down. Alexa thanked me, spoke of the importance of preserving human rights even at the most difficult times, and told the gathering of women that they must do something together. Nazira agreed and asked, What could they do? Someone spoke of a march by women and children, then the word *vigil* was heard.

"A vigil, yes, a vigil, that's what we need!" exclaimed Nazira.

I liked the idea. Everyone else seemed to like it too.

"We'll light candles and gather before Parliament," said a lady. "We'll spread the word, each of us through our families and friends. . . ."

Alexa also promised to help spread the word. I was saying nothing, my heart was beating with joy, at last I had help; I was thanking God: hope had won.

When I said goodbye to Nazira and kept repeating my thanks, she hugged me and said, "Don't worry, keep your chin up."

It was almost three-thirty; Barâa would be getting out of school. I left to pick her up, Nazira's words dancing in my ears.

DECEMBER 10, 2002. I received the report of Consul Leo Martel's third visit to Maher. Ironically, it had occurred on the very day when the United Nations was celebrating human rights. Strange: these reports, which were often accompanied by messages, should have had a soothing effect, but they didn't – quite the opposite. I had become reluctant even to read them. They were ridiculous. According to them, Maher was fine and had everything he needed. I didn't believe those words; I was certain they had been dictated for him. Worse yet, they angered me, reminding me of the injustice done to us, and the uncertainty we were living under; they were only another way to show disdain for us, as far as I could see. However, as I felt time passing, and the visits became less frequent, those same messages became important to me. So I would wait impatiently, yearning to read the phony words that made me grind my teeth but that told me at least that Maher was still alive.

> *Dear Monia,*
> *I hope that you and the kids are doing fine, I myself feel desperate and helpless but when I read your words I see the light at the end of the tunnel. Hopefully my stay in this town is going to be short. Just keep sending me letters and I would like to say that you are the most*

wonderful wife. I love you and I love the kids. Thank you for the money and for the photos. I hope you have passed a good Eid even though I was not there. My hope is to be with you for the next Eid. I will always be a sincere husband. Kiss the kids for me.

If I could not find work, I would soon have trouble making ends meet. I sent off my resumé to Marlene Catterall's office, asking for her help in my search: either I was overqualified or, I was told, other people were better qualified. The result was the same: I was not getting hired. The thought of applying for social assistance embarrassed me. With all my degrees, I told myself, the social workers would laugh at me. One day when I was talking to Marlene, she said, "Why should you be embarrassed? You and your husband both paid income tax when you worked, so now that you're in need, don't hesitate to ask for help." Her words made sense, the words of a politician who knew how things happen, while I was thinking like the immigrant who wants to look perfect and stand proud. With her encouragement, I called the special line to file an application and set up an appointment with a social worker.

Social assistance was handled by the city of Ottawa. At the appointed hour, I presented myself to the receptionist, who took my name and asked me to take a seat in the waiting room. Several other people were waiting in silence, most of them immigrants or refugees. I had all the required papers for the application with me and was praying to God that I would be accepted. I knew that the money I would receive was not a fortune, but it would help me pay the rent and buy food. After a short wait, a lady who spoke French with an Eastern European accent called my name. She led me into a tiny cubicle with a table in the middle, offered me a chair, and sat at the other side of the table. It was as if I were in a cage. The session began with a review of my identification papers, my citizenship status, the ages of my children.

Everything seemed to be going well. I explained my husband's situation and my problems finding work. Then I had to divulge everything about real estate, financial, or other assets. I had a car, I told her.

"What year?"

"1999."

"How much do you think you could sell it for?"

"Uh, I don't know, it must be worth around ten thousand dollars," I replied, not understanding where she was leading. It was not long before I found out.

"Well, madame, to qualify for social assistance, your car cannot be worth more than around six thousand dollars. What you must do now is sell your car and spend the difference; then you can come back and see us."

I was stunned. "I can't sell my car, I have two young children, I can't get around without it!" I said as if trying to make her take pity on me.

She didn't so much as blink; she was used to hearing all kinds of stories, I reasoned, and made no exceptions.

"Then, if I understand correctly," I said, "I should come here almost as a beggar, no clothes, just rags, no car, to beseech you. Is that what I'm supposed to do?"

"Madame, social welfare is for people who have nothing. You must spend everything you have, then apply again."

Then, as if to tell me she had other fish to fry, she stood up. I was seething inside. I wanted to tell her she had no heart; she wasn't a social worker, she was a social policewoman. But I knew I would not say any of this, that I would swallow the pill just as I had swallowed others. Regretting that I'd come in the first place, I left.

"I shouldn't have gone, or even asked for social assistance," I told my mother when I got home.

"Why? Did they turn you down?" she asked.

"Yes, the social worker told me I'd have to sell the car because you can only own a car worth six thousand dollars or less."

"Are they crazy or what?" my mother shot back. "It's not even your car, it belongs to Maher."

Her words struck me like a lightning bolt. For a moment I sat there, gaping. It was true; why hadn't I thought of it before? All the car's papers were in his name. Even far away in his prison, he was helping me! I kissed my mother for her presence of mind and perspicacity, forgot my distress of moments before, and resolved to apply again.

⁓

I couldn't see how Maher was going to get out of prison. The last time I had spoken to Michael Edelson, he had told me practically nothing more could be done to help him, at least from a legal standpoint. All that remained was to speak to the media and win the support of public opinion; but even that was not so easy any more. The journalists' interest was fading; there were no developments, nothing new to report. Bassam, Maher's brother, called me almost every day. He was representing the family and accompanied me when I had important meetings with Mr. Pardy. We would talk on the telephone and discuss ways of getting Maher out of prison, conversations that, above all, indirectly provided mutual moral support and comfort. One day Bassam called to say that the president of Syria would be visiting in England between December 15 and 17 and then would be going on to France.

"How about trying to contact a human rights organization in France to ask for their help?" he suggested. I thought it over for a few moments.

"We could call Reporters Without Borders, or perhaps *Le Monde, Courrier International,* Radio France Internationale, *Libération* . . . Yes, it's a good idea," I exclaimed. "I'll contact them, we can ask them if they're interested in covering the case."

I hung up and went at once to my computer to find a phone number for Reporters Without Borders in France. It was easy, and without a minute's hesitation I called Paris. I wanted to act fast; Bashar al-Assad had finished his visit to London and was on his way to Paris and I didn't want to miss my chance. A Parisian-accented male voice answered. I told him my story, and about Maher's arrest and his disappearance to Syria.

"Do you know where he is being held at present?" the voice asked.

"He is in Syria, I don't know where, but since the president of Syria is visiting France, I thought you could raise the matter with other human rights organizations," I replied enthusiastically, as if I was living in the clouds, as if anything was possible.

"Is your husband a journalist?"

"No, a telecommunications engineer."

"Has he written articles?"

"No," I said, as I felt a lump rising in my throat.

"Well, unfortunately, we can do nothing for your husband; we only act on behalf of journalists."

"Oh, I see, but is there no way you can take up his cause and help him? I can send you information on his case, if you like," I said in hope of convincing the man.

"Unfortunately not. He has to be a journalist. I wish you the best of luck, madame," he said firmly.

It was pointless to continue. "Thank you all the same," I said.

My optimism took a nosedive; for a fraction of a second I would so much have liked Maher to have had a career in journalism, perhaps he would have more chance of being freed. Perhaps I would have better luck calling *Courrier International?* Why not? Maybe they would be tempted to publish an article on Maher, I told myself. Once again, I punched in the telephone number of an office in Paris. I wanted to speak to a certain Jacques Froment, whose number appeared on the website. As before, once connected, I began telling my story. At the other end of the line, I heard only Monsieur Froment's regular breathing; he must have been wondering where I had come from and whether I was normal. When I had finished my story, he said:

"At *Courrier International,* we republish articles published in papers in other countries. Our correspondent in Canada is supposed to recommend or suggest articles. Contact Monsieur Gauthier, he represents us in Canada."

Another slap in the face. The doors were closed; clearly there was no interest in France for our story, so why was I expecting journalists to help me report it? Just because the president of Syria happened to be visiting France? Deep down, I had known it was a long shot, but I had tried; that was all I could do. I sat there at my desk a while, staring at the telephone numbers I had scribbled in my notebook a few minutes before: Radio France Internationale, Agence France-Presse . . . the list was long, but it was a waste of time. I had to think of something else; my strategy had hit a rock.

Winter was on the way. Snow had begun to fall; a mantle of white covered the city. Barâa was adapting to her new life as a schoolgirl. Each day, we spent half an hour reading together. She was beginning to recognize a number of words and was supposed to be reading little stories on her own. I would sit beside her on the big bed while we read. Houd was doing his best to walk but not quite managing it alone. He would pull himself up at the end of the bed, take two little steps, then fall on the floor. He was not fearful any more; he knew my mother, and the two of them would spend hours together when I went out to meet people. My feelings of guilt didn't leave me, but I lived with them as I did with all my other feelings. In my role as mother, I wanted in every possible way to keep Barâa's memories of her father alive, to protect them. But I was wrong; I didn't realize that she didn't need my help. Sometimes, when we were making small talk, out of the blue she would say:

"Oh yes, I know that Toronto is four hundred kilometres by car from Ottawa."

"How did you know that?" I would say, surprised.

"Baba told me, once."

Of her own volition, Barâa was bringing back a word, a gesture, an expression of her father's so that he was always present with us or in her thoughts. One day before going to sleep, she said:

"You know what, today in the school yard, a girl said to me, 'Is your father still in prison?'"

"And what did you say?"

"Nothing, I didn't say anything."

I listened, not knowing what to say, sensing there were tears in her eyes; then she began to sob.

"Maman, I'd like Baba to come back, I miss him so much."

I had never seen her like this before. Now I understood how she was suffering.

"I miss him too, but he'll come back one day, don't worry."

I held her in my arms a while till she calmed down. Slowly, she nodded off. I sat there beside her. Houd was playing on the floor with a thread he had found near the bed. He would pick it up and put it in his mouth, then take it out, covered with saliva; he would drop it, then he would look for it all over again, lost in another world, focused on a little thread. I got up from the bed, took him in my arms, and carried him to the bathroom to give him his bath.

— 3 —

THE BATTLE BEGINS

*I raised my head, saw a grubby old picture of former president
Hafez al-Assad and realized I was in Syria . . .*

DECEMBER 16, 2002. This was the day we had chosen a week earlier
at Nazira's for our first vigil to demand that the government do more
to bring Maher back to Canada. It was snowing and the temperature
was hovering around −20° Celsius. The women who had gathered at
Nazira's had passed on the message to others, but we didn't want it to
be for women only; everyone was welcome. Alexa McDonough's office
had sent an email invitation to all the MPs and their staffs and to other
organizations to join in. I had never before organized a vigil and had
no idea how to go about it, but I was counting heavily on the goodwill
of people I knew or who knew Maher to come. Friends arriving from
Montreal brought candles and plastic glasses to put them in so the
candles would not blow out. I had received several requests from journalists for interviews that day and accepted them, delighted that the
vigil was reviving interest in Maher's story. I was not missing a single
opportunity to speak to the Canadian public.

Barâa announced the vigil at her school. She kept surprising me. Sometimes before going to sleep she would start to cry, she was sad not to see her father, and we would pray together for his return. But sometimes too, as on this day, she showed a great deal of courage and hope. She was proud to stand up in front of the class. It gave her a feeling of doing something; she could demonstrate her misfortune to others and share it with them, and that would heal her wounds and help her bear the pain.

The vigil was to begin at six o'clock that evening in front of the Parliament Buildings near the Eternal Flame. For the occasion, I had arranged to have an enlarged photograph of Maher, Barâa, and me. It was a picture I used a lot, I have to say I liked it; it showed us in our best light. Everyone thought it was taken on Barâa's birthday because, being the only child at the time, she occupied the centre of the picture, as she did our hearts. In fact, it had been taken on my birthday; Maher had bought me a cake and had a little party just for the three of us. I decided to have the picture enlarged and carry it with me during the vigil. A friend in Toronto had volunteered to do the job, and that very morning by courier I had received the beautiful laminated enlargement.

I got the children ready, making sure they would stay good and warm. Especially Houd, who was ten months old and not walking yet; he needed to be well bundled up. I took his little wooden sleigh to pull him in rather than attempt to carry him the whole time. It was like setting out on an expedition.

There was kind of an inexplicable happiness, even excitement in the air. I was naive enough to think that a single vigil would change everything, not realizing that the situation was far more complicated than it appeared. I guess this naivety of mine is part of my nature; it certainly led me to believe that everyone in Canada wanted Maher back. In a way I believed Mr. Pardy when he told me the Department of Foreign Affairs was making great efforts to bring him back. It never occurred to me that there was wheeling and dealing going on to make sure

Maher never got back to Canada. In my mind, the government was not doing enough and had to do more. I simply couldn't see the forces we were confronting, and how strong and effective they were.

When we arrived at the Eternal Flame, we found several journalists already there, waiting for us. Not knowing what to expect, how many people would come, what interest there would be in such an event, I felt a bit reassured. My mother was looking after Houd in his little sleigh. Barâa took up a position next to the enlargement, which we'd propped up against the low wall around the flame. Slowly but surely, people were arriving. Some of them I knew; others were strangers. It was almost dark now and I felt the icy cold settling around us and penetrating down to the bone. Someone suggested we begin to march around the flame and everyone quickly followed suit. Then a voice rang out, shouting: "Bring Maher home!" I took up the words without missing a beat and others joined in. There were about twenty of us, in the cold, marching around the flame, calling for Maher to be brought home to Canada. I had held Houd in my arms for a few minutes, but it was too cold for him and I quickly put him back in his sleigh and covered him with a little blanket. My mother kept an eye on him. Swept up in the whirl of excitement, I didn't want to stop circling the flame. It was a moving experience, with all the little candles twinkling in the darkness and all the people who had come to be with us and support us. Silently, I thanked God. Several journalists took pictures, and interviewed me. I repeated that the government was not doing enough.

Alexa McDonough and Marlene Catterall soon joined us. To my knowledge, they were the only political figures to do so. Their support was vital. Alexa was leader of her party at the time. Ever since her first phone call, when I was still in Tunisia, I had felt she believed in me, that she sincerely wanted to help the cause. It annoyed her that the Canadian government was not doing enough to demand the return of one of its own. Never did I sense in her the glad-handing, scheming politician taking an interest in this affair merely to score points against her political opponents. Her great human and ethical qualities always impressed me. And yet, she was taking an enormous risk in support-ing me. I didn't live in her constituency; she was under no obligation to help me. Since Maher was being presented by the media as a suspect with links to terrorism, it was risky for her to associate with his wife. After all, Maher might really have been a vicious terrorist. Why should she endanger her reputation, her career, and her good name for a cause such as his? I realized as the days went by that Alexa was not only defending the rights of Maher Arar, the individual, but was going beyond that: she was defending her vision of Canada. The true strength of a politician lies in his or her ability to sense approaching danger. The danger in this instance was the erosion of our rights in the name of an illusory and restrictive sense of security. In my case and Maher's, Alexa was looking far ahead, at a time when many politicians were looking no further than the ends of their noses.

There we were, marching in circles in the cold and the dark, but I could feel the warmth of the people around me. Many I had never seen before had come to support our efforts and put pressure on the government. I was grateful and told them so and thanked them. A circle formed around me; I felt I had to speak to the crowd.

> *Dear Friends:*
>
> *Thank you for being here with me, with my kids and with my family. Maher would be so proud to see such support for him and such unity among Canadians around his case. Unfortunately, his basic rights have been violated and I wonder for how long this situation is going to last. For freedom to prevail and for the sake of our democracy, I ask for the release of Maher Arar. I hope that we can meet around the centennial flame every month for a silent vigil, until Maher is released and reunified with his family. Once again, thank you for being here this evening, I will never forget your support!*

Barâa was standing right there beside me, but suddenly I realized I couldn't see Houd. He was not in his sleigh. Frightened, I looked for my mother. She was talking to a lady.

"Where is Houd? He's not in his sleigh!"

"Oh, I was getting worried about him. It was getting colder and colder, so Ahmed took him home with his own children. He'll bring him back to us at the apartment a bit later."

I breathed a sigh of relief; I had panicked, thinking something terrible had happened. A young man who worked in Alexa's office brought cups of coffee and hot chocolate. Barâa took one.

The local television station, CPAC, wanted to interview Alexa and me; the two of us went there together, taking Barâa, who was curious to see a TV studio. Friends drove my mother home. We walked quickly through the streets of Ottawa, which were emptying now, the wind whipping at our faces. We soon arrived at a long building. I knew the place but had never been inside. We took the elevator and stepped into the waiting room. Barâa was so excited that she had spilled hot chocolate on her coat. We found some paper towel to clean it up, and I rubbed vigorously at the chocolate spot while Barâa kept beaming, unperturbed. The makeup artist came to ask if I would like to get ready; I felt a bit self-conscious, since I never used makeup, but she understood and left with a smile. Barâa whispered: "Why don't you put a little powder on your cheeks? It would be so pretty . . ." I pretended not to hear; I was preparing myself mentally for this interview.

Alexa and I both sat on high chairs while the journalists put all kinds of questions to us. My replies were calm and composed. As we left the studio, Alexa said goodbye; her press secretary was waiting and they had another appointment. Barâa held my hand. We were happy, she was starry-eyed over the studio, the cameras . . . and in awe of the young ladies who spent the whole day powdering the noses of politicians and other important people. Deep down, I felt the vigil had been a success: at least the journalists found something to write about;

Maher would not be forgotten. Without admitting it, in my heart of hearts I knew that a miracle was not going to happen, but that slowly, with the simple, sincere, rudimentary means available, my little ship would chart its course through stormy seas.

The next day I called Mr. Pardy; he was not in his office. Soon enough he called me back. I understood from his tone of voice that he did not like the hullabaloo being stirred up in the media over Maher, though he did not tell me directly that I should stop. It was my choice, he said, and he could not prevent it but, clearly, he disapproved. I did not reply, but in my mind the matter was already settled: I would speak out to the media, I would hold vigils, I would keep writing letters, I would visit human rights organizations, I would do everything I could to see justice done. Not just out of obstinacy; I firmly believed that by speaking directly to the public and making people aware, I would help release my husband from his dungeon.

That day, Mr. Pardy announced that Minister of Foreign Affairs Bill Graham would soon be talking to his Syrian counterpart, Farouk al-Shara. Was it just coincidence, or did it have something to do with the previous evening's activities? I couldn't tell, but the news was promising. I wanted to know more, but Mr. Pardy was not about to reveal state secrets and would say no more.

After hanging up, I went to lie on the living room sofa to think over the promised telephone conversation and what it might mean. My natural trust in others had started to give way to mistrust; I had suffered too many disappointments and wanted no more of them. My mother was in the kitchen; she saw me through the little passage way to the living room.

"What's going on?" she asked.

"Mr. Pardy tells me Bill Graham is going to talk to Farouk al-Shara about Maher."

I was telling her because I really appreciated her opinion. She is an open, unpretentious woman of great kindness who has always impressed me with her ability to understand people. When I had a difficult decision to make, I could have complete trust in her instinct.

"That's good news. Let it happen and you'll see."

Ottawa, December 21, 2002.
Dear Maher,
Today is the last day of school for Barâa before the winter holi-
days. I have made some little chocolate cakes for her friends at school.
She is very proud of the idea. Houd is well. For the last two days he
has been crying a lot at night, I think his teeth are hurting him. Today
we had some freezing rain but luckily it is not very cold. Life is so sad
without you. I am impatient for your return. I am sure that sooner or
later Justice will be done to you and you will be able to come home to us.
Take care of yourself, have no worries about us. Be sure of one thing,
that I have just one future goal in life: to see you back here with us in
Canada, and by the Grace of God, I know that this goal will be
attained. We all love you. Monia, Barâa and Houd.

The holidays had arrived and Barâa was on vacation. We spent the long days in the apartment, but sometimes in the afternoon when the sun was still shining, I would take her out to play in the snow. She had a green sled she could pull with a length of rope. Behind our building there was a hill leading to a small park where a lot of children came to slide. The hill was now completely covered with snow. In some places the slope was steep, in others it looked more like a mound of hay. Barâa could spend hours there without getting bored. She would jump onto her sled, I would give her a little push, and off she would go, skimming over the snow all the way to the bottom of the hill. Sometimes the sled would tip over on the way down and Barâa would delight in rolling downhill. I would run after her, my boots sinking into the snow, to help her up, and she would laugh and take off, trying to escape, happy as could be in the one-piece snowsuit that made her look like a teddy bear. These wintry escapades took my mind away from my cares and the dreary life I was leading. In Tunisia, I had seen snow only once in my life, when I was eleven, in my last year of elementary school. Several centimetres fell: it was a huge surprise. Our winters were short, damp, sometimes rainy and windy, but never snowy. My outings in the snow with Barâa brought back the joy-filled memory of that day from my childhood, making snowballs with my friends from the white, almost magical powder that had fallen from the sky.

EARLY JANUARY 2003. As usual, I rose early to take Barâa to school. It was cold and the streets were still covered with snow. Barâa and I took the stairs; my mother would look after Houd. The car was parked in the building's small lot. As I opened the door I saw shattered glass on the back seat; one of the rear windows had been broken. The glove compartment and another compartment for change and other small objects were damaged. What had happened? I was shocked. It looked like a case of vandalism. While Barâa and I stood there staring, my neighbour, Richard, a man in his forties who was bringing up his daughter alone, came out of the building to take his daughter to school. He saw my expression.

"What's the matter?" he said.

"My car has been damaged. The window has been broken and they've damaged the inside too."

We had known Richard for years. In summer, when I took Barâa to the pool in the building to swim, he was almost always there with his daughter, Melanie. He liked to start a conversation and we would spend a few minutes making small talk. Maher knew him too; but all we really knew about him was that he was bringing up his daughter alone. However, he was always obliging and helpful. This morning, finding me in a fix, he said, "Get in the car, we'll drive the girls, then I'll come and help you."

I thanked Richard with all my heart and we left together with the girls. On the way, he told me such things had been happening in the neighbourhood and he had seen a number of similar cases. What could I say? I had begun to feel ill at ease. Was this a random incident, an accident, or an intentional and deliberate act? Was I being targeted? Was someone trying to intimidate me? I said nothing to Richard about my fears, not wanting to make things worse; he knew my story, but I wanted to appear normal and not think of myself as a victim, even though deep down I was feeling sorry for myself. When we returned, I hurried upstairs to make a report to the police and to call my insurance company. Richard waited downstairs, taping plastic over the broken window so I could take the car to be repaired. The insurance company offered me another car and asked me to pick it up at a garage not far away. I was somewhat relieved, but couldn't get it out of my head that secret service agents had done this to me. The fact that I would not keep quiet, that I continued to talk to the media, to hold vigils and to contact politicians was upsetting certain people, there was no doubt about that. Still, I wasn't completely convinced they would go as far as vandalizing my car to frighten me. I became more and more careful, but I didn't by any means give up my way of doing things. When I phoned Mr. Pardy that day for news of Maher, I straightforwardly told him of the incident. He listened to me closely, revealing nothing in his voice, but giving me the impression that he was not taking the matter lightly. Maher's file was progressing very slowly. Sometimes it seemed to me that everything had come to a standstill, that all around us was silence.

When Maher was being held at the Metropolitan Detention Center in Brooklyn, Ahmed and Bassam had sent him $200 American. The money was supposed to be used for long-distance telephone charges, but Maher had never called me in Tunis and I didn't know what had become of that money. Now I wanted to get it back; the matter was rankling me. I had never forgiven his jailers for refusing to let him call me and I wanted the money returned. Instinctively, I thought of Myra, Mr. Pardy's assistant; I called her and asked her to help.

"Could you call the consulate in New York, perhaps Maureen Girvan, who knows Maher's case well, and tell her I'd like to have my $200 back."

Myra was hesitant. She didn't want to refuse but didn't know how to go about recovering the money. "I'll check with our people in New York and get back to you when I have news."

Although I was not yet receiving social assistance, and my financial situation was becoming increasingly shaky, I was not looking for money. I wanted to keep in touch with Mr. Pardy's office; the $200 was a good excuse. But I also wanted to show the American agents that they could not do just as they pleased.

Each day in this new life of mine brought its surprises and disappointments, but I would always find a way, no matter how tortuous it might be, to keep my hopes alive. Sometimes I succeeded and sometimes I failed, but each time I learned to be stronger and more patient. Life, with its multiple facets, was giving me lessons. What I was going through sometimes seemed hard to bear, but I was grateful to God for giving me the courage to keep getting up after I'd fallen, and to keep moving forward.

JANUARY 7, 2003. Myra called to tell me that Leo Martel, the Canadian consul in Damascus, had been able to see Maher. I was surprised because usually she or Mr. Pardy would inform me in advance of a visit and I would write a letter to Maher so that it could be read to him the day of the visit. But this time, for unknown reasons, the visit had come about quickly. Myra promised to forward the letter that Maher had dictated to Mr. Martel, addressed to me.

> *Dear Monia,*
> *I hope you and the kids are doing well. Hope this year will be a*
> *year of peace and prosperity for all mankind. Being far from you, I feel*

very lonely. Every day that goes by feels like a long time. Thank you for sending USD 200. I wanted to inform you that in case I stay in prison longer I will need approximately USD 40 per month (perhaps not every month) and if you can once in a while send it to me. Right now, I have enough money. I send my love. Maher.

It was followed by a short message for Barâa:

Dear Barâa,
Thank you for sending me the Eid card. I hope you are doing well. I miss you very much. Please take care of your little brother and be nice to your mom. Dad.

I was relieved to hear that Maher had received the little greeting card for Eid that Barâa had made for him. He had not said a word about it the last time and I thought it had been lost somewhere between Ottawa and Damascus. But, to my surprise, he had got it. Barâa was going to be happy to know that her father had written a message just for her. The evening of that day when I put her to bed, I showed her the few words her father had written to her. Her face lit up.

"Why didn't he say more?" she asked me.

"I don't know," I replied, "perhaps that's all they let him say."

"Why wouldn't they let him say everything?"

"Sometimes it's hard . . . but when he's here, inshallah, he'll be able to tell you all about it."

"Yes, maybe," she replied without great conviction.

Our little discussion had left me feeling sick to my stomach. All that night Barâa's words kept running through my mind. When I finally drifted off to sleep, I had one single question: would Maher ever come back?

Several days later, I made up my mind to write to Maher even though I knew it would only be read to him on the next visit. I wanted to give him courage, to tell him about our everyday lives. I didn't give many details, since this letter would be read by several people. Everybody didn't have to know everything about my life; enough of it was in the papers already.

> *Ottawa, Saturday January 11, 2003.*
> *Dear Maher,*
> *I hope this letter reaches you and that you are in good health. I have received your last letter. Not a day, an hour or a minute goes by that I do not think of you. Do not think you are alone in your prison, I am with you. I talk to you very often in my thoughts and most of all I pray for you. I know that you are innocent and that by the Grace of God you will return to us. Barâa has read your message, almost all by herself. She is able to read better and better. She talks often about you and believe me, she will always be proud of you. Houd is standing up and walking, holding the edge of the sofa. He is not walking alone yet but I hope he will do it in the months to come. If you need anything at all, let me know. Never will I allow injustice to triumph. This is my daily battle. We all love you. Monia, Barâa and Houd.*

JANUARY 17, 2003. Mr. Pardy called.

"Anything new?" I asked.

"I have some good news," Mr. Pardy replied. I held my breath, thinking of Maher in Syria. Could he soon be coming home? I wondered but said nothing and let Mr. Pardy talk. "Bill Graham, the Foreign Affairs minister, has finally been able to speak to Farouk al-Shara, his Syrian counterpart, and has formally asked Mr. al-Shara to have Maher released or to allow him to defend himself if he is accused of a crime," he continued.

"And what did Mr. al-Shara reply, do you know?"

"It's very rare that a minister replies directly, particularly when a file is as complicated as this one, but we think it's a step in the right direction."

As usual, diplomatic procedure was coming to Mr. Pardy's rescue. He always had a ready answer for my questions. I thanked him for the news, but in my heart, there was nothing to celebrate. It looked to me like another timid poke at helping Maher. But the government, I felt, was still not throwing all its weight behind him. I had pinned my hopes on the meeting; I had expected the Syrian Foreign minister to demonstrate his good faith immediately by promising Maher's release. A cloud of gloom still hung over my head.

MID-JANUARY 2003. The telephone rang. It was Lee Greenberg of the *Ottawa Citizen* calling to say that a journalist from *Time* magazine in New York wanted a copy of the picture of Maher with the birthday cake. He gave me his telephone number. I decided to call the American journalist, Mark Rykoff, right after I'd spoken with Lee. He was quite pleasant, and explained that his magazine was writing an article on Maher. I was happy. I had concentrated all my campaign efforts on Canada until then, for obvious reasons: Maher was a Canadian citizen travelling on a Canadian passport when he was arrested in the United States. Since immigrating to Canada at age seventeen, he had never been back to Syria until sent there by the Americans. He had studied, worked, paid taxes, married, and had two children in Canada. To my mind, it was up to Canada to make an explicit demand for his release. But to my great surprise and profound disappointment, Canada was barely lifting a finger. The United States had washed its hands of the case: the American administration was preparing to invade Iraq and Maher was the last of its concerns. Syria was the big bad wolf. Every time I would ask Mr. Pardy what the Syrians had to say about it, he would reply: "Oh, the Syrians tell us Maher is one of theirs and they have the right to do whatever they want with him."

According to this logic, the wolf had the right to imprison, torture, and eat its victims, but our government, here in Canada, would not lift a finger. It was as if certain people were waiting for the wolf to finish off its victims before complaining and protesting. They might not like the wolf, but they pretended not to see what it was doing to one of their own. And how should I behave toward the Syrians? Was I ready to go to the Syrian Embassy and speak to the authorities there? No, I was not. I was not Syrian, first of all; I would be on foreign ground if I did. Secondly, why should I ask the jailers to free my husband when the real keys were in Ottawa's and Washington's hands? If I approached the Syrians, it would only strengthen their argument and give them the impression that they were in control, while, in fact, they were trying to score political points at my husband's expense. I was not ready to help them do that. Of course I wanted to see my husband again, but I wasn't prepared to grovel, to lose my dignity.

But when I learned that *Time* magazine was going to write an article on Maher, I immediately considered that it was a step in the right direction. I was under no illusions, of course. In the world of journalism, things are not as innocent as they appear. When I asked Mark Rykoff if he could send me a copy of the article, he seemed to hesitate, then said he would try but that he did not have the last word. Finally, he promised to call me when the issue appeared. It never occurred to me that I could be used. In my excitement, I promised to send him the picture. As soon as the call was over, I sat down at my computer, found the picture in .jpg format, and sent it to him, reassuring myself that our conversation had been a good omen; soon things would start moving on the American side. The feeling of success had gone to my head; I'd forgotten that the Canadian consul's visits to Maher had stopped, that I hadn't heard a word from my husband for several weeks now.

Two weeks after that call, I was still waiting to hear from Mark Rykoff, but nothing came. Perhaps they had changed their minds and were not going to publish the article. I was disappointed. Little did I realize the shock that was coming. One day when I was talking to Ahmed, he alluded to the article.

"Have you seen it?" I asked with curiosity.

"Yes, it's on the newsstands," he told me, but he said no more about it.

I understood from his tone of voice that the article was not great. I went at once to the newsstand at the Bayshore shopping centre and found *Time*. I opened it with trembling hands, not knowing what to expect. It was an article entitled "The Challenge of Terror." ("The Challenge of Terror," Steven Frank, *Time*, January 27, 2003.) Of the beautiful picture I had sent, all that was left was Maher's face with his radiant smile. No Barâa, no Monia, no birthday cake. Just Maher the suspected terrorist. His picture was shown alongside those of others suspected of terrorism in Canada. The article was not about Maher; he had been used as an example to show that Canada too had a terrorism problem, that our country had become, according to an expert, "a way station" for terrorists. I knew the theory of course and didn't believe it for an instant. It was a mixture of arrogance and throwing blame on others. But this time the message concerned me personally. I felt betrayed. I was revolted to see how far the search for sensational headlines would go to hide the truth. What was on offer here was not a magazine of news and ideas or a forum for discussion, but a propaganda outlet. In my hands I was holding the perfect example of the theory that "the end justifies the means."

Sick at heart, I returned home. How could I possibly show the article to my mother? Feelings of guilt began to gnaw at me; what a fool I had been to send the picture. It was as if the article had been written with my consent; I had been trapped. How was I going to defend myself? I decided to send the journalist an email. His response was cold. It was not his fault, he wrote, his editor made all the decisions. He sent me the editor's name, and I fired off an email to him. He was more arrogant still. He didn't have any problem with the article, he said, telling me, in effect, to get lost. On top of my feelings of inability to help Maher were regrets at having shared our lovely family photograph with people who didn't deserve it.

On more than one occasion, I had the distinct impression that

Mr. Pardy was trying to humour me. He would try to make me think that things were moving in the right direction to keep me quiet, and to get me off his back. But that was overlooking my nature never to give up. Oh, I would accept things with a certain resignation at first, but I never let despair get the better of me, or accept defeat. Perhaps I had unintentionally made Mr. Pardy feel that I believed what he was telling me. But after I'd taken a moment to look back and analyze the situation with a cool head, I promised myself to keep right on doing exactly what I'd been doing until Maher was back.

For some time I had been thinking about writing an article for the newspapers. I was waiting for the right moment to do it. One day as I was reading the *Globe and Mail,* I was startled to see one of my family pictures. It had been taken in Tunisia, at El-Haouria, a tiny, remote village on the northeastern coast; I was holding Houd in my arms, Barâa was proudly displaying a fish a fisherman had just given her, and Maher was sitting with brows knit against the rays of the sun. I had given the picture to a *Globe and Mail* journalist earlier, but it had never been used. Now, the same newspaper had published it alongside an article on another person arrested in Ottawa on a national security certificate, even though that had no relation to our story. It was a grave error; the paper apologized and promised to give me space for an article when I had written it. I was delighted and decided to write as soon as possible. My article would be factual, it would speak about me and my husband, but it would also inspire people to act, to do something. I didn't want to look like the weepy victim lamenting her fate; I wanted to write of hope and action. I needed solitude, time by myself, to do it. In the apartment there were always other things to be done: a bottle to prepare to soothe Houd's crying, homework to help Barâa with, dirty laundry to take down to the washing machines in the basement. I made up my mind to go to the library nearby where I took the children every week to borrow books. This time I went alone. I found a table on the second floor near a window and thought. First I wrote in French, then translated my words into English. After several attempts, this is what I wrote:

GLOBE AND MAIL, JANUARY 18, 2003. *Barâa, my eldest daughter will be six in one month. Yesterday, she told me that she is going to travel to Syria by helicopter: "I will open the door of the jail where Dad is being kept and get him back to Canada. If I cannot take him out of there, then I will ask the guards to keep me there with my Dad in the same room. You can join me with Houd (my little one), Grandma, and Grandpa . . ."*

I was amazed by her imagination and her logic. Unfortunately, she does not understand how far removed the world of adults is from her innocence.

It has been now more than three months since the children and I have seen Maher. The last time I saw him was September 25th. One week later, he called from the Metropolitan Detention Center in Brooklyn, New York, to let us know that he had been arrested. He asked for a lawyer. One week later, I received a call from an official at the Canadian Consulate in New York . . . I have sad news for you," she said, "Maher has been deported to Syria."

However, I failed to receive any official notification about the whereabouts of Maher. For thirteen days, he disappeared from the planet, vanished from the world of myself and my children. Then, on October 21st, he appeared in Syria, the land of miracles.

Every moment since has been one question after another: Will I be able to see him again? Will our children ever enjoy his presence and feel his affection?

When I came to Canada twelve years ago, I dreamt of a country of freedom and democracy. On September 26th, 2002, I woke up to live a daily nightmare.

I feel bitterly deceived. Every day is a new adventure for me. I have to be the caring mother for my children, answer the probing questions of my eldest and pamper my ten-month-old baby, Houd. I have given countless interviews to journalists and pressed the Canadian government for answers about my husband's situation. In the past, I had only heard of the "Superwoman ideal;" today, it seems I live a distorted image of it.

It is terrible to live in uncertainty. I had been taught early on during my graduate studies in business that planning and strategy form the core of a sound company. Later, I applied many of these principles to my life. I realize now that I was too idealistic. I have to introduce what we call in financial mathematical models, a "stochastic element" to capture all the unknowns of my current state.

This new life has taught me of the fragility of our most precious human assets. One day, Maher was a loving husband, a devoted father and a brilliant engineer. Then, he was turned into a file number. I still cannot accept that a Canadian citizen, who left Syria at 17 – whose unused Syria passport still shows the face of an adolescent, can be thrown into jail, interrogated at length, threatened with deportation, denied proper access to a lawyer, denied a transparent trial, and then deported to the country of his birth.

Furthermore, he had been "sent" from the U.S. to Jordan, then to Syria, without his consent.

For days, we labored in Syria to find out where he was. But the U.S. authorities refused to offer us even that courtesy. Maher ceased to be as a human being in the eyes of some. Instead, he was regarded as a parcel sent to whichever country would accept him.

When I read Voltaire's "Candide" for the first time at the age of 17, I did not really understand the beauty and depth of this novel, Voltaire criticized the government for its illusory security and intolerance. Two centuries later, it seems that a few governments have failed to heed his words of advice.

Maher has done [a lot for] his country Canada. He studied in Canada, founded a family, raised his children, and established his business. Unfortunately for him, the U.S. authorities did not judge all this sufficient proof of his loyalty to Canada his country. Instead, they decided to send him elsewhere . . . .

If these are the conditions surrounding this very strange case, how can we still believe in countries claiming to be defenders of democracy? How can we still trust their legal system and at a first place their Justice?

I am always proud and happy to present myself as a mother of two children. Children are our eternal source of youth, energy and hope. Every day through my deeds and my words I would like to raise good and proud citizens. I do not like them to live in shadow or with bitterness. When my daughter Barâa, shares her thoughts with me, I feel that I am strong. In her eyes, I can read innocence — and I can still believe that one day our family will reunite.

When I had finished, I was emotionally drained; it was as if my soul had become part of the words, as if it didn't want to return to my body. I gathered my papers, stuffed them into my briefcase, and went home.

Translating the text took me another few days, then I sent the English version to Riad Saloojee at CAIR-CAN for his opinion. His comments came back quickly and I was able to send the article off to the *Globe and Mail* on time. I had learned that I could also send the French version to *La Presse,* which would definitely publish it. Our story would not be forgotten; I was succeeding in sharing my dreams and my disappointment with the country's readers. I very much liked the idea of communicating with the public; it reminded me of the vigil we had organized the previous month. It also made me want to keep up the contact, not sporadically but regularly. That was when the idea of a website popped into my mind. Yes, why not create a site where I would talk about Maher's case? It would be a way for me to keep all the people I knew informed about the case, but it would also be a window to make the case known to more people, and to seek their help. It could include all new information along with articles and coming events. As I didn't have a clue about how to set one up, I began by organizing all the information I wanted to put on the site. I found the published articles, saved the photographs – in short, I gathered all the material together before finding someone to help me. Websites were an unknown field for me; I knew next to nothing about them but was eager to get involved. This new stage of my life was teaching me a precious lesson. It was not enough to reflect and observe: now I was learning to act.

I was in constant contact with Ahmed and his family. I spoke often to his wife, Racha, and I visited them from time to time. I kept them up to date on the case and Ahmed was always ready with suggestions. He knew more people in the Muslim community than I, and did all he could to win support and urge organizations to put more pressure on the government. He didn't always tell me what he was doing, but I quickly figured out that he was doing a great deal without making much noise about it.

I sensed that people were forgetting about Maher, however. The best way for me to overcome my fears was to get my teeth into something. There was nothing worse than feeling useless and doing nothing. So I made up my mind to share my plans with the people around me, and proposed to Riad and Ahmed that we meet to find a way out of the impasse. The meeting was set for Riad's office in Kanata. We all arrived on time at around six o'clock and went to the conference room. My plan was to float my idea of a website and get their opinion, but also to see if they were ready to help me with the project. The meeting was businesslike and the atmosphere was very fraternal; I came away happy. There I was with two men, one who had known Maher for years and the other who barely knew him, but both were moved by a thirst for justice and each was offering his help in his own way. Both had their professions, their own lives and families; the job would only make life more difficult for them. But when I brought up the idea of a website, Riad and Ahmed liked it.

"We know a website designer in Toronto," Riad said. "I'll speak to him. He might help you set up the site."

Ahmed had another idea. He wanted me to prepare a brochure that would outline all of Maher's accomplishments to date: "You can include copies of his diplomas, testimonials from his former colleagues, letters of support from prominent people, everything you can find in Maher's favour." It was a wonderful idea, but I had trouble imagining what such a brochure would look like. "You can take the pamphlet with you any time you go to see a politician or other important person," Ahmed said. "It will be an important document for the work we're doing."

We all agreed that I should work at the two projects, and both men were ready to help. So I threw myself wholeheartedly into them. They would take me an enormous amount of time, but I felt relief to know that, in spite of the diplomatic silence, I was doing everything I could to have our family reunited.

A few days after our meeting, Mr. Ramzi called. He was the Toronto website designer who would help me create Maher's site, which he agreed to do without compensation. He asked me to send him all the material I wanted to appear on the site. We would call it "FreeMaherArar." Although I have always preferred direct contact over virtual presence, I will never regret this idea. When I saw a preliminary version of the site, I was very moved; I felt I had reached out my hand toward another world. Since the website's launch, I have received emails from Canadians all over the country. I don't recall getting a single hateful or doubtful message; all have been from people shocked by the Canadian government's slowness to act and especially generous with their words of support and encouragement. We feel the need for an extended hand like this in our most vulnerable moments; the website made me realize that I was no longer alone in this fight, that I had many new friends by my side. The messages of support I received helped ease the doubt that was welling up in me and re-established the equilibrium I needed to survive and get on with my life with a semblance of normalcy.

My article for the *Globe and Mail* was published in both English and French, but it had no effect. There was neither comment nor reaction. Still, I was not discouraged. Writing it had given me a chance to be alone with myself, to draw on the best within me, on my deepest thoughts and emotions. This time of inner peace and self-examination brought me the calm I had been seeking. Since Maher's arrest, I had been deluged with news, one report after another; I had been taking blows, one after another. Day and night I dreamed of a miracle; it was the only way I could pull myself out of the pit. How I wanted things to get better fast! My faith was strong; my relationship with God had helped me to survive, to keep my head up. But this time I was caught short: the wave was too big and I was swept off my feet and into a new life. Everything happened so fast. Every day I prayed to God, but I was not finding any time for reflection, to be alone with myself, to concentrate on my spiritual life. My days were too full; I was always carrying out my tasks in haste for fear of not finishing, always getting back to work on Maher's case because I was afraid he might never return.

The day I sat down in the library, I looked deep inside myself and saw that beside the person I had become, I still existed. I had feelings, hopes, and above all I had my faith. Before Maher's arrest, my life had been a relatively easy one. I had no major problems to disturb or upset me and I knew how privileged I was; I could only thank God for giving me everything. But the sense of continuity, the wellspring of happiness had suddenly dried up on September 26, 2002. Of course, as a believer I saw a sign from God in what had happened. I found consolation in the thought that God was testing me, but I no longer had time to meditate or think deeply. The opportunity to write was like taking a fresh look in the mirror; I was learning to know myself again, taking the time to nourish my faith and recreate the deep, intense, spiritual bond I had been neglecting or failing to see. Yes, I was being tested, but my reaction to the test was going to change. I wanted to learn from this new life as I had learned from the old; in this test I wanted to see myself not as a victim but as an active participant. I would accept the new role that had been assigned to me and would pray fervently to learn. When I was still a child, I always wanted my father to give me more responsibility; my parents had spoiled me a bit, and I was always anxious to prove to everyone around me that I could be independent and strong. Those were just a young girl's wishes and dreams, of course. Then, suddenly, I had lost my stability, my happiness, my family life; all I could dream of was to return to peace and quiet again. But I understood that I could not pick my dreams to suit my wants. Today, I had to confront my new life with patience and conviction, sure that my faith would accompany me along this road in spite of all the obstacles.

My MP, Marlene Catterall, paid us a visit in our little apartment. At first I thought there might be something new, but that was not the case. She had come simply to visit and get to know us a bit better. Her visit also roused Barâa and Houd's curiosity. Barâa began talking to her and showing Marlene her toys and the gifts she had received for Eid, but Houd, who was not talking yet, stayed sitting on my knee, smiling shyly now and then. When Marlene talked about her grandchildren, I felt my children were reminding her of them. I would have liked her to talk more about the case, but she was very careful to give me no false hopes.

"Have confidence in Mr. Pardy," she told me. "He's been a diplomat a long time. He can slither through the intricate paths of diplomacy like a snake."

"Yes, but I don't see any concrete results. There are practically no visits any more. We've put ourselves at the mercy of the Syrian government. I don't see any way out."

Marlene listened but said nothing. Houd was now on her knee, I don't know how she had wooed him, but he was clearly happy and not complaining. My mother brought us green tea and biscuits; Marlene served herself. The discussion was no longer about Maher, we were talking children and families. Barâa demonstrated her new crayons that were like glue tubes that gave out a kind of gelatinous fluid full of sparkles.

"You've given me a fantastic idea, Barâa. I'm going to buy some crayons like that for my granddaughter."

Barâa looked proud. She loved to discover new kinds of coloured crayons and would sing their praises to her friends and relatives. Marlene spent an hour like this; her natural way with the children and her manner of speaking about her family made me forget that many people saw us as a family suspected of terrorism. For an hour I forgot how we were perceived and thought only of the present moment.

When she stood up and prepared to leave, she said, "The minister, Bill Graham, has read your article. Everybody thinks it's very moving."

Flustered and without thinking, I said, "Thank you," as if I needed to say something in reply. I would have liked to ask some more questions but held back. Marlene's expression had told me the visit was over.

The FreeMaherArar.com website was up and running now and I was logging on daily. I continued to gather documents for the brochure that would present Maher not as a terrorist but as a successful engineer. When I had worked on my doctoral thesis, I had spent whole days reading articles, writing programs, finding recent articles, and understanding their implications for my subject. At the time I thought that once I was a professor I would continue this work. I never thought that one day I would be searching for articles and gathering documents, pictures, and statements attesting to my husband's innocence. When I had radio interviews or was talking to journalists, the most difficult question to answer was "Yes, but why do you think your husband is innocent?" It was a difficult question not because I doubted his innocence but because no wife, mother, or other relative of a prisoner can possibly give an objective answer. How could I convince people around me that my husband was not a terrorist? Would my words be enough, my love, my confidence? Why would they believe me, especially when he, Maher, was not here to defend himself, when he had been arrested and then deported in mysterious circumstances? How should I answer? As a faithful, loving wife, and risk having people scoff at my naivety and simplicity? Or as a good tactician, replying with shrewdness and cool judgment? Is the truth all that hard to put across? I found myself busy stacking up Maher's diplomas, displaying his business cards, unearthing all the articles written in support of him so that people would at last listen to me. I was convinced it would be more effective for people to listen to me in person, to meet me, to pay attention when I told them loud and clear that my husband was not a member of al-Qaeda, not a terrorist, and had never plotted anything against anyone. But that would be forgetting how the world we live in works. Still, I was not giving up my way of seeing things. In fact, the moment I came before a camera or microphone, I would forget all my arguments and feel as if another person were speaking in my place, and it would be my heart, a voice more profound than mine, taking over and expressing itself; whatever I had inside me would come out, naturally. So what if my English sentences were grammatically correct or not. My despair and sadness were equalled only by my enthusiasm and faith once I found myself in front of a microphone, voicing my bitter disappointment at the government's efforts, and my hopes of seeing my husband back with us in Canada.

— 4 —

THE SILENCE OF WORDS

hold on tight, I'm going to do all I can to get you out of there . . .

FEBRUARY 5, 2003. Every day on the news, the invasion of Iraq was drawing closer and closer. War had spared my homeland; conflict had always seemed far away. People's suffering was something we saw on television, or read about in newspapers and books. But this time, it was different. Maher's arrest had brought home to me just how close events happening far away could be; my interest in the Middle East had taken on a personal aspect. Even though today's wars couldn't be called "world" conflicts, they affected far more people than those who lived in the countries directly involved.

After the invasion of Iraq, would Syria be next? Could Maher possibly become a political hostage, trapped by the flames of war that now threatened the entire Middle East? Those were the questions that kept running through my mind as I lay on the living room sofa watching Colin Powell, the U.S. secretary of state, addressing the United Nations General Assembly, lecturing like a university professor, with a slide presentation to make his point.

Closing my eyes, I saw myself as a newlywed in our little apartment on Place Decelles in Montreal. My doctoral studies at McGill had just begun; I divided my time between my lectures and studying at the library or at home. The work was demanding; I had to submit reports and summaries, program econometric methods, and make oral presentations. Maher was also a McGill student, completing his B.A. in computer engineering, while selling computers he would assemble himself. At home, we each had our own study space, he in the kitchen, I in the living room. The upstairs neighbours would often play loud, hard-rock music or come in late at night and tramp around noisily. To get some relief from the stress of our studies and the noise of the apartment, we would often go for walks on Mount Royal, strolling in silence, hand in hand, taking in the natural beauty around us.

I had been brought up to believe that a solid academic background was the key to success in life. It had been my father's constant refrain, and it was to become my mission: to be successful academically, to make my parents proud of me. Life in Canada had given me the opportunity to finish what I could not in Tunisia. When I completed my B.A. in commerce at the Institut des hautes études commerciales, I had come first in my class, which normally would have made me eligible for a Tunisian Government scholarship to study in Canada. But the Tunisian Ministry of Higher Education never approved my application, pretending that one document or another was missing from my file. One day, while I was waiting to see the head of the institute from which I had just graduated, the secretary, a kindly looking woman, cast a maternal eye on me and said, "My dear girl, don't you realize it's your head scarf that upsets people? Don't you realize your scholarship file will never be completed in time?"

I looked at her, wide-eyed with astonishment. Official policy in Tunisia discouraged the head scarf, and deep down I knew that wearing it would hurt my prospects, but I had pretended that everything was normal. The secretary's straightforward words shook me out of my state of denial.

If they wouldn't grant me a scholarship, my mind was already made up: I would go to Canada and find some other way to pay for my studies. My brother helped me financially through my master's program at Montreal's École des hautes études commerciales; then I won a J. W. McConnell scholarship for academic excellence from McGill for my doctoral studies. As the years passed, I gradually reached my goal. Receiving that doctorate was the greatest joy of my life. I saw the doors opening before me; the future was bright. Then suddenly came Maher's arrest and imprisonment, and our lives were turned upside down.

Here I was, still sitting in front of the television; Colin Powell was still talking, but I could no longer understand a word of what he was saying. But I could feel the fear. War was coming. I shivered.

At last, my letter to Prime Minister Jean Chrétien was ready. I was counting on Alexa McDonough's good offices to get it into his hands, which she promised to do during question period in the House of Commons. I was naive enough, and optimistic enough, to believe that he would read it himself and give me an answer. Up until then, the prime minister had mentioned Maher only once, in Beirut, at the 2002 Francophonie Summit, stating that there was little Canada could do to help him. "We cannot go and pick him up and bring him back." ("Canada can't help Ottawa man the U.S. deported to Syria, PM says: While officials have protested the U.S. action, they still have no idea where Maher Arar is," *Ottawa Citizen*, Mike Trickey, with files from Patti Edgar, October 18, 2002.)

With my letter, I hoped to get him personally involved in the case. When I'd asked Gar Pardy if Prime Minister Chrétien could intervene and call for Maher's release, he had replied:

"He can't do it for two reasons:

"First, all diplomatic channels must be exhausted before getting the prime minister involved. If President al-Assad says no to Mr.

Chrétien, it will be a definitive no, which will be very difficult to get around later.

"Second, Mr. Chrétien has already intervened in the past, in the case of Ahmed Said Khadr when he was arrested in Pakistan as a suspect in a bomb attack. Pakistan agreed to free Khadr, but the United States then accused him of terrorism. The Canadian intelligence agencies have never forgiven Chrétien for getting involved. They certainly don't want him to be involved again."

Always the same old arguments. I knew them by heart. But I wasn't going to let that get me down. I was obsessed with the idea of getting through to Mr. Chrétien. Mr. Pardy knew all the ins and outs of diplomacy, but in my mind, I would find a way. I wanted to open doors on all fronts: politics, public statements, the media, letters, public personalities, the Internet, diplomacy: I had to try everything.

***

Barâa and Houd were both born in February: Barâa would soon be six years old and Houd, one year old. I wanted to have a little party for them, to let them know that life went on, that even though their Baba was not there, they were growing up. Meanwhile, January had gone by and I hadn't found the time to organize a second vigil. I decided to hold it in February, on the same day as my children's party. This second vigil was easier to organize. I alerted all my acquaintances and asked Alexa's and Marlene's offices to help spread the word. Unfortunately, the relative silence on the media front over the last few weeks had created confusion. In chance encounters I would hear people say, "Oh, your husband is still in prison? I hadn't heard anything. I thought the whole thing had been settled."

I was counting on the vigil to get our story back into the news.

***

FEBRUARY 24, 2003. I chose the same place: the Eternal Flame, in front of the Canadian Parliament. The day was cold, but not the −20° Celsius of the previous vigil. I got there at around six o'clock with my mother, Barâa, and Houd, and found several people already waiting.

The day before, I had baked two cakes: a chocolate one for Barâa (she had chosen the recipe herself from of one of my cookbooks) and a simple white cake with cream icing, decorated with tiny coloured candies arranged in a rainbow. They had taken some time to make, but the thought of the children's pleasure at seeing their respective cakes was uppermost in my mind. Cake baking was one of my favourite hobbies; I enjoyed making them and discovering new recipes. I had been baking cakes since age twelve. When I was making and decorating a cake, I could put my worries aside, a kind of culinary escape that recharged my emotional batteries.

But standing there before the flame whipping back and forth in the wind, I forgot the cakes and creams and icings and began to wonder if more people were going to arrive, and if the journalists would turn up. My brother-in-law Bassam had come from Montreal. Shyly, a few more people joined us. Alexa was there, accompanied by Jack Layton, who had become the NDP's new leader a month before. She introduced us; he was wearing a red beret and seemed open and pleasant. His party would stay focused on Maher's case as long as it took, he assured me. His words were encouraging to me.

There were around fifteen of us altogether, a few journalists came and took pictures. But this vigil was different; there was none of the emotion and warmth of the first one; people seemed gloomy and sad. Was discouragement getting the better of us? Still, I was grateful for the support, even if it was fragile and hesitant, and saw a great gift in it. My husband was accused of terrorism. I knew people were whispering, "Why take risks? Why help someone we don't know? What if Maher Arar turns out to be a terrorist, then what will we look like? Better to keep our distance." But the people standing there with me had ignored the cold, the rumours, and the prejudice. It was a magnificent display of courage and support that would remain in my heart. Words of gratitude came naturally and I thanked everyone for coming. Calmly, I repeated what had become our standing demand on the Canadian government: bring Maher home. The small crowd dispersed immediately afterwards and I went home quietly with my mother and the children.

Back home, our party was simple and quick. The children were merry. I took photos: Houd, his face smeared with cream, and Barâa savouring a slice of chocolate cake. How I would have loved Maher to be there with us.

<hr />

The Canadian consul's visits to Maher seemed to have stopped. The first had taken place on October 23, and three more had followed at one-month intervals. This time, almost six weeks had passed without a word. When I called Gar Pardy, he told me that diplomatic notes to Damascus were not being answered and he didn't know the reason why. I was concerned that something serious had happened to Maher, but at the same time I took the opportunity to remind Mr. Pardy that the Syrians were not to be trusted. He didn't appreciate my comments; he firmly believed that the forceful approach would never work, that we should use positive reinforcement by showing gratitude at the opportune time. I could understand his reasoning, but as far as I was concerned, my husband's jailers wanted to show Canada that they could do whatever they pleased: Leo Martel's visits to Maher Arar could easily become a kind of good-behaviour "carrot" they could dangle in front of our nose. I hated this situation; if only Canada would show more backbone.

FEBRUARY 18, 2003. Myra, Gar Pardy's assistant, sent me a message to say that another visit had taken place without any advance warning. The Syrian agents normally responsible for organizing the meetings had apparently informed the consul they hadn't been able to organize a visit earlier because of a heavy workload and certain statutory holidays. At the end of Myra's message, I once again found a few words from Maher.

> *Dear Monia,*
>
> *I begin by wishing Houd and Barâa a happy birthday. Not a single minute goes by that I don't think of you and the kids. Life without you and the kids is not worth living. I hope justice will be done as soon as possible and I hope we will soon be reunited. Please convey my salutations to my family. I love you all. Maher.*

I still hadn't found work, and almost nothing was left of the savings that Maher and I had put aside after we'd finished our studies. My mother was helping out with her own social assistance, but things were getting more and more difficult. The apartment had really become too small for the four of us too. We needed a larger place, but I couldn't afford it. Even though I felt scarred by my first experience, I applied again for social assistance. But what if they turn me down again? I wondered. What would become of us?

The social worker I encountered at the Ottawa municipal welfare office was businesslike, but polite and smiling. As she put me through the same routine, my heart was pounding. Would there be a problem? What about the car? Was she also going to ask me to sell it? To my surprise she said not a word; things went better than I could have hoped. I told her my husband was in prison and far from the country, but her expression remained unchanged, as if everything were quite normal. When at last she told me I would soon receive my first social assistance cheque, I was suddenly overcome with joy. She continued: "You don't have to look for work because you have a very young child. I'm giving you an exemption, which you can renew."

Touched, I thanked her for accepting me, and then explained that I might soon be changing my address.

"Bring me the new lease, that's all I'll need," she said.

I left the building with a light heart and hurried home to tell my mother the good news.

The next morning, I began looking for a new apartment, something with two bedrooms, within walking distance of a shopping centre where I could take the children when the weather turned cold. I began my search in the Bayshore district – where we used to live – which had a large number of apartment blocks. With my modest budget, I knew we would have to put up with simple lodgings and frayed carpets. Most of the neighbourhood buildings were managed by a firm called Minto. The Minto agent, a scrawny little man, took me to see several apartments. I followed him from one building to another, up and down elevators, down long windowless corridors with faded, threadbare carpeting and fluorescent lights that made the buildings look like cheap motels. I hoped to find something on the ground floor because I was afraid we might have complaints about the children from downstairs neighbours. When we lived on Van Horne Street in Montreal, our upstairs neighbours had two girls five or six years old. Whenever they came home, it was as if a tornado had struck; the floor shook and the windows rattled. I didn't want to inflict a similar experience on our new neighbours.

The next day, I visited a two-bedroom ground-floor apartment; from the balcony I could see the Bayshore shopping centre. I decided then and there to rent it, and followed the agent to his office to settle the details. Considering my low income, he asked me to find a co-signatory to guarantee the lease. Taken aback, I had no idea who to call on, who would not be afraid to sign his name alongside mine. But I signed the lease, assuring the agent that I would return it with the missing signature. After all, it was a simple enough condition: just a signature, a little matter of confidence. Except that in my situation, everything had become complicated.

I went home, ticking off names of people I knew. That was when I thought of Ammou (Uncle) Jalal, a friend of Maher's who worked in Montreal. He was fond of Maher and the children and was close to retirement, so not really concerned about his career as other acquaintances might be. As soon as I got home I called and spoke to his wife, Wanda, who assured me he would be happy to do me the favour. There wasn't a hint of hesitation in her voice, which told me that my fears were unjustified. I faxed her the request and she promised to send it to the rental office at the end of the afternoon as soon as her husband had signed it. I was delighted. The next day when I called the rental agent, he told me everything was settled and I would be getting my copy of the lease soon.

～～～

March was nearly over; spring was coming. Houd had just wakened from his nap. I prepared his bottle and took him in my arms. When he had finished, he stood up and took a couple of hesitant steps, fell down, got up holding the edge of the sofa, then suddenly, without warning, started to walk.

"Houd's walking, he's walking! Barâa, Mama, come and see, look, he's walking!" I called out. I was overjoyed to see him stand up alone and stride out on his own. It was the same pride parents feel when their children finish their studies and receive their degrees. To me, this was a step toward independence and it brought tears to my eyes. We all looked on with amazement and delight, while Houd laughed to have discovered the age-old art of walking.

～～～

The days went by in monotonous succession. I would take Barâa to school, come home, play with Houd a little, then sit down at my computer. Since the creation of the FreeMaherArar.com website, I read and responded to all the messages I received every day. A lady in Newfoundland wrote regularly; she told me she had spoken to her congregation about the case and promised to keep sending letters herself to the minister of Foreign Affairs. Often people who sent letters to the prime minister or their local MP would send me copies. The site kept me busy and never failed to give me a daily dose of encouragement. There were other websites to check too, where I hoped to read everything I could that was being said about Maher and his case.

One evening as I was clearing the supper table, the telephone rang. It was a woman's voice, speaking in Arabic. She introduced herself as Samah; a friend, whom she didn't name, had given her my number.

"I know someone by the name of Bill Skidmore who teaches a course on human rights at Carleton University here in Ottawa. He would like you to come and talk to his class on your husband's case."

"Yes, umm, why not . . . ," I stammered, caught off-guard. "Yes, I'll take his number . . . I'll call him, I promise. Thank you so much."

Funny, I said to myself, now people are asking me to talk about my husband, and about the implications of his case; who would have thought? But was I ready to do it?

It didn't take long for me to realize that the invitation was a turning point. Up until now, I was the one organizing events such as the vigils to stir up public opinion. But now someone else had taken the initiative. More and more people outside my immediate circle were taking an interest in Maher's case.

"What's the use of talking to students?" my mother asked when I told her the news. She didn't understand how important public opinion was, that letters to government ministers could build a kind of political pressure over time.

"Talking is all I have and I'll keep on doing it as long as I'm alive," I replied, making up my mind to call the professor the very next day.

Bill Skidmore's office was on one of the upper floors at Carleton University. The room was full of books, old and new; children's drawings and political caricatures were pinned and taped to the walls; cardboard boxes full of documents crowded the floor; and it had a stunning view of Ottawa. Our conversation was short and to the point. Bill would begin the session with a lecture, then I would follow. The idea, as he put it, was to combine theory and practice, and give the students insight into the major issues of the day. His dedication as a teacher was plain to see; he was a man constantly seeking to learn. As I was about to leave, assuring him that I would go ahead with the presentation, he blurted out:

"I know a lady named Kerry Pither. We met years ago when she was working on the East Timor issue. She's an impressive person: dedicated and very dynamic. I think it would be a good idea for you to meet her. She may be able to help you. I'll put you in touch with her."

I left the office with a spring in my step.

❧

MARCH 19, 2003. Today was my debut as a university lecturer. I parked my car, took Carleton's underground corridors, and promptly lost my usually reliable sense of direction. I reached the lecture hall too late to hear Bill's lecture. Some students were standing around outside the door during the break, waiting for my presentation to begin. I hurried down the stairs into the amphitheatre, being careful not to fall on my face. Bill was standing in front of the class; when he saw me his face lit up. He explained how the portable microphone worked, and I attached it to the belt of my skirt. There must have been at least a hundred students in the audience; I felt a tinge of stage fright. Though

I'd spent several hours preparing my presentation, I wondered whether I would be able to hold their attention, to explain everything that had happened without sounding boring, or like a victim lamenting her fate. As all those concerns were running through my head, I noticed a stocky, middle-aged man take a seat a few rows up from the front. He looked Middle Eastern, perhaps an Arab; he didn't really look like a student, and his presence intrigued me. He pulled paper and pencil out of a briefcase and prepared to take notes.

In the lecture hall, there were curious looks, interested looks, blasé and skeptical looks; a few looked bored and half asleep. Bill introduced me and, all at once, there I was, alone before the students. Speaking softly, I began. At first I read from my notes, but then started to improvise, speaking to the audience as if we'd known one another for weeks. I told my story, I described my anguish and my pain; I spoke about my decision to speak up and speak out against injustice. I talked about my new life, about the lengthy silence ever since the consular visits to Maher had stopped. The interested expressions on the faces of some of students buoyed me up and made me feel at home. Suddenly a young man seated at the back stood up; he was wrapped in an American flag, and he moved quickly down the stairs toward me, saying nothing, all the way to the bottom, and left by the door closest to the desk I was standing by. I stopped, stared, at a loss. I heard muffled giggles in the hall and turned toward Bill, who clearly had no idea of what was going on. I tried to smile and couldn't, then pretended that nothing had happened and continued my presentation.

When I finished, many of the students broke into applause. Bill stood up and came over to me, thanked me, and asked the students if there were any questions. We had forgotten the flag incident; once again I was immersed in questions and answers, doing my best to satisfy the curiosity of my audience. The Middle Eastern–looking man I had observed taking notes during my talk was no longer there. I felt exhausted but didn't want to stop, it was such a wonderful experience;

I loved interacting with the students and envied Bill his job. When it was all over, several students came to me at the desk to learn more and ask how they could help.

"Write letters. Visit the website FreeMaherArar.com. You'll find all the information you need there," I told them.

Engaging the students in dialogue had lifted me out of the doldrums. As we left the hall, I thanked Bill for the opportunity to talk about Maher's case and about the threat to our freedom, then went off in the darkness to find my car. This time I walked above ground; the cold wind was better than the underground corridors.

⌦

The next day, to my surprise, Marlene Catterall called. She told me she was preparing to go to Syria with Sarkis Assadourian, one of her Liberal MP colleagues, an Armenian of Syrian origin. For a moment, I was speechless. Then it hit me. In November, I'd read an article about Canada-Syria trade in fields such as petroleum, gas, communications, and lumber. It quoted the commercial attaché at the Canadian Embassy in Syria as looking forward to a visit to Damascus by a Canadian trade delegation in May 2003 ("Canada projects future business co-operation with Syria," Syrialive.net, November 15, 2002). The article had startled me. My husband was in prison in Syria, and meanwhile here was Canada, doing business with his jailers. I caught the scent of betrayal. That same day I called Marlene and shared my frustration with her. To my surprise, her first words were:

"If there's a delegation, I'll be part of it."

Her reaction had taken me aback. As far as I was concerned, we should be boycotting Syria, not trading with it. But Marlene had seen it as an opportunity to let the Syrians know just how important Maher was to us.

Our discussion had ended there. Marlene had said no more and I thought the whole thing had been shelved – until her call. The planned trip to Syria had resurfaced. The details were scanty, but it was clear that the sole reason for her going was Maher. Finally, I began to understand that it wasn't such a bad idea after all. Knowing that she would be meeting Maher gave me something to look forward to. It wasn't long before I was imagining that soon I would see Maher, that Marlene would bring him back with her, as a surprise. Everything around me suddenly seemed fresh and new and full of hope. I stepped out onto the balcony. There was still a wintry nip in the air, but I could see a few early buds on the trees; spring could not be far away. I prayed to God that my nightmare would end, that we could begin to live a normal life again.

The delegation was to leave on March 24, which gave me a few days to write a letter for Marlene to deliver. Barâa drew a picture for her father, and I picked out some recent photos of the children. I stuffed everything in a big envelope and dropped it off at Marlene's office on Carling Avenue.

Ottawa, Monday March 24, 2003.

Dear Maher,

It is now almost six months since the last time I saw you. I still remember the day you kissed Barâa, Houd and me before going to the airport, expecting to see us again soon. Our lives have turned upside down since then. Every day I live in hope of seeing you again and seeing our dear family forever reunited here in Ottawa. But as I keep repeating in my letters, be patient and one day Justice will be done to you. It's springtime here, the weather is milder all the time. Barâa talks about you a lot. You know, she has happy memories of the good times we had together when you took us to the park or the playground. Even she believes that she is going to see you again soon. And you know what, Houd started walking two days ago. He still falls down but he stands all alone and walks. I have sent you their photos. Don't give up hope, be sure that I am doing and will do all in my power to see you back

safe and sound with us. Here is where your place is, near your children,
your wife and your family. We love you very much. Hold on tight.
Monia, Barâa and Houd.

In the meantime, Ahmed's wife, Racha, and I had planned to take
the children to a sugar shack. Off we went, with her two sons, age
three and four, along with Houd, Barâa, and my mother. Our destination was the pretty village of Pakenham, west of Ottawa. The children
were delighted to be with their friends. No sooner had we arrived than
they ran off to inspect the rusty old agricultural machines that had
been left on the farm. Big brown patches of mud were starting to
appear, contrasting with the sparkling white of the snow. The smell of
maple syrup was rising from the big boilers where the sap was sim-
mering. I bought Houd a stick of maple candy, which he sucked peacefully while he watched the other children at play.

Soon it was time for the sleigh ride. Drawn by two hefty draft
horses, the sleigh swayed from side to side and the children laughed
as it moved through the forest. All we could hear was the sound of
the horses' hooves sinking into the soft snow and the children's
laughter. As the sun shone onto my face, I savoured the moment.
Everybody was light-hearted; spring was in the air, a scent of renewal,
but a part of me was still in mourning; I was afraid I would never
see Maher again. In silence, I admired the beauty of the majestic
maple trees.

I wanted to speak with Marlene before she left for Syria, and I wanted
Ahmed to be there with me. He believed, as I did, that the Syrians
should be told in no uncertain terms that Canada wanted Maher back.
"Marlene has to understand that," he said. I wanted his voice added to
mine to make sure the message got across.

We were to meet at Marlene's parliamentary office. Gar Pardy would be present, and I had let him know that Ahmed would be present, which he accepted cheerfully. When I reached Marlene's office after clearing parliamentary security, Mr. Pardy was already there with another official whom I hadn't met. His ID badge indicated that he was from the Department of Foreign Affairs. Ahmed had not yet arrived. Sarkis Assadourian was already sitting at the table, and Marlene was speaking on the telephone in another room. There was a glum look on everybody's face. After the usual pleasantries, Mr. Pardy announced laconically: "The trip to Syria has been cancelled. Our MPs have not been issued visas for Syria. The war in Iraq has complicated things. I'm awfully sorry . . ."

I thought my heart would stop beating. For a second, I thought it was all a joke. But it was no joke. Someone, somewhere, must have pulled strings to prevent the delegation from reaching its destination, but I didn't dare say what was on my mind. As Marlene was ending her call, Ahmed arrived and I told him the news. I could see the disappointment on his face, but he recovered quickly. Addressing all those present, he said: "Canada must continue to insist that Syria return Maher. They have to understand that his return to Canada is an important issue!"

Unfortunately, our hosts had already begun to think of other things.

I fought back my tears; the last thing I wanted was to cry in front of these very important people. Once again, I'd let myself be carried away by the hope of seeing Maher again. I was ashamed of my stupidity, ashamed of myself. The meeting ended abruptly and I went home and shut myself in the bedroom.

We would be moving into the new apartment on the last day of the month; I was packing our belongings into cardboard boxes. Everything could be moved by car except for a few big pieces of furniture and the freezer, for which we would need a van. My mother called one of her friends who had a small van; she agreed to help us when we were ready.

Preparing for the move brought back memories.

When my parents married, they lived in a small apartment that my father owned in a nearby Tunis suburb where many middle-class families were beginning to settle. The neighbourhood was just becoming fashionable. At the time, the government was contemplating building a large sports complex there for the 1967 Mediterranean Games. The building we lived in was called Le Caroubier, after the heat-resistant tree that grows widely in Tunisia and throughout the entire Mediterranean area. Carob beans, the fruit of that tree, are now used as a substitute for chocolate, something I only learned years later in natural food shops in Canada.

When I was born, five years after my brother, what was already a cramped apartment in that neighbourhood became outright tiny. My father decided to sell it and move the family to a roomier one, with three bedrooms and a large balcony overlooking the Rue Maillot, in the section of Tunis called Le Belvédère. I can still remember the place, where we spent ten years of our lives.

My brother and I attended private schools. Mine was called École Jeanne d'Arc, and in those days was still run by the Sisters of Saint Joseph. Some of our teachers – all women – were Arab and others were French. A few of the nuns still taught piano or French, but most worked in the school administration. Instruction was in both languages. The school was a large, two-storey building with a dormitory for the nuns and a canteen in the basement for the girls who ate lunch at school, like me.

Being a civil servant, my father was not rich. But he insisted that we have a good education. He spent nearly half his monthly salary on school fees, the rest on rent and food; at month's end he would have to ask for an advance on his next month's salary to make ends meet.

When I came home I would have a quick snack, then hurry downstairs to play with Najoua, the caretaker's daughter, who was my age and went to the neighbourhood public school. We played hide and seek, hopscotch, and skipped rope while the boys played soccer or marbles. The streets were quiet in those days; Tunis had not yet been invaded by the automobile.

In the summer of 1978, my father bought a small house with a garden in a new district, called El Menzah 6, which was just being developed. That was the only move I remember from my childhood in Tunis; how happy I was that day to see the moving truck pull up in front of our building. But what I remember best about it was a minor mishap. It was summer and I was wearing wooden clogs at the time. Somehow my foot twisted and I fell to the sidewalk, cutting myself above the eyebrow. At the sight of blood, my friends ran off to call for help, more from alarm than any real danger. At the corner pharmacy, the pharmacist cleaned the wound with alcohol and put a small bandage over it.

Almost twenty years later, I was about to move house again, this time far from Tunisia – in Ottawa, and without the least fear or anxiety. On the contrary, I was happy to be able to live in a bigger place with my mother and the children, even if I knew things would be strained financially.

⁓

A few days after the move, Gar Pardy's assistant, Myra, called. Usually, her tone of voice was neutral, but this time she sounded happy.

"I've got good news for you," she exclaimed.

Every time I heard the words *good news*, my heart would start pounding, thinking of Maher of course. Were they going to see him at last? I wondered. Or maybe even send him back to Canada?

She went on: "I've just received confirmation from our consulate in New York. You'll soon be getting a cheque for two hundred dollars in the mail."

Flabbergasted, I didn't know what to say. But I quickly snapped out of it and thanked Myra for following up on a point of principle we'd been insisting on. Within a week, there was the cheque in my mailbox. The money that Ahmed had sent on my behalf for Maher to use to make long-distance calls from his New York prison – something he'd never been authorized to do – came back to me six months later.

Two months had gone by since the last vigil. There simply hadn't been time to organize another one, what with looking after the children and keeping on top of Maher's case. The two meetings in front of the Eternal Flame had been, for me, like a window opening, like a breath of fresh air that brought me the courage I needed to ask for help. But finally the vigils came to stop just as they had begun: quietly.

EARLY APRIL. We were settling into the new apartment. Barâa and Houd shared one bedroom, the other bedroom was mine. In addition to holding the big futon, where I slept, the room did double-duty as my office. My mother slept in the living room. We were all happy with our new arrangements; the apartment was sunny and clean and it wasn't long before we felt right at home.

The cancelled trip to Syria was still weighing on my mind. I was fuming at Marlene and at Gar Pardy, as if they were somehow responsible for the setback. Enough false hopes were enough. I felt like writing to Mr. Pardy to tell him just how disappointed and frustrated I felt. Maybe I was being mean, but I wanted to force him to explain himself. Still, I hung back. Finally, I made up my mind to send him an email in which I said that by turning down the request for visas from our MPs, Syria had humiliated Canada; clearly it was the stronger of the two countries.

I had no idea how he might react. In fact, I didn't expect him to take me seriously, but I had misjudged Mr. Pardy. Several days later he sent me a long reply that stopped me in my tracks. To this day, I can't tell if he, a career diplomat, had thought his message through before sending it or if he had just dashed it off. For in it, he revealed things that I, the wife of Maher Arar, should not have known. Whatever the case, I shall always be grateful to him for opening my eyes – inadvertently or not – to a reality that I had suspected but for which, until then, I had no proof.

> *April 12, 2003*
> *Ms. Mazigh,*
> *I do not agree with your analysis of the relationship between Syria and Canada, or Syria and any other country on this subject. A major part of the problem here is that not everyone within the Canadian government is in agreement with what we are doing to support Maher's cause. The Syrians are well aware of this situation and without any doubt this influences their willingness to cooperate.*
> *(. . .)*
> *Gar Pardy*

I read the message a good dozen times over. So Mr. Pardy's hands were tied because he didn't have the backing of "everyone in the government." But who was opposed to Maher's return? Was it the police? Was it the secret service? American sympathizers within the government? Who? I was at a total loss. The situation reminded me of a set of Russian dolls, each one nested inside the other. Mr. Pardy's words had not only made a lot of things clear, they had also opened the door to another series of questions I was not finding answers to.

What possible use could I make of the head of Consular Affairs' "admission"? Leaking it to the press was out of the question. After all, it was personal correspondence between Mr. Pardy and me; I couldn't abuse his confidence by leaking it to journalists. I decided to send the message on to Ahmed. He couldn't believe his eyes either.

"Perhaps by 'government,' Mr. Pardy meant the Conservative opposition," he said.

I smiled bitterly, remembering the vicious falsehoods uttered by Diane Ablonczy, a Canadian Alliance MP (Calgary-Nose Hill), in November 2002:

"Mr. Speaker, it is time the Liberals told the truth: that their system of screening and security checks is pathetic. Arar was given dual Syrian and Canadian citizenship by the government. It did not pick up on his terrorist links and the U.S. had to clue in. How is it that the U.S. could uncover this man's background so quickly when the government's screening system failed to find his al-Qaeda links?" (The Edited *Hansard*, Monday November 18, 2002).

"No, no," I said to Ahmed. "'The government' means all the departments concerned with Maher's case. If it's what you think it is, why wouldn't he just have said 'the opposition'? Why did he say 'the government'?" I was emphasizing the word *government*. Ahmed was now convinced that Mr. Pardy was trying to clear himself of blame and impress me with all he was doing to win agreement between the various elements of government.

Later in the same email, Mr. Pardy informed me that Marlene Catterall and Sarkis Assadourian would soon be travelling to Syria. I was astounded; nothing seemed to make sense any more. Still, I dashed off an angry letter to Marlene, saying, "Today I feel that my husband has been betrayed by his own country."

❦

Marlene and Sarkis Assadourian were scheduled to travel to Syria on April 22 and 23, 2003. Marlene herself telephoned me to say that they had finally obtained visas for Damascus and in a few days she would be able to see Maher in person. Now my despair changed instantly to joy.

I counted the days and nights. Images spun round and round in my mind. I imagined Marlene's voice telling me that Maher would be set free; I imagined Maher, Marlene, and Sarkis sitting together, talking. Maher would be smiling, motioning as if to say "see you soon!" I was now in a state of constant expectation. This time, there were no limits to my hope.

> *Ottawa, April 18 2003.*
> *Dear Maher,*
> *Seven months have passed. Seven months of loneliness, sorrow and . . . hope of seeing you back with me and Barâa and Houd one day. The children have got bigger and it breaks my heart to see them growing without you. But keep up your courage, I'm sure they'll see you again and will be proud of their papa. Never will I accept the injustice done to you, and I will do all it takes for you. You are not alone but always in my thoughts every moment of my life and I promise you it's true. Barâa is good at school, she's making a lot of progress in reading and writing. Houd is walking better and better, he's very cute, still stubborn the way you know him, but adorable with his winning smile. I hope you'll come back to Canada and together we'll be able to put this terrible nightmare behind us. We all send you a big hug.*
> *Monia, Barâa and Houd.*

APRIL 24, 2003. When I called Gar Pardy to find out how the trip had gone, he was tight-lipped.

"Marlene would like to speak to you personally, I was to tell you that," he replied. Mr. Pardy could be talkative, but that day the conversation came to an abrupt halt; I could get no more out of him. I didn't know what to make of his attitude; it certainly didn't seem promising.

When I went to meet Marlene in her riding office on Carling Street, I asked Nazira Tareen of the Ottawa Muslim Women's Organization and my brother-in-law Bassam to go with me. Marlene had a downcast look on her face as she described the visit.

"Everything happened so fast. Sarkis and I were with the Canadian ambassador to Syria when the Syrian authorities advised us that they were ready to take us to see Maher. We accepted at once and set off. I had no idea where we were; they took us from place to place. Finally, as we were standing in a room talking, I saw Maher coming toward us; he seemed confused and disoriented. When he saw us, he realized we were a Canadian delegation, and that we'd come to visit him. I told him my name and that I was his MP, I told him about you and the children, about how fast they were growing." She seemed touched, and stopped for a moment. "Maher was shaken; he stood there and cried, and when I handed him the photo of the children he cried even more. It was heartbreaking. I started to cry with him."

Marlene wiped a tear from her cheek with a trembling hand.

"I didn't know what to do," she said. "It was unbearable. A political attaché from the embassy suggested that Maher might dictate a letter for you and started to write at once."

I gave the piece of paper she handed me a quick glance; the writing was untidy and hurried. I wanted to read the letter later, alone, so I stuffed it into my purse.

"Did the Syrians say whether they might release him?" I asked Marlene.

She shook her head. "The Syrian agents I talked to were totally intransigent. They kept insisting that they were going to try him before a military tribunal for membership in al-Qaeda."

I was stunned. What did al-Qaeda have to do with it? Mr. Pardy had told me earlier that Maher was suspected of membership in the Muslim Brotherhood. The organization was a real political threat to the Ba'athist regime of Hafez al-Assad, who died in June 2000, and of his son Bashar, who succeeded him. Being a member was a capital crime. But whether it was al-Qaeda or the Muslim Brotherhood, Maher's situation was getting worse. There was nothing we could do, Marlene said. As far as the Syrians were concerned, Maher was one of theirs and they could do with him whatever they pleased.

My blood started to boil. I was sorry the mission had even taken place, and that Marlene had gone. Bassam started explaining to her about torture in Syria and the cruelty of the notorious secret police, the Mukhabarat. I was feeling sick to my stomach and asked Bassam to take me home.

If Maher was going to be tried by a Syrian military tribunal, I knew I might not see him again for years. I just couldn't believe that our life, mine and Maher's, could have changed so dramatically. When I married Maher, I never for a fraction of a second doubted his honesty and goodness; I knew just as certainly now that he was no terrorist. I would not let him down, but every day new obstacles were springing up. Every day he spent in Syria, far from his family and friends, complicated my mission.

APRIL 28, 2003. Ever since the *Time* article, I'd given up knocking on American doors. Admittedly, I didn't have the time to take on both the Canadian and American governments. What could I hope to achieve in a country where I knew neither politicians nor officials, where I was not even a citizen? It made much more sense for me to concentrate my efforts in Canada. But after much hesitation, I decided to write to Paul Cellucci, the American ambassador to Canada. After all, Maher had been arrested and held in New York before being sent off to Syria. I knew from the media that the ambassador was a controversial figure who tended to stick his nose into Canadian politics, so why not try to get a reaction or comment from him on Maher's case.

Besides, the U.S. secretary of state, Colin Powell, would soon be going to Syria; I wondered if the Americans could raise the question of Maher. I was daydreaming, of course, but there was nothing to lose by trying. I was prepared to meet the ambassador and give him my version of things if he was ready to listen.

APRIL 29, 2003. Nazira Tareen had twisted my arm to attend a fundraising event she was organizing; several political figures would be there. On the way, I picked up Rose, a friend of hers. We were chatting about politics, children, and education when Rose changed the subject.

"Did you know that John Manley will be the guest of honour tonight? You should take the opportunity to approach him."

Manley was then deputy prime minister of Canada, with special responsibility for security matters following the events of September 11, 2001.

"I'll do it," I said. "All I need is to find the right moment."

The event was being held at the Lebanese Orthodox church. Its shiny copper dome was glinting in the rays of the setting sun as I parked the car and Rose and I entered the reception hall, in which hundreds of tables were set with white tablecloths. Many guests were already seated. Nazira, who was hostess for the night, wearing her customary sari, greeted us briefly. We found our places at the rear of the hall. I sat down, not knowing anyone except Rose. Our table began to fill; a lady sat down beside me and introduced herself.

"My name is Selma," she said.

Rose explained who I was. Selma recognized Maher's case immediately. Her smiling face put me immediately at ease.

During the meal we were treated to Indian dancing, brief presentations, and awards to local dignitaries. Finally, it was John Manley's turn to speak, which he did without notes. I listened attentively in spite of my nervousness. As he was concluding, Selma reached over and touched my arm.

"You've got to catch him as soon as he finishes," she said.

Rose, who had understood, nodded in agreement. Now Manley was cracking jokes about his days as Foreign Affairs minister; the audience was in stitches. My hands were moist and my heart was beating fast. At last I heard applause, then Nazira took the microphone and thanked him. He waved to the audience once more, then left the stage.

I moved to stand up; my tablemates Selma and Rose threw me encouraging glances. John Manley, holding his wife's arm, was heading straight for the exit, which was just beside our table. Slowly I stepped forward and addressed him:

"Good evening, Mr. Manley, my name is Monia Mazigh. I am the wife of Maher Arar, the Canadian citizen detained in Syria. Marlene Catterall, the MP for my riding, has been to Syria. She saw my husband and discussed his case with the Syrian authorities. They told her that he would soon be tried by military tribunal. Canada has done very little for Maher Arar. I beg you, as deputy prime minister, to do something. My husband must be returned to Canada, his place is here . . ."

The words had come naturally, without missing a beat. Mr. Manley's piercing blue eyes registered surprise, while his wife looked at me with a kindly expression and listened with interest. There I stood, tiny in front of two tall people; I was not about to budge. After a minute of silence, Manley said, "I promise I'll discuss the case with Marlene and I'll see what I can do." Then, with the natural ease of a practised politician, perfected over time, he said goodbye and left. I thought I heard a furtively whispered "good luck" from his wife.

It wasn't long before the event ended. All I could think of was my brief conversation with John Manley. Who knows? I thought. Maybe he'll actually do something.

I took a deep breath. I had done what I set out to do. I had spoken to John Manley and his wife had witnessed it. Then and there

Our wedding day, in 1994.

At home, in Bayshore, winter 1999.

In Al-Haouaria, Tunisia, with Houd (left) and Barâa in the summer
of 2002.

The vigil, December 2002. From left to right: Alexa McDonough,
author, Nazira Tareen.

Julie Oliver, Ottawa Citizen

Above: The birthday photo that appeared in *Time* magazine in
January 2003.

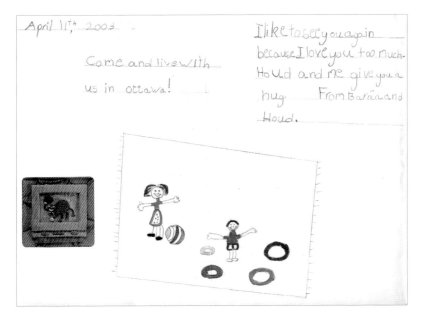

April 11th, 2003

Come and live with
us in ottawa!

I like to see you again
because I love you too much.
Houd and me give you a
hug. From Baraa and
Houd.

The giant passport for the march on September 25, 2003.

Courtesy of Amnesty International

The press conference at
Montréal–Dorval
International Airport,
October 6, 2003.

Rod MacIvor, Ottawa Citizen

Shaun Best / Reuters

At Montréal–Dorval
International Airport, on the
day of Maher's return.

At the press conference on November 4, 2003, in Ottawa.

Jim Young/Reuters

Maher, Barâa, and Houd at home in 2004 or 2005.

I resolved to write him a letter to make sure he kept his word. Selma and Rose were waiting with anxious eyes. They had seen me speak to the minister; now they wanted to hear everything. I sat down, my face felt flushed and my eyes were wet. It took me a few moments to collect myself. As I was driving Rose home, we talked about him. I'd done the right thing in approaching him, she said. When I got to our apartment, the children were sleeping peacefully. I turned on the computer, sat down, and wrote to John Manley to remind him of his promise. When I had finished, I performed my prayers and went to bed, proud of what I'd done.

POLITICIANS GET INVOLVED

*I could barely open my eyes, at last saw
the light of day, I was breathing again . . .*

EARLY MAY 2003. My decision to find an apartment near a shopping centre had been a good one. It was only a few steps – and a few
minutes – from all the shops. Houd could practise his walking in
complete safety, Barâa and my mother could window shop to their
heart's content, and I could do last minute shopping if we were short
of something. But it was springtime, and we spent more and more
time in the park right next to our building, with its two play areas, a
small hill, and sandboxes, where Barâa and Houd loved to spend
hours on end.

Over the last months, my confidence in my fellow human beings
had been at a low ebb; I was overcome with sadness. The more I
thought of Maher, the guiltier I felt. I slept in a warm bed, in a heated
apartment, eating three meals a day; for all I knew, and feared, he was
sleeping on the floor, shivering with cold, starving to death.

But recently, I was feeling a gradual change in my outlook. Life
had to go on, even if Maher was not here with us, and only patience

would help me surmount the obstacles that lay ahead. Perhaps I was getting used to things as they were, or perhaps my period of mourning was drawing to a close. Whatever it was, I was full of hope, and ready to face whatever might come. A sense of serenity now seemed to flow in my veins: the life force itself, perhaps. Or perhaps my faith had guided me. I'll never know for sure. But I did know that, surrounded by my children, my mother, and a few friends, I was becoming accustomed to separation.

Since Marlene's trip to Syria, I'd not had a word about Maher. Each morning I woke up expecting the worst even though Marlene's news, that Maher would be tried by a military tribunal, had not been confirmed. Anything could happen.

My letters to Paul Cellucci, the U.S. ambassador to Canada, and to John Manley had gone unanswered. Nothing had come of my letter to Prime Minister Jean Chrétien, the one Alexa had left on his desk in the House of Commons; I'd received a note from his director of communications made up of the usual polite formulas that said very little. Fortunately our website, FreeMaherArar.com, kept me busy and brought me new hope every day. Messages of support kept coming in. It was as if hundreds of people who didn't even know one another had set up a support network for Maher and me.

A few days earlier, Riad Saloojee had let me know that Jeff Sallot, a reporter for the *Globe and Mail,* was working on an article about RCMP and intelligence service involvement in Maher's case. Riad also told me that a colleague of his had met Paul Cellucci at a reception and had asked him just where the Americans stood. The ambassador's answer was that the Canadian authorities had wanted Maher deported, which put the ball in Canada's court. The more pieces I gathered, the more unlikely it seemed that I could ever solve what had become a monster puzzle.

I had long suspected that the Canadian police and intelligence authorities were involved in some way in Maher's arrest and deportation. Surely their visit to our house and their insistence on meeting

Maher were more than simple coincidence. After Maher had made it clear to the agents that lawyer Michael Edelson would be accompanying him, they had never set up a meeting. As for the RCMP file on Maher, I had no idea of what it might contain. For all I knew, they wanted to ask him about the investigation they were conducting. And if they really wanted to ask him questions, they surely could have done it in Edelson's presence.

MAY 9, 2003. Bassam, my brother-in-law, and I were scheduled to meet Gar Pardy. It would be a "routine" meeting like all the others. I would ask if the government was working on a strategy to bring Maher back to Canada, while Mr. Pardy would assure me that it was doing everything it could.

Sometimes Mr. Pardy would tell me: "I don't have the slightest doubt that Maher will be set free one day." I would hold my breath in anticipation of a surprise announcement, but he would quickly continue: "But I can't tell you how or when."

Bassam arrived from Montreal, and we drove off together to the Department of Foreign Affairs, where Myra and Mr. Pardy were waiting for us. I immediately mentioned my brief encounter with John Manley and my follow-up letter. Mr. Pardy seemed pleased, and I promised to keep him informed. As expected, the department had no more news of Maher than I did since Marlene Catterall's trip. But Mr. Pardy seemed worried that the Syrians would actually bring Maher before a military tribunal.

"They're saying that Maher went to Afghanistan in 1993," he said.

"But he never went to Afghanistan! Who's claiming that?"

"The Syrian authorities say so," he answered.

"But didn't they claim that Maher belonged to the Muslim Brotherhood, then to al-Qaeda? Today it's Afghanistan. What will it be tomorrow?"

As the meeting was ending, Mr. Pardy informed me that Deputy Minister of Foreign Affairs Gaëtan Lavertu would be travelling to Syria at the end of the month. While not wishing to reveal the purpose of the deputy minister's trip, he led me to understand that he was preparing a letter on Maher's case for the Syrian authorities. He would have to discuss it with people from the Solicitor General's office for permission to use certain terms. Both of us knew that it would take an official document to establish that Maher had no connection with terrorist activities in Canada. Last fall, Michael Edelson had not been able to convince the RCMP brass to give him such a letter. This time, Gar Pardy was trying the diplomatic route, by adding a sentence that would clear Maher of all suspicion in the eyes of the Syrians but that would not irritate certain people in the police and the Canadian intelligence services.

I didn't get it. On the one hand, some members of the Canadian government recognized that Maher had suffered an injustice, but on the other hand, the police refused to co-operate. Why? Their refusal left a dark cloud hanging over Maher's head. No one could tell me why the RCMP was acting as it did. If they believed that Maher was innocent, what was to stop them from giving me a letter that said so? But if they believed that he was guilty of something, why hadn't they arrested him right here in Canada? As for me, I was certain that Maher was no terrorist; he'd never belonged to any terrorist group, had never gone to Afghanistan. Where did these accusations come from, and, more crucially, how could they be disproved? Mr. Pardy knew that the letter idea might fail, but he was still hopeful. I couldn't help thinking the same thing.

꩜

Bill Skidmore hadn't forgotten me. As promised, he had contacted Kerry Pither. It had become clear to me that I needed help in finding my way through the social and political complexities of the case. Up to now, I'd been getting short-term, occasional assistance, and relying a lot on the availability and goodwill of my friends, or of Alexa's office. But it wasn't enough.

Kerry and I met for the first time in the tiny downtown Ottawa office of the non-governmental organization (NGO) network she worked for. She showed me in with a broad smile that won my confidence. If you were to judge by appearances, we had nothing in common. She was an atheist, I, a believer; she was tall; I, small in stature; she came from an English-speaking background, mine was French-speaking and Arab. But it didn't take us long to find common ground: she was well aware of Maher's situation, and believed it was time to put an end to the injustice. She listened attentively as I explained what steps were already being taken, without committing herself to our working together. First she would need permission from the board of her organization. But I left her office with a light step.

When I got home, my mother told me that a gentleman called Irwin Cotler had called, and that he would call again. Cotler, a McGill University professor and now a Member of Parliament for a Montreal-area riding, was well known as a defender of human rights. I'd heard of him when he took the case of a Canadian of Tunisian origin from Montreal who had been arrested and jailed while on a trip to Tunisia. Cotler had won the case, and the man had been released. I'd already attempted to reach Cotler at his Ottawa office or in Montreal. Each time I called, he was either away from his office or busy; he never called back. Now I would be speaking with Irwin Cotler himself.

Later that day, he called again: he was determined to take up Maher's case. And what's more, it would be without charge, pro bono. It was all I could do to contain my excitement. This was more than I'd ever expected. His was a name to reckon with in the legal world. I couldn't have hoped for anything better. I had just won significant new support.

But my joy was short-lived. When I checked my mailbox a few

minutes later, I found a letter from the American Embassy. In it, Ambassador Cellucci's secretary affirmed that as Maher was a Canadian citizen, the United States had no authority to intervene on his behalf with either the Canadian or the Syrian authorities. That last sentence puzzled me: after all, the Americans had deported him in the first place without taking account of his Canadian citizenship. It just didn't make sense.

LATE MAY 2003. I phoned Myra to ask if Gaëtan Lavertu's trip to Syria had taken place, and if Mr. Pardy had given him a letter absolving Maher of any connection with terrorist movements. Myra seemed embarrassed. Mr. Lavertu had indeed left for Syria, she said, but without the letter.

"Mr. Pardy couldn't get authorization to write what he wanted," she explained, and then added that he would be taking up the matter with his Syrian counterparts "in the context of human rights."

I was disappointed but not surprised. Certain people were doing all they could to block Maher's release. Still, there was the off chance that Mr. Lavertu might raise the matter with the Syrian authorities. Myra promised that she would keep me up to date. But I'd forgotten to make sure that Mr. Lavertu would bring back news of Maher. I hadn't heard a word since April, when Marlene had returned from Syria. According to Mr. Pardy, the Syrians no longer authorized consular visits since they had announced their intention to put Maher on trial.

A few days after our conversation, Myra called to tell me that Mr. Lavertu had met the Syrian authorities, but that Maher's case had not come up. My heart missed a beat.

"Why was that?" I said.

"We're told that Mr. Lavertu didn't have time to raise the matter."

I didn't get it. Myra had to be joking. Yet I knew that she was quite serious.

"What does that mean, 'didn't have time'? What could be more important than a Canadian rotting in prison?" I asked.

By now, Myra knew the ropes after months of working on the case. She was only telling me what was in her notes; there was nothing else she could do. As usual, I regretted having believed for an instant that Mr. Lavertu's trip would amount to anything. I didn't know who to believe or what to do: trust Mr. Pardy and the Department of Foreign Affairs or go about my business on my own.

Fortunately, Kerry Pither called a few days later to tell me that the more she studied Maher's case, the more certain she was of its political implications. She was determined to help, and the board of her organization had given her the green light to go ahead. We began to meet and to talk by phone regularly.

Together we drew up a timeline of the events related to Maher's case, with all the key dates, beginning with the RCMP visit to our house in Bayshore, and including all the consular visits and my meetings with political figures. The object was to prepare a factual document that would clearly illustrate what had happened, without passing judgment on the facts themselves.

For months I'd been requesting that Mr. Pardy arrange a meeting with Bill Graham, the minister of Foreign Affairs. But each time, he sidestepped my request with the aplomb of the wily diplomat that he was. "The honourable minister is very busy right now," he would tell me. "He's travelling constantly. He's on holiday." Still, I kept on pressing the issue every time we met.

One day in early June, I was at home when the telephone rang. Foreign Affairs Minister Graham's office was on the line: the minister was prepared to meet me on June 13, at one o'clock. I couldn't believe my ears! There must be some mistake, I thought at first. But I took hold of myself and agreed to the meeting then and there.

I didn't inform the media of the meeting. Mr. Pardy may have had the impression that I spent most of my time talking with journalists, but it just wasn't so. From the start, I preferred to give the government and the civil service the time they needed to act and do their job. But when it became clear that nothing was happening, that I was getting nowhere, I would let the media know.

Even though my mother didn't utter a discouraging word about my upcoming meeting, I could tell she didn't really believe it would change anything. She wasn't alone. Several of my friends and family members felt the same way. They'd already made up their minds that Maher would not be coming back, but when they saw me fighting on against insurmountable odds, they didn't want to let me down. I was convinced they felt sorry for me. It was as though everyone else knew something I didn't – that Maher would not be coming back – and they were hiding the truth from me. But I was learning to be patient; even with the emotions of others.

I called Kerry to tell her the news. Without missing a beat she switched into "operational" mode: "You've absolutely got to bring people with you; you've got to have witnesses, and support."

We agreed that Riad would be present as a representative of the Arab and Muslim community, Alex Neve of Amnesty International as a human rights representative, Paul Purrit, an official of the Canadian Labour Congress, and of course Kerry. We wanted to convey the impression that Canadian public opinion was on our side.

⁓

JUNE 13, 2003. The meeting was to take place at Mr. Graham's office on Parliament Hill. Kerry and I were the first to arrive at the main entrance, where we waited for Riad Saloojee and Paul Purrit. Alex was travelling but had insisted I tell the minister that he would have liked to be with us. We passed through the security check without incident and made our way upstairs to Mr. Graham's office. It was impossible to predict who would be present with the minister, but I was curious to see the expression on "their" faces when they saw me walk in with my "support committee." The first person I saw in the waiting room was Marlene Catterall. I had no idea she would be there, and I don't think she was too happy to see me there surrounded by a delegation. Instead of a friend, the friend had brought the whole family along!

Then Mr. Graham arrived, shook my hand, and showed us into his office. There were already three other people waiting there: his personal secretary, another adviser, and Myra, who was probably filling in for Mr. Pardy. Luckily I was not alone; five against one would have been tough. This was the moment I'd been waiting for; I would not get another chance. It was a battle I had to win.

The minister opened the meeting by thanking Marlene Catterall for organizing it. I just about fell off my chair. Marlene had never breathed a word to me. Then, without missing a beat, I handed Mr. Graham the fact sheet I'd prepared about Maher and his career; I also gave him Alex Neve's two appeals to the members of Amnesty International along with the U.S. ambassador's answer to my letter. Then, in a soft voice, I began to speak. I was baffled by the Canadian government's position, I said, before slipping in Mr. Pardy's remark that not everybody in the government was in agreement with our efforts to repatriate Maher.

The time was ripe to use what amounted to inside information. Better that Mr. Pardy was not present. He might have interrupted or tried to explain his words away. I glanced at Myra; she was impassive. For fear of compromising Mr. Pardy, I added how much I appreciated his frankness and the quality of his work. With a nod, the minister acknowledged the compliment.

I was determined to stick to my plan, to put the minister on the defensive, and to throw every possible argument I could at him to prove that there was sharp disagreement within the government over Maher's case: that on one side, the Department of Foreign Affairs was working for his release, and on the other, some government agencies, such as the intelligence services like CSIS, and the RCMP, were doing everything they could to derail it.

"Look at this example, your Excellency. Last month, the deputy minister, Gaëtan Lavertu, went to Syria. In the beginning, when Myra and Mr. Pardy told me about his visit, we discussed a letter that would help liberate Maher. At the time, they told me that they would make every effort to coordinate their efforts with the Solicitor General's office. One week later, to my great dismay, the whole idea had fallen through. Apparently the intelligence services wouldn't authorize it," I told him.

The minister listened, apparently with interest. His expression gave me courage. I continued.

"Even the Americans have insinuated that the Canadians are behind Maher Arar's deportation," I said, looking toward Riad.

Marlene Catterall, who was sitting opposite me, broke her silence: "That's not exactly what I've heard . . ."

Speaking calmly, Riad joined the discussion, recounting what the American ambassador had said: "One of my colleagues heard the ambassador state that certain people in Canada wanted Arar deported," he said calmly.

Marlene disagreed with him. For her, it was a case of "certain people in Canada looking the other way when Arar was deported."

I added, "Whatever the words they used, it looks as if the U.S. has put the ball in Canada's court, and it's time for our government to take a stand."

The minister picked up on my remarks, admitting that the world of intelligence was a murky one, and that getting to the bottom of things and learning the truth was no easy matter. Not only did he give me his assurance that he would keep on working on the case, he also stated that he was prepared to write a letter to his Syrian counterpart to ask for Maher's release. It would include a sentence to the effect that "there is no obstacle to Arar's return to Canada." I suggested that it should include a few phrases to indicate to the Syrians that Maher had no connection with terrorist activities in Canada.

"After all," I said, "a police state wouldn't put much credence in diplomats; it would be more inclined to listen to what its police colleagues had to say."

The minister seemed convinced, but he was not prepared to commit himself to the famous letter. He was all for it, but he didn't know if "everybody else" would agree to co-operate. Still, the meeting ended on a hopeful note.

My friends and I left Mr. Graham's office together. We all felt that it had gone well. Kerry and I would go over the notes she'd taken later. I thanked the others for coming, and we all went our separate ways.

The trees were all green by now, new grass had grown up, and the gardeners were busy planting red, purple, and white flowers in front of their buildings. What a contrast with the white, miserable winter that had just ended. With every early summer, I marvelled at the transformation of nature in Canada. There had been precious little green in Tunisia. Even Belvedere Garden, which had been established during the French protectorate, was no longer as green as it was when I used to play there as a little girl. The last time I'd seen it, just before Maher's arrest, the grass had turned yellow; many of the majestic trees I remembered from my youth had been destroyed either by lightning or sickness. In the past, the residents of the capital called the garden "the lungs of Tunis." My father would bring us there several times a week. The garden changed with the seasons. In the springtime, thick green grass, poppies, and chamomile covered the ground. I would turn somersaults and run this way and that until I was out of breath. There was a tiny merry-go-round with rusty old yet brightly painted cars that I just loved to ride in.

Later, when I grew up, parks and public gardens were no longer a part of my life. Promoters in the suburbs where we lived were more interested in building stores and shopping centres. But when I began my university-level studies at the Institut des hautes études in Carthage, I struck up contact with nature once more. The institute, which had once been a church painted blue and white, was situated on a verdant hillside overlooking the Mediterranean. Between classes my friends and I would stroll through the trees, listening to the songs of the many birds that lived there. Now, these images from my life in Tunisia would often enter my mind, and mingle with the ones that every early Canadian summer would bring to me.

At home, life went on. Barâa had made great progress in reading and writing, and was busy learning a song that she and her friends would sing for the year-end ceremonies. As for Houd, he was still not talking; he would make strange sounds when he saw a squirrel or a cat, but I knew what he was saying. By keeping our expenses under tight control, we were able to get by on my monthly social assistance cheque. For the children's new clothes, we shopped at the second-hand cloth- ing store; the outfits were still in good shape, and prices were low. Every so often Ammou Jalal's wife, Wanda, would send us a sack full of children's clothing she would pick up in neighbourhood bazaars not far from her house. She would buy anything she thought we could use: dresses, skirts, and blouses for Barâa, and shorts or jumpers for Houd. The kids just loved trying on their new clothes: they turned our house into a costume party, dancing around holding on to the table, running off to look in the mirror, then coming back, laughing.

At Houd's age, Barâa had begun to call her father "ba-ba-ba," but Houd couldn't even remember him. Barâa would talk about him, but only occasionally. She would look at our old photos, talk about her memories, and often in the evening she would tell me how much she missed her Baba. And I would comfort her, hold her tight in my arms, and tell her that one day he would be with us, while deep down I prayed that my wishes would be granted.

MID-JUNE 2003. A few days after the meeting with Bill Graham, as I was working at the computer, someone knocked on the door. I was startled. Surprise visits were a rarity; generally I knew who was coming. I opened the door; it was the letter carrier. With one hand he gave me a letter and with the other a pen to sign as proof of receipt. It was from the Privy Council of Canada. I'd never sent them a letter; what did the Privy Council want from me? My heart had begun to beat faster as I tore open the outer envelope; inside was a white envelope with the seal of the Prime Minister's Office in gilt embossed letters. I opened it in turn: inside was a two-page letter from Prime Minister Jean Chrétien.

Finally, almost nine months after Maher had been detained, the prime minister of Canada had finally deigned to recognize me. I read the letter again and again; it contained words of happiness and words of sadness. Words that made me feel pessimistic, and words that almost made me jump for joy. Mr. Chrétien repeated what the Syrian authorities had told Mr. Pardy: that Maher had received military training at a camp in Afghanistan. But he also assured me that Canada would continue to do all it could to bring Maher back to Canada. His last words made me happy. For the first time, it was as if a strong, sure hand stretched toward me. But the remark about military training in Afghanistan worried me. Where had that allegation come from? Why was Canada telling me that the Syrians had provided them the information? Why did they believe them and not me, when I'd been telling them all along that my husband was innocent, that he was not a member of al-Qaeda? All this by way of saying that the prime minister's letter, the one I'd been expecting for months, had a mixed effect. It was clear that the accusation of terrorism would not go away; I had no idea how we would ever be able to put it behind us.

Alexa McDonough called to see how things were going. As

always, I felt that her concern was genuine. Though she was no longer party leader, she had become the NDP Foreign Affairs critic, so it was quite normal that she should take an interest in Maher's case, in addition to her initial and ongoing concern for our situation. She had heard of Marlene Catterall's trip to Syria, and the news that Maher was to be tried by a military tribunal. But we hadn't spoken for some time, so I took the opportunity to tell her about my new supporters. Halfway through our conversation, Alexa told me that a person she could not name wanted to meet me in her office, and encouraged me to come. It was clear that I'd entered a world where mystery and secrecy had become part of daily life.

We would meet in Alexa's office in the Parliament Buildings.

It was summer and Ottawa was swarming with tourists; the lineup was long and getting longer by the minute. As I waited my turn, I observed the happy, carefree crowd inching its way forward to get a look at Parliament. People were laughing, bantering; no one even bothered to wonder what I was doing there, silent and alone. When I got to Alexa's office, she was waiting for me, gave me a hug, and showed me into her study. Seated there was a woman I'd never seen before. She smiled, held out her hand.

"Monia, I'd like you to meet Senator Mobina Jaffer," said Alexa. "Mobina has been hoping to meet you for some time now. I hope she can help you."

I'd heard vaguely of Mobina Jaffer, a Liberal senator appointed by Jean Chrétien. The three of us sat down around a table in Alexa's spacious, sunny office. I gave Senator Jaffer a detailed account of Maher's case, and clarified several points for her, including the prime minister's letter, while she took notes. She made no great promises but assured me she would do her best to help. That was enough for me; any additional support was most welcome. The flow of support seemed to be moving faster now, and deep in my heart I prayed that it wouldn't stop. After the senator had left, I stayed on for a few minutes with Alexa.

"I'm happy she came," Alexa said. "We don't want partisan politics, and Senator Jaffer will be a precious ally on Maher's case."

⁂

My social life was very rudimentary. We saw Ahmed and Racha and their children regularly, but most of the time my mother and the children and I lived pretty reclusively. Many of our old friends didn't seem to be speaking to us any more; perhaps they were afraid, or perhaps it was just that our phone number had changed and they couldn't reach us. Part of it was my own making; I didn't have time to have guests and go visiting, and besides, I'd always liked the peace and quiet of being alone and avoiding big family gatherings. What had happened to Maher made some people curious, confused, embarrassed, or pitying, which, however genuine, I found hard to take. Sighs and teary eyes almost made me ill. Better to stay home by myself, or go out with the children for a change of scene.

⁂

The previous fall I'd met Hanen through a mutual friend; she later introduced me to her husband, Issam. Over time, the two became regular visitors. Their stories of newcomers trying to fit in reminded me of our own early days in Canada. They were quite familiar with our situation; Issam had made some effort to help me find work, which I hadn't been able to do thus far. I could sense their compassion, their willingness to help.

⁂

June was almost over; it wouldn't be long before summer vacation began. In a few weeks, Barâa would be at home along with Houd. I would no longer have to walk Barâa to and from school, but I was a bit apprehensive at the prospect of looking after both children the whole day, calming one down and cajoling the other, or asking Barâa to be more patient with her little brother. For all my motherly concerns, which were probably excessive, I was looking forward to the summer months.

People in Canada naturally assume that since I was born in a warm country I prefer summer to winter; but that would be like claiming that all Canadians love the winter! In Tunisia, I actually detested the summer months. When I was four or five years old, my father would rent a little house in Marsa or Kram, seaside villages not far from Tunis. Often, we would only be a few hundred metres from the beach, where my mother would take us daily and we would spend the entire day. My father would take the commuter train to work in the morning, and in the afternoon when offices closed he would join us. During the week only the locals would come to swim, take the sun, or play ball. There were always plenty of children our age to play with, while the adults stayed under their beach umbrellas. Strolling vendors would sell roasted peanuts in little cones made from old newspapers. Those tall, skinny vendors, with their dark, almost black skins, were from Tataouine, a southern Tunisian town in the desert, where there wasn't much work. They would spend their summers trudging up and down the hot sand for kilometres on end, trying to save a pittance selling almonds, peanuts, or sunflower seeds.

On weekends we'd stay at home; the beaches would be flooded with waves of humanity pouring out of packed buses and railway cars; there were men, sometimes carrying fat green watermelons under their arms, women and children with their beach buckets, everyone escaping the stifling heat of Tunis for the cooling waters of the Mediterranean.

A few years later, my father couldn't afford the rent for a seaside bungalow and we would spend the entire summer at home. He never owned a car; he would send us to the beach by commuter train or taxi. Occasionally, one of his friends would take us by car to a beach a bit farther away where we would spend the whole day. But most of the time I was bored silly. I read my way through book after book, and waited for September, when school would start up and I'd see all my friends again. All things considered, summer in Canada was better: the weather wasn't too hot, the lakeside beaches weren't packed elbow to elbow with people. Sure, I missed the sight and the smell and the feel of the sea, but I learned to do fine with a lot of other childhood memories, and missing the sea didn't bother me all that much.

LATE JUNE. Issam and Hanen dropped by for a visit. She was expecting her first child, and was soon to give birth. She would have to give up her job teaching French at a language school for adults; how would I like to take over for her during her maternity leave? she asked.

"You mean I would be teaching French?" I said, startled.

"Yes. I've already put in a word with the principal. If you're interested, let me take her your resumé and she'll get in touch with you."

I'd given up looking for work months ago. Not one of my applications had even been answered. The monthly welfare cheque covered our basic needs.

If I went back to work now, my routine would be thrown off, the welfare cheques would stop coming, and I might not have enough time to help Maher. But there were plenty of advantages as well, especially getting rid of the embarrassment of being on welfare. And at least I'd have an opportunity to use my education. I promised Hanen I would send her the resumé.

But first I had to talk to my social worker, which I did the very next day. She explained that I was entitled to work a certain number of hours per week and still draw financial assistance. Her answer reassured me; I could take a job and continue to receive my welfare cheques because my income would not be very much. I might be away from the children for most of the day, but at the same time I'd be rubbing shoulders with new people and getting some satisfaction from teaching others a new language. I began to feel better. All things considered, going back to work would be a good idea.

A few days later a call came from Marissa, the principal of Hanen's school. I explained my financial situation, and she offered me a part-time teaching position, to begin in the coming weeks. I accepted her offer on the spot. True enough, it wasn't a job that matched my real qualifications, but like just about everything else, it was better than nothing. My Ph.D. in finance, my knowledge of econometrics, the sleepless nights spent mastering the sophisticated models used to evaluate financial derivatives such as options and futures, was none of it to be of any use at all? Women working in these fields were few and far between. Several of my colleagues from the doctoral program (where I had been one of the two women in the class) were now working in the top universities or in major international institutions such as the World Bank.

And here I was, almost twiddling my thumbs. Every month I waited impatiently for my welfare cheque, worried that I wouldn't be able to pay the rent. I wrote letters to the prime minister and dreamed of once again seeing my terrorist-suspect husband who'd been thrown into a Syrian prison. The prospect of teaching French gave my morale a boost, but in truth, I was still in a deep pit, with no idea how and when I might eventually get out.

— 6 —

TORTURE AND LIES

Bring my father home . . .

EARLY JULY. CBC journalist Lawrence Morton called. He worked for *Disclosure,* a television program that probed behind the headlines of intriguing stories, seeking an often elusive truth. The show was planning a report on Maher's story, but the project was still in an embryonic stage. Lawrence asked if I had heard that an American journalist was writing an article about the case.

"What's his name," I asked.

"Seymour Hersh."

"I've never heard of him. Do you have any idea what he's saying in his article?"

Lawrence wouldn't say any more. But it was clear that someone had handed him the information and I would soon know all about it. When the conversation was over, I sat down at my computer and did a search on Seymour Hersh. He was a highly respected American journalist, a Pulitzer Prize winner specialized in investigative reports on military and security matters. What would he say about Maher? I wondered.

As the days went by, I forgot about Seymour Hersh. The children were now at home all day. We would often go to Westboro Beach on the Ottawa River, not far from home. Barâa was like a fish, diving into the cold water and coming back up with a proud smile on her face. Houd was more cautious; he was curious about the water but didn't dare venture into it. As a practising Muslim, I couldn't bathe in public, so I would wear a light skirt and walk with Houd at the water's edge, trying to persuade him to go into the water. But he preferred to play in the sand with his buckets and shovels and cups.

The prime minister's letter had not made me forget the promise his minister of Foreign Affairs, Bill Graham, had made me when we met, about writing a letter to his Syrian counterpart, including a statement that Maher was not involved in terrorism in Canada. Since my conversation with Myra about Mr. Lavertu's visit to Syria, I no longer felt like talking to her or Mr. Pardy. From now on I would devote all my energy to making my own contacts, to gathering more support, and without any high hopes let Mr. Pardy go about his job. I felt like a bird growing up and wanting to fly on its own.

The next day, I called Robert Fry, Bill Graham's secretary, who had been at my meeting with the minister and had given me his business card. He was not available, but left me a message that the letter project had fallen through. Clearly the minister had been unable to persuade all the government departments to adopt a common position toward the Syrians. But now Mr. Fry had gone even further: the Canadian security agencies, he said, were even opposed to such efforts because they had more questions than before about Maher. His message hit me like a slap in the face. I sat there stunned in front of my computer. But instead of replying right away I pulled out Jean Chrétien's letter and reread it several times over. The prime minister of Canada had assured me that Canada would spare no effort to bring Maher back, yet at the same time, Mr. Fry's message told me that "certain persons" in "certain agencies" were not working to this end. Mr. Pardy's words in his email of June 12 came rushing back into my head. How frustrating it must have been to see his efforts come to nothing each time he tried a new approach to bringing Maher home! Strangely, for the first time, I almost felt sympathy for Mr. Pardy.

⁓

JULY 7, 2003. I told Kerry Pither and Alex Neve about the failure of the letter plan. Since Kerry and I had begun working together, we often talked to Alex, who was still working for Amnesty International but was spending more and more time on Maher's file. He never hesitated to give us advice or opinions and kept writing letters to government departments requesting that they take action on the case. We would meet in Amnesty's big conference room and discuss short- and long-term strategy. In the beginning, I had been working alone with the help of a few friends; now there was a structure taking shape around me. The list of people helping and advising us kept getting longer. Kerry had introduced me to Marion Dewar, the former mayor of Ottawa, who was retired but still active, dynamic, and eager to lend her energy to causes dear to her. Bill Skidmore, from Carleton University, would also join us and give us his opinion. Surprisingly and unexpectedly, we had become a small, functioning organization. Kerry and I communicated by phone or email; she reread my letters and contacted journalists; she was my right hand.

But even this was not enough. Ours was an uphill struggle, and we needed a lot of support. Kerry wanted to get more non-governmental organizations working with us, as well as individuals, to convince the government that Maher Arar must be brought home. So we drafted a letter, to be co-signed by human rights organizations, unions, and other NGOs – the broadest possible representation of signatories – requesting a meeting with the American ambassador to Canada, Mr. Paul Cellucci. Alex wrote the letter and sent it in the name of Amnesty International with all the other signatories supporting Amnesty's request. I remembered well my disappointment over the letter I had written myself to the ambassador, but I had all but forgotten the reply. Now I had friends supporting me; I felt stronger, and more confident.

꧁꧂

JULY 14, 2003. It was hot that summer; one heat wave followed the other in quick succession. By the end of the day, our apartment was like an oven. I would open the balcony door and sit at the dining room table, trying to catch a cool breeze. The caretaker of our building often watered the lawn with an oscillating sprinkler that sent little droplets of water flying to one side and then the other. Our balcony directly overlooked the lawn, and Barâa and Houd always wanted to jump over the railing to go and play under the sprinkler. Sometimes other children would come to play in the spray until the caretaker spotted them and moved his sprinkler or just shut off the water.

I was woolgathering over things like this late one afternoon when the telephone rang. It was Marlene. I was surprised to hear from her at this hour; she usually called during the day. After the usual greetings, she said, "Monia, I have some important news for you." My heart was beating a mile a minute. What can it be now? I wondered. She continued.

"Senator Pierre de Bané, Mr. Chrétien's special envoy, will soon be travelling to the Middle East. He is scheduled to meet with the president of Syria. He will raise the question of Maher's case and give the president a letter from Mr. Chrétien. As yet there's no confirmation of this meeting, but I hope it will happen." The blood pounded in my temples; what was I going to do with this news? I thanked Marlene for the information.

"Not a word to the media, now. No one must know," she said. I promised not to breathe a word to the journalists.

Before ending the conversation, Marlene asked, "Are you happy?" I didn't know what to say. Why was she asking me this?

"I think so," I said. "I hope it all goes well."

That night I couldn't sleep a wink, unable to believe that Prime Minister Chrétien was really going to send a letter to the President of Syria about Maher. Was it really a victory that the Canadian prime minister was getting involved personally? Could I really be pleased and optimistic? Or was this another trial balloon that was going to burst like so many others? But this was exactly what I had dared hope for – wasn't it? – that Mr. Chrétien would intervene personally in Maher's file. So why was I being nagged by all these doubts and fears?

The next morning I sent an email to Kerry, Alex, and Riad about the latest news. I had confidence in all of them, knowing that they would take it seriously and be ready to help with their ideas and their time. I was sworn to silence, I told them. Then, as if to reassure myself, I wrote that even if the outcome were positive, we would not let up. It was my way of telling my subconscious that I must take nothing for granted. Their response told me that this latest development could only be a step in the right direction, although we had no idea when the letter would be delivered or what impact it would have on the Maher Arar affair.

Seymour Hersh's article appeared in the July 28 issue of *The New Yorker* and, to my great surprise, it said not a word about Maher. ("The Syrian Bet: Did the Bush Administration burn a useful source on Al Qaeda?" Seymour M. Hersh, *The New Yorker*, July 28, 2003.) Hersh had an intriguing theory: Syria, a country officially at war with Israel, had played on the theme of terrorism ever since September 11, 2001, to ensure that it would have a key role in any peace negotiations involving the United States, Israel, and other countries in the region. The Syrians, he maintained, had given many signs of "cooperation" over the files of al-Qaeda terrorists as a friendly gesture toward the United States, even helping the CIA foil an attack on the American Embassy in Ottawa with timely information. He seemed to have developed a remarkable talent for extracting confidential information from anonymous sources. He described the case of Mohammad Haydar al-Zammar, a Syrian-born German citizen suspected of being a major recruiter in the September 11 attacks, who was arrested in Morocco in 2002, then deported to Syria, where he was still being held by Syrian intelligence. But for all the talk about Syria, al-Qaeda, and plots foiled at the last minute, there was not a word about Maher Arar. So why had the journalist Lawrence Morton told me that Hersh was going to write about Maher? Had it been his own supposition?

⁓

JULY 24, 2003. I was about to leave for work. The children were still in their pyjamas. When Houd saw me at the door, he began to whimper as usual. Barâa, who loved to play the big sister, tried to take him in her arms to comfort him, but he wriggled away from her and ran to me. My mother came to the rescue and took Houd to see the squirrels on the balcony; magically, he forgot his woes. I kissed Barâa and left, almost on the run, for the parking lot.

It was almost the same scene every morning since I had begun to work part-time at Marissa's language school. Marissa and I had hit it off immediately. She was dynamic, always there bright and early, and ran her school with rare dedication. I wasn't working full-time because I didn't want to be away that much from the children, or put such a big responsibility on my mother's shoulders. Marissa never talked to me about my husband's case. It was as though there was an understanding between us. Our eyes would meet and I sensed that she knew everything; an exchange of smiles was enough.

I would spend the morning at work. I had a single student, a middle-aged civil servant who was anxious to pass her French exams in order to advance and get the promotion she was hoping for. I would have her read in French, conjugate verbs, take dictation, and we would review certain rules of grammar. Sometimes I could see myself as a child again, sitting at my desk, copying verb endings in the different past tenses. Who would have thought back then that I would be teaching French one day? But my life had taken a turn that no one could have predicted, and I was more than happy to have found a little job that gave me a smidgen of pride and a chance to meet new people. Since Maher's arrest, my life had been focused only on how to get him home; my new job was giving me a kind of respite and allowing me to see and think more clearly.

On that particular day, after the first session I went downstairs to the computer room to check my messages. I found an email from Kerry, who would forward articles that mentioned Maher. An article written by Robert Fife at the *Ottawa Citizen* left me in shock. I couldn't believe what I was reading. Fife claimed that, according to Seymour Hersh, the Syrians had relayed confidential information to the Americans that helped them foil terrorist attacks; Fife speculated that Maher's arrest had been linked to one such attack, creating the impression that Maher had been involved in the alleged plot to attack the American Embassy in Ottawa. ("Terror threats in Ottawa: Two kinds of fear: Report says Syrian intelligence helped U.S. to foil al-Qaeda plot on target in Ottawa," Robert Fife, *Ottawa Citizen*, July 24, 2003.) Yet Hersh had never mentioned Maher's name, merely citing the American Embassy case as an example of the Syrians' efforts to curry favour with the Americans and carve out a more important role in Middle Eastern peace negotiations.

I felt the blood run cold in my veins. When would these speculations end? Why were people so determined to make Maher out to be a villain? Why had Robert Fife not called me to get my point of view and comments? I was always available to the media, wasn't I?

The break between sessions was almost over and my head was spinning. I went to the public telephones, wanting to talk to Kerry, wanting desperately to talk to someone to share my pain, sadness, and fury. Kerry was at home; she often worked there.

"Do you know Robert Fife?" I asked her. "He's never written

about Maher before. Why didn't he speak to me before writing his article?" I bombarded her with questions, giving her no time to answer. Then I slowed down. "What do you think?"

"I don't know. We must talk about it with cool heads, and in the meantime I'll contact Robert Fife. Call me from home when you're through at school."

I went to the classroom where my student was waiting. I hid my emotions and pretended nothing had happened. I don't know by what miracle or willpower I managed to deliver the dictation I had planned; I had to force the words out of my mouth. All I really wanted to do was go home and finish talking to Kerry.

Once home, I called her. She told me she had contacted Robert Fife and suggested he speak to me. I waited impatiently for him to call, and when he did, the first thing he said was: "How's it going?"

"Very badly since I read your article," I retorted. I don't know how the words came to my mouth, but I immediately felt better. Fife had nothing to say in reply. I told him he should have spoken to me before writing his article, and that I knew my husband was innocent and had never been involved in a terrorist plot. We continued the discussion, I not knowing whether he intended to use my comments but wanting to give him my perspective. I was afraid that the article he had written, which smeared Maher insidiously and linked him to a plot that never existed, according to the RCMP, would destroy any progress I had made toward helping my husband. In fact, it had the reverse effect: journalists who had had nothing to report since Marlene's visit to Syria were now back covering the Maher Arar affair. Besides, after the adjournment of Parliament for the summer, there was not much else of interest happening.

Several days after our first conversation, Fife called again, asking if I knew about Pierre de Bané's mission to Syria and the letter from Prime Minister Chrétien that he was to deliver to President al-Assad. I was cornered. What was I going to say? Marlene had made me promise not to breathe a word, and here was this journalist asking me if I knew about it. If I said no I would be lying and if I said yes I would be breaking my promise. Then he would want to know how I knew and there was no way I wanted to mention Marlene's name. All this flashed through my head and I ducked his first question with my reply:

"That's very positive and promising news. Will it be enough, though? Will it convince the Syrians to release Maher; I don't know . . ." Fife didn't press me further; perhaps what he wanted was my reaction, and information about the visit was not important for the story he was working on. When I had hung up the telephone, I thanked God for giving me the words to escape this little trap. In the context, keeping a secret had turned out to be harder than walking on sheer ice.

LATE JULY 2003. I had not had any news of Maher since Marlene's trip to Damascus on April 23. Mr. Pardy had stopped calling to tell me if there had been consular visits. I was sorry now for being so ungrateful when I received reports of these visits; at least they told me that Maher was alive.

Since I had begun to work closely with Kerry, Ahmed was much less involved with our work, though he and his family were still fast friends of mine. In the meantime, Ahmed had lost his job and was working from home, creating some pressure in the family; I certainly didn't want to add to it. One day Ahmed phoned to tell me he had read on the website of the Syrian Human Rights Committee (SHRC), based in Great Britain, that Maher was being tortured.

I was horror-struck.

As soon as I had found out that he was being sent to Syria, I suspected he might be tortured, but I tried not to think about it. The country was notorious for serious human rights violations. When the Canadian consular reports said that Maher "was well," I knew the little act staged by the Syrian authorities must have covered up another reality. The site Ahmed referred me to was appalling: it gave detailed descriptions of torture of prisoners and political opponents: electric cables, beatings, sleep deprivation, isolation, and so on. And there, amidst this shocking information, was Maher's name. It made my flesh creep. At times I couldn't take any more and would stop reading, then, as if driven by an invisible power, I would start again. There was a big difference between suspecting something might happen and having proof of it.

What was I going to do? I had to tell Mr. Pardy, had to talk to Kerry and Alex. Amnesty International might be able to help; this was their field. Kerry said I should start by getting a letter from the Syrian Human Rights Committee. Amnesty Canada confirmed through Amnesty London that SHRC was a serious, reliable organization. I wrote to its executive director, Saleem al-Hasan. I didn't have high hopes of receiving more information, presuming that such organizations must be careful not to reveal their sources. Mr. al-Hasan's reply came promptly, however, offering to give me in writing what his organization had learned of the torture inflicted on Maher.

Now I was truly torn. I wanted written proof that he had been tortured, which would be vital to the process of getting him released. But I wanted most of all to find out if my husband was well.

I received the letter from SHRC describing Maher's dreadful treatment at the hands of the Syrians: it confirmed that Maher was really suffering while the Canadian government here in Canada was doing precious little to obtain his release.

❧

JULY 30, 2003. In a new article by Robert Fife in the *Ottawa Citizen,* I learned, for the first time since Maher disappeared, that "rogue" elements in the RCMP might have fed information to American authorities leading to Maher's arrest and deportation ("Chrétien wants to know who gave up Ottawa man to CIA, Syria," Robert Fife, *Ottawa Citizen,* July 23, 2003). This astonishing revelation had come from the

Solicitor General of Canada, Wayne Easter, minister responsible for the RCMP and intelligence agencies! How could the minister say such a thing when the RCMP had steadfastly refused to make any comment whatever on the case? In a way, it might even prove to be a source of grim satisfaction for me. For the first time, the possibility was being raised publicly and officially that Canadian public servants were behind Maher's woes, and mine.

There could no longer be any mistake: someone, somewhere in Canada, had helped the Americans deport my husband and send him to be tortured! I was relieved to read, at least, that my suspicions were not just the fruit of my imagination or my paranoia. But the reality was the same: Maher was still in prison, the Syrians were not budging from their position, the Americans were turning a deaf ear, and Canada was twiddling its thumbs.

Fife's article raised a question that no one had dared ask before: what role did the RCMP or CSIS play in Maher's arrest and deportation? The data from the Syrian Human Rights Committee and the news that "rogue" elements in the RCMP might be involved opened the door to questions from organizations such as Amnesty International. Voices were beginning to be heard demanding a parliamentary inquiry. So it was no longer just I, the tearful wife, who was seeing secret agents behind every tree and wanting at all costs to find an offender; now there were many of us looking for the truth about Canada's real role in this affair.

***

Since I had begun working at the language school, my life was strictly ruled by the clock. I would spend my mornings teaching and my evenings, after the children were in bed, preparing for the next day's class. As soon as I came home from work, my time was divided between the children and phone calls with Kerry or with journalists. My mother looked after the children when I was out or on the phone, and prepared most of our meals. When the weather was fine, I would make some sandwiches and we would all go to the park or the beach; we would stay outdoors for hours, Barâa riding around on her bicycle and Houd in the sand or on the swings.

As I watched the children at play, happy, innocent, and carefree, I thanked God for the gift He had given me. But I also felt a twinge in my heart. Both of them were growing up without their father, Barâa having known him and remembering him and Houd not having known him at all. How would this affect their future? They might not ever see their father again. I didn't know if, later, they would agree with the choice I had made to speak publicly about what had happened to us. It weighed constantly on my mind. Where once I had been a woman who made plans for life, who considered herself fulfilled and happy with a husband and two children, I had now seen my life turned upside down. But I no longer felt the despair of the first days; instead, there was bitterness and an almost gentle grief. I closed my eyes and drew a long breath; I prayed that all my fears would be unfounded, and that I would remain sure of what I was doing.

Preparations were underway to hold a press conference to announce publicly that Maher was being tortured in Syria, as documented by the Syrian Human Rights Committee. This had been a difficult decision; I would rather never have Barâa hear of such a terrible thing, but if I was to obtain massive public support, there was really no choice. Kerry, Alex, and I agreed that our strategy should be to go public with the torture letter, but also to ask Mr. Chrétien to recall Franco Pillarella, the Canadian ambassador to Syria. I had already suggested this to Mr. Pardy in the past, but he had been against it.

"It would serve absolutely no purpose to recall the Canadian ambassador," he had said. "Relations between the two countries would only get worse, and what will we do when we no longer have an ambassador in Syria?"

Mr. Pardy had a good point. Still, I could hardly tell people that my husband was being tortured and not insist that Canada harden its attitude toward Syria. I was no diplomat. I was suffering, I was the wife of a man who was suffering, and I had to use all the weapons available before it was too late.

AUGUST 7, 2003. I went to Kerry's office in downtown Ottawa. Kerry was putting the final touches to the kits we were going to hand out to the journalists. Everything was there: a press release; a chronology of events, the letter from the Syrian Human Rights Committee, and a letter from Amnesty International denouncing torture and demanding that the Canadian government obtain Maher's release or assure him the chance to defend himself in a fair trial. I helped Kerry finish the photocopies and put all the documents in cardboard boxes. The evening before, I had prepared notes of what I was going to say in English and French, and now I went into an empty office beside Kerry's and practised. Then Kerry came for me and we left on foot, our arms laden with boxes. Parliament was only a few minutes' walk away. I was nervous and my stomach hurt.

Alex Neve and Marion Dewar were waiting for us at the entrance to the Parliament Buildings; both would also be speaking at the press conference. We passed security with no problem. The room we had reserved was crowded with journalists. I went to the podium with Alex and Marion beside me. Alex spoke first. Maher Arar must be released immediately, he insisted, and if he was accused of anything he must be given the right to defend himself.

Though I knew Maher was innocent, I liked these words. They expressed the idea of fundamental justice and should answer the skeptics and those who had already made up their minds that Maher was guilty. What could be more obvious than the right to defend oneself against allegations? When my turn came, I was feeling better. I went to the microphone and spoke calmly. As soon as I had finished, the journalists asked a number of questions and I answered them. Then

Marion spoke to demand, along with Amnesty, that the Canadian government take action.

Afterwards, I had many requests for radio and television interviews. The interest was encouraging, but I was anxious above all to see how the government would react to my demands and those from Amnesty. The reaction was prompt. The next morning, a spokesman for the Prime Minister's Office told the media:

"We believe that the ambassador should remain in Syria. It would do no good to recall him." I was not surprised by this reply; I had expected it. From the comments I read in the press, however, it was clear the government was in a predicament. It was taking the "allegations of torture" (these were the terms it used) seriously and promising to take the matter up with the Syrians.

But the Syrians were still refusing to give access to Maher. Was it a tactic to demonstrate that they were in charge, or was Maher's condition so bad that they dared not let him be seen? Four months had passed since the last visit, which had been Marlene's. Since then, there had been nothing but silence. In spite of the success of the press conference, I was terribly afraid that something dreadful had happened to Maher.

The Syrian Human Rights Committee letter on torture had set off a kind of media frenzy; overnight, it seemed, everyone wanted to talk about Maher Arar. While for months I had not been able to persuade one journalist to write a single line on Maher's story, now the "news" of a plot targeting the American Embassy together with the torture report had generated an almost continuous flood of calls to me and to Kerry. Journalism has become just like high fashion, I said to myself. It only takes one to dare to do something different to make all the others start doing the same thing.

AUGUST 14, 2003. For once I was not teaching; I was planning to stay at home and do some housecleaning instead. The children were playing in their room. In recent weeks, I'd observed that they were becoming quite close. They were five years apart and relations between them were sometimes tense, especially since Barâa liked to talk and Houd could only babble a few words. So when I saw them playing peacefully together I would avoid disturbing them until I heard shrill voices or crying. On this particular day things were going pretty well and I had begun to clean the bathroom when the telephone rang.

It was Myra. Gar Pardy had not called me for a very long time, nor had I made an effort to call him either, ever since the plan for a letter to the Syrian minister had fallen through. I knew he was not responsible for that failure, but I no longer had much confidence in his diplomatic network. Had he realized this or was he very busy with other things? In any event, it was Myra I was talking to at the moment. She told me that the Canadian consul at Damascus, who was still Leo Martel, had finally obtained authorization to visit Maher. I thought, Oh, that means he's still alive, at least. Myra expected to receive the consul's report within hours and promised to send it to me at once. I thanked her and hung up.

I intended to keep cleaning the bathroom, but my mind was now elsewhere. After four months of silence, what was I going to hear? That all was well? That Maher was in excellent health? That the Syrians would give us greater visiting rights? Perhaps, but I wanted to know where he was being held, if he was going to be released, and when. With these things leaping about in my head, the loud voices of the children squabbling brought me back to reality. A few hours later, Houd had just begun his nap, Barâa was alone, happily playing in peace again, and I turned on my computer to find a message from Myra:

Monia: Further to our telecom of today . . . I now have the report of the visit. Maher has passed a message to you: Monia: I just miss you and the children very much. Hope to be with you soon. Maher.

He will also be allowed a lawyer of his choice at the civil court trial next week, and has asked for you to take care of his defence through family. Given his wish for not attracting adverse media publicity, he has asked for this to be done discreetly. He said that this was possible through a cousin of his father.

Gar and I will call you later today.

I didn't know what to think. The message seemed to be written in code; I had never received anything like it. First I was being told that Maher would shortly be brought before a civil court, but without a word about the charges against him. And what was this about adverse publicity? Why should that worry him? Everything published recently in the Canadian press had been sympathetic to him, or at least neutral. Were these his words, or were the Syrians dictating them? I knew accusations of torture were the worst publicity a country could have. Was that the message I was supposed to get? And who was this lawyer Maher spoke of? I remember vaguely hearing talk in the family about a distant cousin who was a lawyer in Syria, but why would Maher want him as his lawyer? I couldn't make sense of it; I was getting more and more upset.

At this juncture, Kerry called me on her cellphone; she was short of breath, walking fast in the street.

"Guess what? Bill Graham is giving a press conference in Toronto. I heard about it from journalists who called me. He's going to talk about Maher."

I told Kerry what I had just heard. I was angry. Why had Myra called me just a few hours before this press conference without telling me about it? Kerry was in a hurry and had to hang up.

"I'll find out what Bill Graham says at his press conference and call you back," she promised.

I wracked my brain. Why hadn't they notified me? Were they afraid I would talk to the media before the minister did? And why hold the press conference in Toronto? The journalists who knew Maher's file were in Ottawa, not Toronto. How could uninformed journalists ask pertinent questions and report correctly? So the Maher Arar case had become a political football and the minister wanted to score points in the wake of the torture report of the previous week.

I didn't know what to think. Yes, I was happy to know that Maher was still alive, but no more than that because I was told nothing about his physical or mental condition or about where he was being held. And talk of a civil court in Syria, what did that mean? The unanswered questions were piling up.

The day dawned hot and humid. Since morning, I had kept the living room curtains closed in hopes of preserving some coolness in the apartment, in vain. Waiting for Kerry to call and let me know what Bill Graham had told the media, I lay down on my bed but couldn't relax; the children were running in all directions.

Finally, she called: "The journalists tell me that Graham said Maher has not been tortured. He was well and will soon be brought before a civil court."

So the government was dismissing the charges of torture with a wave of the hand, even though they were documented by a Syrian human rights organization. I would have loved to believe it, and could have if there had been an independent doctor present during the visit in question, or if the visit had taken place in a known location and without Maher's Syrian jailors. But the minister had simply refuted the allegations without offering anything to support his position. It was impossible for me to believe Mr. Graham's assurances. Originally I'd been a rather naive young woman; but the past months' events had given me a lesson in the value of caution and clear thinking. I could see neither in what the minister had said.

Kerry suggested I talk to some of the Toronto journalists who were going to report on Bill Graham's press conference and gave me their names and phone numbers. Bottling up my despair as best I could, I agreed, sat down at the table, and called one of them. After the first few words, I realized that the young woman knew practically nothing of the case. She wanted to have me believe that my husband was fine. After all, that was what she had heard from the minister's mouth. I of course tried to change her mind, explaining the case so she could put things into perspective. But she persisted, and I was beginning to lose patience when suddenly there was nothing but silence at the end of the line. At the same time I heard the refrigerator motor stop. There was a power failure; that was why my cordless phone was not working. Expecting everything to return to normal soon, I waited in the living room in the darkness.

My mother turned on her little transistor radio; we quickly learned that a massive blackout had struck the entire northeastern power grid of North America. I thought back to the ice storm that had struck Quebec and parts of Ontario in January 1998. At the time, Maher and I were already living in Ottawa, but I had gone to Montreal for a few days to consult with my Ph.D. thesis director at McGill. I was staying at my parents' with Barâa, who was ten months old. After the power went off, the apartment became colder and colder and I could no longer warm Barâa's milk and food. We were stuck for two days like this before Maher could come and take us back to Ottawa.

What if the blackout lasted for days? I was afraid of losing all the food in the fridge. Now Barâa came to me with questions; she was afraid of the dark. I went to get candles and matches that I kept in a plastic bag for emergencies and we prepared for the night in the stifling heat.

When we woke the next day the power was still off, but I left for work anyway. I wondered if the article by the journalist I'd talked to the day before had been published, curious to see how she had treated the story of the consular visit. During the morning break, I phoned Kerry, who had no power either. I told her about my conversation with the journalist and asked her if she had read her article.

"I'm going to the office. I'll send you all today's articles I find," she replied.

I was very worried by the thought of Maher being brought to trial. I still had no idea of the charges against him but wanted to be prepared for the worst. It was imperative to find a lawyer as soon as possible. Putting his defence in the hands of "a cousin of his father's" who had been long established in Syria didn't appeal to me. Was that really Maher's wish or his jailers'? I was determined to find a human rights lawyer in Syria who was recognized in his field and independent. I wrote an email to Saleem el-Hasan of the Syrian Human Rights Committee asking him to give me a list of names.

When I came home from work, I phoned the parliamentary office of Irwin Cotler, the MP and lawyer who had offered to defend Maher free of charge. He was not there, but I left him a message. I wanted to bring him up to date and ask for his help finding a good lawyer in Syria. I was aware that the country's judicial system was not independent of the political authorities; everything was in the hands of the president and his circle of cronies. Even if Maher was defended by the best lawyer in the world, I knew there could be no real justice in Syria because the judges were politically influenced and even the most upright of them had their hands tied by directives from above. But that was no reason to leave him alone without a lawyer to defend him. We had to demand a public trial, and if the Syrians agreed to such a thing, I knew that Maher would be found innocent. In my mind, however, the whole court business was farcical: what were the charges, when was the trial to be held, where would it be held? I wasn't even sure the trial would take place, but I was behaving as if it would.

That evening, when I read Kerry's email with the articles published after Mr. Graham's press conference, the one I was looking for was not there. I called her.

"There was only one article on the consular visit," I said. "The reporter I was talking to just before the blackout didn't write hers."

Kerry burst out laughing. "So it was the hand of God that brought about the power failure! Perfect timing . . . !" It was something that Kerry, who was not a believer, loved to tease me about. "Don't you see, when the power was cut that journalist was foiled, the one who didn't know a thing about her subject but wanted to write an article anyway." I had to smile in spite of the tension that was nearly stifling me. I appreciated Kerry's warm-hearted humour.

Saleem el-Hassan responded with two lawyers' names: Haytham al-Maleh and Anwar al-Bunni. The same two were recommended by Amnesty International's London office. Irwin Cotler also confirmed that a Syrian acquaintance spoke highly of both lawyers. I read the information on the two and chose Haytham al-Maleh, who had been imprisoned in Syria for his work on free speech and his support of political prisoners. He impressed me, although I had not met him. But before phoning him, I wanted more information about the trial, and I thought Mr. Pardy would be the only one who could help me with that. I called him and he confirmed that the Syrians were preparing for a trial soon, and without hesitation agreed to meet me. I called Kerry and asked her to come along.

⌒

AUGUST 19, 2003. Ever since we'd heard that Maher would be brought before a civil court, I had not known which way to turn. My hope was that Mr. Pardy would be able to give me some pointers. I picked up Kerry at home and parked behind the Foreign Affairs building. Myra and Mr. Pardy were waiting for us. Mr. Pardy seemed to be in a good mood, which was reassuring. He began by telling me that, four days earlier, the Department of Foreign Affairs had asked the Syrian ambassador, Ahmed Arnous, to state the charges against Maher, the date of the trial, and whether Syria would grant me a visa to attend the hearings. I was very surprised by this last request, because I had never even raised the possibility myself. But this was not the time to interrupt; I kept quiet. Mr. Pardy also told me that he wanted to obtain a visa for James Lockyer, a lawyer known for his defence of people wrongly accused, so that he could attend the trial as a legal observer. The Syrian ambassador had taken note of the requests but had not yet responded.

"Why do you think the Syrians have changed their tactics and are now talking about a civil trial instead of a military tribunal?" I asked Mr. Pardy. "The president never even bothered to reply to Prime Minister Chrétien's letter!"

"In my opinion," he replied, "everything that's happening now is precisely the result of the letter we sent to President al-Assad. It could very well be that, by going through the motions of a trial, the Syrians want to wash their hands of Maher's case and release him. They may just want to save face." My heart began to pound, then I sharply reminded myself this was probably another false hope. I pretended not to have heard and let Mr. Pardy keep talking: "On the other hand, I'm not very optimistic about your choice of lawyer. Haytham al-Maleh is not much appreciated by the Damascus regime and people there could be pretty annoyed."

"But I never wanted a trial in Syria," I retorted. "My husband will never be able to defend himself there, and defend himself against what, besides? The charges aren't even known yet. With Haytham al-Maleh, I'm not taking any chances. And if the Syrians try to be really nasty, then Haytham al-Maleh is the man to see through their dirty work."

Mr. Pardy's tone of voice and expression changed. "We have to know what your aim is, Monia: to get your husband out of prison or to keep fighting just for the sake of fighting. If you choose the first, well, you have to go along with this trial and do it as discreetly as possible.

It's your choice." Then, as if to change the subject, he went on to talk about James Lockyer. I didn't know him, though I had heard of him. I knew that he had taken the defence of several prisoners and succeeded in clearing them of all suspicion and having them released. "James Lockyer is not only a very good lawyer," Mr. Pardy continued, "but he also understands politics. The Syrians have not yet replied about his visa, but we can also discuss your trip to Syria."

I wanted to shout no! but held back. Then I asked, "What guarantees will I have if I go to Syria?"

Mr. Pardy seemed exasperated this time. "There won't be any. You will be with the people from the Canadian Embassy in Syria at all times, but if the Syrians want to arrest you, there's nothing we can do about it."

I thought at once of the children and told myself I would never be crazy enough to go and risk leaving my children alone. I would rather wait here with my children for Maher's return, even if that might take years.

Throughout the meeting, Myra was taking notes, not saying a word.

Kerry asked Mr. Pardy: "Do you know where the last consular visit to Maher was held?"

He replied that it was held at the office of Major General Hassan Khalil, the head of military intelligence. My eyes widened; this was the first time I had heard this kind of detail.

Kerry continued, "Who was present at the visit?"

Mr. Pardy didn't seem surprised: "General Khalil, an interpreter, two Syrian agents, and Leo Martel, the Canadian consul. The Canadian ambassador to Syria talked with General Khalil for two hours after the consular visit."

So tongues were loosening. Immediately I asked if there were things in the report I had not been told. Myra turned to Mr. Pardy with an inquiring look as if to say: May I? Showing no expression, Mr. Pardy nodded. In a low voice, Myra read:

Arar was able to express himself freely and said the press will know the truth when he gets home and that the long detention had destroyed him mentally. He said that he was not being treated any worse than the other prisoners.

In shock, I listened to words I was hearing for the first time. I glanced at Kerry; her expression had changed. I didn't know what to do, what to think. I had been sent an incomplete report a few days earlier. Now I was getting the other part, much harsher, closer to the truth than I had ever imagined. I had nothing more to say. The trial, the lawyers, and all the rest had disappeared. Maher was suffering, I knew it. My heart had told me from the beginning, now the words Myra had just read confirmed it. Kerry and Mr. Pardy continued to talk, but I wasn't listening, I wasn't interested; I just wanted the meeting to end so I could talk to Kerry alone.

But there was another surprise coming: Myra told us this was the last time we would see Mr. Pardy. He would be retiring at the end of the month, to be replaced by Conrad Sigurdson.

"I've been working for too long," Mr. Pardy said light-heartedly. "It's time I took some rest."

I didn't say anything. It was too much to swallow all at once. Kerry and I thanked Myra, wished Mr. Pardy good luck, and left.

The meeting left a bitter taste in my mouth. I couldn't forget what I'd heard about Maher's mental state and about his treatment as a prisoner. Mr. Pardy could have prevented Myra from reading the original report of the consular visit, but he didn't. Why? Was it because he was soon to retire and could soon enough wash his hands of the whole matter? Or hadn't he been able to keep it in?

That night I couldn't sleep. I tossed and turned in the heat of my airless bedroom. My skin felt sticky, my pillow wasn't comfortable any more, I hated it. My life since Maher's arrest passed before my eyes: the first meeting with Mr. Pardy, the hopes, the doubts, and the disappointments, Marlene's visit to Syria, the letter that was never authorized by the RCMP and Canadian intelligence services, the letter from Jean Chrétien . . . and now the civil trial that was fast approaching and could either be the key to Maher's release – or the trap that would mean he would never come home.

I tried to rest, to forget, and to hope that things would get better, but my head was throbbing. I longed to get away, far away, to escape this tension that had hold of me. I got up and went to look at the children; they were both sleeping peacefully in their little beds. For a few minutes I watched them breathing gently and it calmed me. Then I went to the kitchen and drank a glass of water.

— 7 —

INTEREST GROWS

once an orderly, rather intellectual person,
I became a human rights activist . . .

SEPTEMBER 2, 2003. September began on a positive note. In an op-ed article published in the *Globe and Mail,* Irwin Cotler, the lawyer and professor of law who had volunteered to defend Maher, had pin-pointed six measures that Canada must adopt in order to obtain his release ("Six Steps to Freedom: What Canada must do to secure justice for Maher Arar," Irwin Cotler, *Globe and Mail,* September 2, 2003). Cotler's excellent analysis was written with great intellectual discipline; the fact that he was also a Liberal MP gave it even more weight.

I was delighted, especially since I had been wondering what a lawyer could hope to accomplish when his client, a victim of injustice, was being held endlessly in prison and didn't even know the charges against him. Now, however, Cotler had given me the arguments I needed to make the Canadian government get involved. So far, I had run up against a stone wall: the civil trial that Minister Bill Graham and the officials at Foreign Affairs kept talking about seemed to be going nowhere, which only magnified the very real danger that Maher would be held indefinitely in that secretive country, Syria.

༄

SEPTEMBER 3, 2003. A month earlier, I'd learned that Gar Pardy, head of Consular Affairs at Foreign Affairs, would soon be retiring – but I had no idea of the reasons for his unexpected (and to me, rather sudden) departure. Could it have been a consequence of his email of April 12, in which he described the Canadian government's ambiguous position on Arar's case, giving me a "lead" that I would later use to put the government in an awkward position? Whatever my conjecture, it meant that I would now have to learn to work with his replacement, Conrad Sigurdson. Myra Pastyr-Lupul, Mr. Pardy's assistant, was still on the job, which meant that at least I could look forward to a certain continuity in my relations with the department. Even though I'd often been annoyed with Mr. Pardy, I was genuinely sad to see him go. I'd always hoped that he could carry through with his work and see the promise he'd repeatedly made me – that Maher would be back one day – come true.

Unfortunately, Mr. Pardy's departure only deepened my feelings of uncertainty. So when I called his replacement, Mr. Sigurdson, I hardly knew what to expect. Over the phone his voice sounded timid, almost inaudible. What a contrast with Gar Pardy, who knew how to fill every minute of a conversation, and who had the gift, each time we spoke, of boosting my confidence. This time, Myra joined the discussion. She who had always taken a back seat, letting Mr. Pardy occupy the foreground, was now helping Mr. Sigurdson and spoke of the case with confidence.

Not only was I thrown off by the new situation, but the news I was about to hear disturbed me even more: Maher was not going to be brought before a civil court, Myra informed me, but before the

175

Supreme State Security Court. *Supreme, security, state:* the three words echoed in my head. I thought back to my teenage years in Tunisia, when I'd heard of the State Security courts there, a parallel judicial system whose primary function was to muzzle the government's Islamic opponents. One didn't trifle with "state security" in Tunisia. Nor in Syria, for that matter. People would tremble when they heard the words, words that were whispered furtively, almost superstitiously, as if to keep such a misfortune as tangling with "state security" from befalling them. In those courts, there was no appeal against the verdict, which all too often led to a life sentence or the death penalty.

"What do you know about that court?' I asked Mr. Sigurdson, to verify my suspicions.

"We know that the procedures are summary, and that the sentence cannot be appealed," he answered as though he'd expected the question.

"But weren't the Syrians talking about a civil court?"

"Yes, they were. We've just heard the news."

But that wasn't all. Mr. Sigurdson also told me that Maher was now being held in Sednaya Military Prison, which Saleem el-Hassan of the Syrian Human Rights Committee had also mentioned in his report. But Mr. Sigurdson was not yet aware of the charges, nor the trial date. We were back at square one, but this time the spectre of the Supreme Court seemed to be sending a signal that things had taken a new, ominous turn.

"Do you know if the ambassador will be able to attend the trial?"

There was a moment of silence, then Myra spoke up:

"The ambassador, Franco Pillarella, will be leaving on September 12. His replacement will be Brian Davis. According to our best information, he should be arriving in Syria soon."

Speechless with consternation, I listened without a word. What more could I say? I waited for the conversation to run its course and hung up. I needed to be alone to think things through.

Just what was going on at Foreign Affairs? Gar Pardy, the head of

Consular Affairs, was retiring while Maher's case remained unsettled. Canada's ambassador to Syria was leaving on the eve of a major trial, just as the Foreign Affairs minister, Bill Graham, was boasting to journalists in Toronto that Maher had the right to be tried by a civil court. Now Conrad Sigurdson was telling me that my husband was to be tried by the Supreme State Security Court.

In my dismay, I'd forgotten Irwin Cotler's article and his six measures. I sat down at my computer and did a short search, hoping to learn more about this Supreme Court. I wanted to find out for myself if my fears were justified. I found my answer in the U.S. State Department's 2002 Country Report for Syria: "[The Court] did not observe constitutional provisions safeguarding defendants' rights." The report also stated that defendants were not allowed to attend preliminary hearings or the investigative phase of the process, trials were generally closed to the public, defence lawyers were forced to submit written rather than oral pleas, the state's case was based on confessions, and defendants could not argue in court that their confessions had been coerced.[*]

The more I read, the more sick at heart I felt, seeing Maher trapped in a dreadful labyrinth from which he couldn't escape. My own sense of helplessness deepened; it was as if I were sinking down into a bottomless pit. I'd had some sorrows in my life, but all those had faded away, leaving only pangs in my heart. But the wound that Maher's imprisonment had inflicted on me gaped open, and what I was hearing only tore it wider.

"Mama, when are we going to the shopping centre? I need a new school bag. And this year, I want a backpack."

---

[*] This 2002 Report was replaced by a 2003 Report. See http://www.state.gov/ p/nea/ci/80195.htm.

Barâa, who would be starting grade two in a few days, was insisting that we go shopping for school supplies. Gone was the little girl intimidated by the teacher and the other children; now she was a big girl waiting impatiently for the first day of school to see all her old friends and meet her new teacher. Houd, still too young at nineteen months to go to school, didn't know what she was talking about.

"All right," I agreed. "Let's go right now."

I was happy to get out of the apartment and get my mind on small, unchallenging things; Barâa was jumping for joy. In minutes we were ready to go. Houd had retrieved his stroller from the closet, brought it to the door, and was sitting in it patiently.

It was a fine day, and the short walk to the shopping centre gave me a welcome chance to bask in the warmth of the sun's rays. Not surprisingly, the shops were thronged with parents and children looking for clothing, shoes, backpacks, pens, coloured pencils, and whatever else you could think of. Houd swung his little legs up and down in his stroller as he loved to do and looked curiously at the people around him. I let Barâa drag me from one shop to another. Suddenly, it was love at first sight between Barâa and a denim skirt in a window.

"I can keep my old school bag, it's still good, but I really adore that skirt. I've just got to have it!"

Naturally, I bought it, along with a few other items, and we returned home. Our little outing had brought me back to earth; I felt better. So when the children insisted on going out to play again, I went along gladly. The park was crawling with kids; it seemed to be welcoming us with open arms.

⌒⌒⌒

Imagine my surprise when I learned that the request I had made in July to meet the U.S. ambassador to Canada had been accepted! Except that we would not be speaking with Ambassador Paul Cellucci himself, as we'd hoped, but with his political counsellor, Robert Flora. This was the first time the U.S. Embassy had agreed to discuss Maher. My colleagues and I decided that Alex Neve of Amnesty International, Riad Saloojee of CAIR-CAN, Flora MacDonald, a former minister of Foreign Affairs and now a representative of the International Civil Liberties Monitoring Group, and I would make up the delegation. I didn't know Ms. MacDonald personally, but we had spoken by telephone and I had a great deal of respect for her experience as a politician and her dedication to many humanitarian causes. I was delighted that she'd agreed to lend us her support.

I was thinking about what I would say at the meeting when the phone rang. It was Alex. Usually he was bright and cheerful, but that morning he seemed hesitant, embarrassed.

"What is it?" I asked him.

His answer came slowly: "It's about the meeting at the U.S. Embassy . . ."

I was expecting the worst. The Americans were going to let us drop . . . But he went on: "Well, Robert Flora, who runs the political section of the embassy, whom I know pretty well – we've worked together on a number of cases – he doesn't want you to be part of the delegation."

Alex was upset; he wondered if we shouldn't cancel the meeting. As far as I was concerned, it had never occurred to me that a meeting could take place without me; it seemed preposterous that I couldn't be a part of a delegation that was visiting the embassy to talk about my husband. But I was comforted to know that I was the only one being excluded.

"We've got to meet the people from the embassy," I told Alex without missing a beat. "It's an opportunity we can't afford to miss."

Yes, I wanted the meeting to take place, with or without me. I wanted the Americans to rectify their error and help us bring Maher back to Canada. Even if it was unlikely that my wish would come true, I wanted to try. With a note of relief, Alex told me: "I'll call the embassy and let them know that we'll be there as planned, Flora, Riad, and I."

A question popped into my head: "What about the American dip-lomatic official? Did he say why he didn't want me in the delegation?"

Embarrassed again, Alex replied, "He told me he didn't want the meeting to be too emotional . . . at least that's what I thought I heard."

I was startled by the official's answer. I'd never cried in public. It was ironic! The suffering I might be expected to feel as the wife of a man who was in prison and subjected to torture was turning out to be a handicap, undermining my efforts.

Ever since I'd learned that Maher was to be tried by the Syrian Supreme State Security Court, I had been doing everything I could to alert the people around me. Kerry Pither and I wanted to gather together as much information as we could about the court and its injustices, and share what we learned with the Canadian public. We were convinced that our first task was to warn people in Canada – citizens and politi-cians alike – about the perils Maher was facing in Syria. Amnesty International put its information centre at our disposal. We quickly learned that several Syrian dissidents or opposition politicians had been tried by the court. We had strong evidence of the irregularities that had taken place. But what really frustrated me was that no one knew what Maher was accused of. Even Haythem al-Maleh, the Syrian lawyer I'd chosen on the recommendation of several human rights organizations, could not learn the answer.

SEPTEMBER 9, 2003. I called Mr. al-Maleh to find out if there was any news. The telephone connection was bad; I was afraid we'd be cut off at any moment.

"Have you been able to meet Maher?" I asked.

"No," he said with a note of sadness and resignation in his voice. "I keep insisting on meeting with him and seeing his file, but they refuse. They say I cannot speak to him before the trial begins, and that the file is not yet completed."

There was a moment of silence, then I ventured: "Is that normal?"

I thought I heard faint laughter at the other end of the line, then Mr. al-Maleh said, "I don't know any more what's normal and what isn't . . ."

I thanked him for his efforts and promised to keep him up to date on what we were doing.

It occurred to me that the Syrians might be bluffing. Their refusal to make any specific accusations might be a positive sign; it might mean that they had nothing on Maher. Maybe it was their way of washing their hands of his case. Or perhaps they were trying to whip up public opinion by showing that Maher really was a dangerous terrorist. I wanted to believe that it was all a put-on, that they were looking for a way to release him. But I couldn't count on it, knowing well Syria's reputation for ignoring political pressure. Ultimately, I had to choose between trusting my intuition and relying on the facts. Once again, I found myself torn between hope and fear, between light and darkness.

A day or two later, I was waiting in line at the post office when I noticed a stack of blue pamphlets featuring the Canadian passport. I picked one up for a closer look. On the first page were the words: "The Canadian passport: a trusted document." When my husband travelled from Tunisia to Montreal with his Canadian passport, with stopovers in Switzerland and the United States to change planes, there had been no doubt in his mind that his Canadian passport was indeed a trusted document. Now, a year after his arrest in the United States and his deportation to Syria, I can only presume that he no longer thinks so.

One thing is certain: the U.S. authorities didn't consider the Canadian passport to be a trusted document when they removed my husband to Syria, where he was born, rather than to Canada, where he has lived since age seventeen.

Who is going to defend Maher Arar now? I wondered. Three countries owed us an account of what they had done – or had not done: the United States, Syria, and Canada. The American authorities, the very people responsible for his plight, with not the slightest consideration for his basic rights, had so far refused to co-operate, claiming they deported him with the blessing of Canadian police authorities. That left us with Syria and Canada.

In Syria, my husband had received no medical care and had not been allowed to speak with any member of his family. He was accused of belonging to the al-Qaeda network, a crime for which they wanted to bring him before a military tribunal. For months, the consular visits had been suspended and no Canadian official had been allowed to see him. It was as if he had simply vanished. And now, all of a sudden, they wanted to try him before the Supreme State Security Court – truly terrifying news. There would never be justice for Maher in Syria, I was convinced of it.

My only hope of bringing my husband back, of bringing Barâa and Houd's father back to them, was the Canadian government. Tragically, a year after the start of our ordeal, even that hope, once so tenacious, had all but vanished.

Maher's six-year-old daughter would cry herself to sleep, thinking of the father she had not seen for twelve months, an eternity for her. School would be starting once more, but as with last year, her father would not be with us to share her enthusiasm and delight.

Time and again she asked, "When will Baba come back?"

I didn't know what to answer. The Canadian passport – "trusted document" that it is – had not protected my husband.

SEPTEMBER 11, 2003. I made my way to the offices of the International Civil Liberties Monitoring Group. This was where our little delegation was to gather before making its way to the meeting at the

U.S. Embassy. Flora MacDonald was already there; it was my first encounter with her. She welcomed me cordially and asked me several questions with a view to sharpening her grasp of Maher's case. As Canada's then-minister of External Affairs (as it was called at the time) during the 1979–80 hostage crisis in Tehran, she had a fascinating negotiating argument: since the Canadian Embassy in Iran had helped several members of the U.S. Embassy staff to flee, she would suggest to "our American friends" that they do the same, by helping Maher Arar to get out of Syria. To me, the idea was a brilliant one.

When Alex, Riad, and Kerry arrived, the five of us went off on foot toward the U.S. Embassy, a fifteen-minute walk. It was a hot day and I'd made the mistake of wearing a dark jacket; it felt as though I was crossing the desert – which, in a different sense, I'd been doing for the last year. A handful of journalists who'd got wind of the meeting were waiting for us in front of the embassy gates. Alex, Flora MacDonald, and Riad went in; I watched as they spoke to a security guard, then entered the building. Meanwhile, Kerry and I waited outside. I was still fuming at being shut out of the meeting, but I had great confidence in our delegation. Little by little the journalists – who were just as impatient as we were to find out what the Americans had to say about Maher – gathered around us; I didn't even notice the time go by.

Then I caught sight of Flora MacDonald leaving the embassy, followed by Riad and Alex. The journalists rushed off to meet them, each trying to pry from them a statement about the meeting. I waited off to the side for the little crowd to disperse, and Flora quickly came over to inform me of the results of the discussion: the United States was not prepared to so much as lift a finger. Its position was that, in diplomatic terms, it was a matter between Canada and Syria; there was no way they could intervene. I had known that our initiative was unlikely to succeed, so I felt no severe letdown. Still, it was hard news to swallow.

But there was a new element: the embassy now recognized the full responsibility of its government in the decision to arrest Maher and deport him; the Canadian government had played no role in those events, they claimed. That, at least, cleared the air: there had been an admission of responsibility. But that was of no help to Maher.

⁓

There I was, alone at home, drafting a French text for my new student. Barâa was at school while my mother had taken Houd to the shopping centre to buy him a pair of running shoes: it was about time, as he'd begun to run by now. The phone rang. It was Anthony, Alexa McDonough's assistant. Alexa was now the NDP International Development critic and a member of the House of Commons Standing Committee on Foreign Affairs and International Development. Anthony told me that I would soon be receiving an invitation to testify before the committee about Maher's case. The words popped out spontaneously: "I can hardly believe my ears!"

"Alexa has already talked to almost all the committee members. They're all in agreement. So you should be receiving an official invitation from the Clerk's office."

Of course I had no way of knowing what the committee members would think, but I was more than pleased to hear the news. Especially since others would also be invited to testify, including, so Anthony believed, civil servants from Foreign Affairs and high-ranking RCMP officers. If nothing else, this indicated that things were moving inside the government. Could it possibly be shaking itself out of its lethargy? I quickly called Kerry, who saw it as a positive development.

At the time, Kerry and I were working to put together a pamphlet to distribute at our upcoming public events. We agreed that it should contain an update on Maher's situation in Syria, along with a list of the things people could do to aid his cause, such as writing to the prime minister to insist that he intervene in person with the Syrian president to stop the Supreme State Security Court trial. We wanted to give all our sympathizers ideas and advice on how to help defend Maher.

Meanwhile, I was in regular contact with Haythem al-Maleh; every time we spoke, I would ask him if he'd been able to meet Maher, or even consult his file. And each time the response was the same, in a tone of bitter resignation: "I can't do a thing."

No solution seemed to be in sight, no way of cutting through that monstrous knot. But I was still not convinced that the wretched trial would ever be held in the first place.

SEPTEMBER 18, 2003. Today Anthony told me over the phone that it was being said that some members of the Standing Committee on Foreign Affairs were not in agreement with having me testify. And since the committee clerk had not yet officially invited me, I was afraid the whole thing had fallen through. It was all I could do to keep from pushing the panic button, which over time I'd developed a tendency to do.

Kerry and I were to meet at her house that day before going on to a meeting at Amnesty International. I adored Kerry's house; it had a particular charm about it, and I felt safer there than anywhere else. Maybe it was the massive exposed wooden beams that reminded me of the mosques I used to attend with my father when I was a little girl. Or maybe it was the calm that seemed to emanate from the old walls that created a sense of peace and calm. I took a seat in the living room and waited there, enjoying the silence, while Kerry was making final preparations upstairs.

I closed my eyes: I was tired, sad, and feeling all alone. I saw Ahmed and Racha rarely now; I knew they cared for me and prayed for me, but Ahmed had gone into business for himself, and his life had become more complicated. Hanen and Issam's baby had arrived, and they were caught up with looking after the new arrival. More than ever, I was left still thinking I could do it all alone, along with my mother and the children. Solitude was weighing more heavily these days. When I'd heard that the Foreign Affairs Committee would hear my testimony,

I'd forgotten my troubles; for several days my spirits had soared. But Anthony's most recent call had dashed my hopes once again.

There stood Kerry in front of me, brushing her hair. I told her Anthony's latest news. She stopped and looked at me. I don't know what happened at that instant, but I began to weep. I had never cried in front of her, out of modesty perhaps, or perhaps because I simply hadn't felt it. But this time it swept over me, and I couldn't stop. Sobbing, I blurted out: "I'm at my wits' end. There's nothing to be done. They don't even want me to testify before the committee. Why is everyone against me?"

The tears just wouldn't stop. Kerry was at a loss. She handed me some tissues; I dried my tears and blew my nose. She did everything she could to console me: "Everything is going to be all right, you'll see."

I wanted to apologize. "I don't know what came over me, but suddenly I felt so powerless! I've got to prepare myself never to see Maher again."

For a moment longer I remained seated, with Kerry sitting beside me now. Then I got up: "I'm going to wash my face."

Later in the day, when I thought back to that incident, I was still shaken by that powerful surge of emotion. Finally I was beginning to understand the stress I was under, and how little it took for it to come to the surface and break through the protective shell of coolness that I'd built up around me.

SEPTEMBER 25, 2003. The meeting of the Standing Committee on Foreign Affairs was confirmed. At last, I would be able to testify before the politicians. By some unbelievable fluke, the meeting would be taking place on the anniversary of Maher's arrest. Call it coincidence!

I'd written out my testimony, but my stomach was churning. After picking up Kerry at her house, I parked in the underground garage at the World Exchange Plaza, a few steps away from Parliament Hill, where the committee would be meeting. Just as Kerry and I were climbing the steps to the Parliament Buildings, a car with tinted windows stopped close to us, the uniformed driver got out and ran around to open the rear door; a man got out. It must be Richard Proulx, I thought, the assistant commissioner of the RCMP Criminal Intelligence Directorate, who was scheduled to testify as well.

We entered the hearing room in the West Block where the committee was sitting. I recognized some of the MPs present: Alexa McDonough, Marlene Catterall, and Irwin Cotler, but many of them were unknown to me. There were also many journalists on hand. Richard Proulx (it had been he) spoke first. He refused to answer several questions from the MPs, irritating them in the process. His behaviour gave the impression that he had something to hide. Then came Irwin Cotler, who was wearing two hats: that of a sitting MP and that of a lawyer active in support of Maher's cause.

His presentation consisted primarily of the arguments he had already made publicly in his *Globe and Mail* article. But he also underlined the legal errors that had already been made, and insisted that Canada could correct them. From my seat, I could see the journalists taking notes. Soon it would be my turn, and my heart was beating rapidly. I prayed for courage, and when my time finally came, I began to read my prepared text in a calm voice:

> *Ladies and gentlemen,*
>
> *First of all, I would like to thank you and all the members of this committee for giving me this opportunity to come and talk about what I have been through with my two children and all the family since September 25 of last year.*
>
> *Today it's exactly one year since I saw my husband for the last time. I've never seen him, I never talk to him, and my 6-year old daughter Barâa, who goes to grade 2 this year, has never been seen by him at school. My 19-month-old baby son hasn't seen his father for one year; he was only 7 months when he saw his father for the last time. Now he's a*

baby of 19 months, he walks, he runs, he's even started talking, but he doesn't know his father.

Let me tell you, it has been 12 months of sorrow, 12 months of disappointment. However, I am more than ever determined to bring justice to my husband, Maher Arar. I believe in the Canadian values of justice. I will try to educate my children to believe in them, and I hope that one day they will be proud to see Canada doing all it can to bring their father back home. I feel that it is very important to do that. I am not a politician, I am a mother of two children. However, it's very important to me to do it. It's very important, not only for me or for my husband, but for my two children and for many other Canadian citizens who are watching this case and are very concerned about the future of our country. Many Canadians who are from Arab and Muslim backgrounds are very concerned about what happened to Maher Arar, about the meaning of their Canadian citizenship today.

In two or three days — I don't know, but I know it's coming very soon — my husband will be facing an unfair trial . . .

Suddenly the tears began to flow and I couldn't stop them. I'd wanted to impress the MPs with my courage, and now my body was betraying me. Later, I overheard Marlene Catterall saying that this was the first time she'd ever seen me cry. It was if my tears had been held prisoner for these long months and all at once, in front of the MPs, the journalists, and the parliamentary officials, they were set free, as if to show everyone present that I was a human being.

I took hold of myself and continued:

My husband will be in front of one of the worst courts in the world. He will be in front of the Syrian Supreme State Security Court. This is not a civil court, this is not an open trial; this is almost a military court for someone who has been living in Canada for 15 years without going back to Syria, aside from being deported there. The

Syrian lawyer I hired very recently has been denied access to him. He has been refused access to the file, and he has not even been able to know what are the charges. This court was set up 40 years ago. There is a lot of documentation about it from the U.S. State Department. This court does not accept any appeal. The Government of Canada must stop this trial.

My questions are the following for you: Why should he face such an unfair trial in Syria if he has spent the last 15 years of his life here in Canada? If he decided in 1991 to become a Canadian citizen, if he did all his studies in Canada, if he came to Ottawa, worked for high-tech companies, and participated in the economic growth of Canada, why should he be today held incommunicado in Syria, coming to trial in a few days? Why should he face an unfair trial if he was forcibly deported to Syria? He was kidnapped, taken to Syria, and kept incommunicado for the past 12 months, reportedly being subjected to severe torture.

Today I would like to help stop this injustice, to help stop this large threat to our human rights, to our Canadian values. I think as members of an elected government, you can make a difference and you can be very proud to show it to all Canadian citizens. Maher Arar is a test for all Canadians, and I, as well as my two children, hope we are going to pass that test, we are going to see him back one day. I came with personal suggestions, and I think they will be helpful. I hope you will do more than welcome them in trying to help this Canadian citizen back to Canada.

First, I would like to see the Prime Minister make it clear to the Syrian President that this trial is not acceptable, that Maher Arar must not face trial in Syria. He doesn't belong there; he belongs to Canada, he belongs to his children, and he belongs to his parents, who have been suffering for one year. Mr. Jean Chrétien must make it clear to the Syrian President that he must be brought home. If the Syrian President and the Syrian authorities continue to ignore the Canadian government, which they have since day number one — they never replied to Mr. Jean Chrétien's letter, they never replied to all the diplomat's notes sent by the Department of Foreign Affairs, and they don't count on their replying — then Syria must know that Canada will suspend its ongoing efforts to accelerate trade and investment in Syria. We have relations with Syria. They are willing to be part of the international community. They need Canada, as well as many other countries in this world. Why don't we use that leverage? Why have we been so reluctant? Why have we been so timid, so shy? Why? Doesn't he deserve more than this?

Second, the Canadian government must ask the United States to take responsibility for what they have done. There has not been any contact with the Americans, except at the very early stage of this case, to ask them why they deported a Canadian citizen without official notification to Canada, why they decided to deport him to Syria.

The U.S. State Department acknowledged on their website that Syria is a state sponsoring terrorism. It is a state where human rights do not mean a lot. The United States must be asked to intervene on my husband's behalf.

Third, it's very important that the Canadian government launch an inquiry. I think you are watching today what happened in the first part of this committee, how shaky and how contradictory was the answer of the RCMP involvement in that tragedy.

If there is any role of the security agency, I have to know. My children have the right to know. In 10 or 15 years they will be adults. They will start asking questions. My daughter of 6 years is starting to ask questions. She would like to go to Syria. She said to me that she would like to live with her father in the jail cell.

Canadians have a right to know if our own security agencies are choosing to use the courts in authoritarian regimes instead of our own justice system.

If they didn't find anything on Maher Arar, they should say publicly today to the Syrians that Canada doesn't have any evidence to *link Maher Arar to terrorist activities. I have asked them on many occasions. They didn't want to acknowledge it.*

They can keep on refusing, but I think today they have a moral obligation, if not a legal obligation, to say that Canada doesn't have any evidence and to participate in all our efforts to bring this citizen back to justice, because he has been refused justice.

Today I have only [one] request. Our nightmare must come to an end. The Canadian government must use all its efforts — and I know their efforts are tremendous. They can make a difference and stop this injustice and bring this citizen back to his country as soon as possible.

I think my children, my husband, and I deserve more than we have received for these past 12 months. We deserve justice.

Thank you.

When I got back to the apartment, Barâa was sitting on the floor among her coloured crayons. She was working on a poster for tomorrow's demonstration to commemorate the day of Maher's arrest in the United States one year ago. Many people were supporting the event. For all my discouragement, I couldn't help seeing how, over time, more and more people had rallied to Maher's cause. With time, my pain had grown; but support was growing as well. Our little informal committee was learning to work in a more organized way, and we were making substantial gains.

Amnesty International had obtained a permit for our march through the streets of Ottawa. We planned to hold a press conference in front of Parliament, then proceed to the American Embassy, to the Prime Minister's Office, and finally to the Syrian Embassy. For the occasion I'd written three letters: one for George W. Bush, one for Jean Chrétien, and one for Bashar al-Assad, the president of Syria. Each of them demanded that Maher be returned to his family, in Canada. I wanted to hand each letter to a representative of the respective governments.

Kerry, who was handling our overall communications strategy, had thought up the idea of creating a huge Canadian passport, made of cardboard. It was a brilliant idea; the message was simple and convincing: Maher Arar had been deported to Syria in spite of his Canadian passport. It was up to the government to save the reputation of its passport. Alex had got permission for us to march in the street, Bill Skidmore would look after the loud-hailer and distributing the leaflets. I felt empowered now, and with the support of so many people, I was confident the march would be a success.

By now Barâa had finished her picture; proudly she came over to show it to me. It depicted a little girl, a little boy, a woman wearing a head scarf, and a man.

"It's my family," she explained. "You, Baba, Houd, and me."

Tears welled up in my eyes. In her picture I recognized all the love and devotion a child could be capable of. Praising her work, I hugged her close to me.

How does a mother feel when her children are put in such trying circumstances? I would have done anything to spare them. But I was discovering how we, as human beings, have an immense capacity for adaptation and for courage. How would Barâa reconcile herself with her father's tragedy? How could she believe in the people and the institutions of her country? I wanted her to grow up to be proud of herself and her family. And now, with her little picture, she was showing me that she wanted only one very simple thing: for the four of us to live together. I knew then that, just like me, she, too, would do anything she could to help her father.

SEPTEMBER 26, 2003. I'd asked my mother-in-law, who lived in Montreal, to come to Ottawa to take part in the march. I wanted the women of our family from all generations to be there: my mother-in-law, my mother, Barâa, and I. Each one of us had lost Maher, each in her own way; each of us had a story to tell. I wanted to take the opportunity to reveal the hidden side of the affair, all those who had been so deeply affected by his tragedy.

That morning, I drove to the bus station to pick up my mother-in-law. I found her thin and frail. She seemed to have aged ten years since the last time we'd met. We went home for a bite before leaving for the demonstration. Barâa, who insisted on participating, had not gone to school. I could see the excitement and determination in her eyes; she wanted to protect the memory of her "Baba" and to feel useful. Then the five of us went off.

On the way, we stopped at Kerry's office, which was buzzing with excitement: several people were putting the final touches to the giant passport while Kerry was taking a last look at my three letters. Another woman made photocopies of Barâa's drawing, then helped her glue the original to a piece of cardboard and hang it from her neck with a length of string. I looked at my daughter, who was beaming, displaying her artwork on her chest the way people once carried sandwich boards. When everything was ready, we set off on foot toward Parliament Hill. Leaving my mother, mother-in-law, and the children on the lawn, I went inside with Kerry and Alex Neve.

The room where the press conference would be held was packed with journalists: the case had now begun to draw serious attention. Alex, representing Amnesty International, followed me to the rostrum, as did Svend Robinson of the NDP. We emphasized that a whole year had passed since Maher's arrest and demanded, once again, that the Canadian government do whatever it took to repatriate him. Then I answered questions from the journalists, never missing a chance to denounce the government's inaction.

Afterwards, I went outside to join my family for the march. Kerry and Svend joined us, and our little procession set out. Perhaps a dozen people fell in behind. My mother-in-law and I held the giant passport open: on the first page was a photograph of Maher, a smile on his face. Barâa, with a serious look, marched along directly in front of me. Suddenly, I felt a shiver running through my body; it was all I could do to hold back my tears. Journalists were scurrying this way and that, filming us from different angles. Our little group came to a halt in front of the U.S. Embassy, and I pulled the first letter out of my handbag. Alex asked the security guard if someone from the embassy would come outside to accept the letter, and we waited for a few minutes in front of the wrought-iron main gate. No one came. Then one of the demonstrators had the idea of taping the letter and a copy of Barâa's picture to the black bars of the gate. As luck would have it, someone had brought a roll of tape, and in a matter of seconds the letter and picture were firmly attached to the gate, fluttering there gently in the breeze.

The Prime Minister's Office, located in the Langevin Block, was our second stop. When we got there, Houd, who'd been quietly seated in his stroller during the first part of the march, began to whimper. My mother decided to let him stretch his legs, and he toddled forward toward the steps that led up to the entrance. At that moment a government employee stepped forward to take the letter. When I handed it to him, I noticed that his hand was shaking. He promised me that he would hand it to those responsible for the case and quickly vanished inside. I turned to run after Houd, who was trying to negotiate the steps, and put him back in his stroller. He understood that recess was over and didn't utter a peep.

No more than fifteen people were marching with us. One of Bill Skidmore's students was handing out leaflets, and another chanted through the loud-hailer: "Bring Maher home!" Some people stopped to ask us what it was all about, while others went about their business without even pausing to throw us a glance.

The Syrian Embassy, our last stop, was not far from the Langevin Block. The demonstration had begun with the United States and ended in front of Syria, stopping off at Canada on the way. For me, it represented Maher's involuntary wanderings, from the United States until his detention in Syria, with Canada playing a central role. Next to the building that housed the Syrian Embassy was a small parking lot;

our little procession stopped there. A police officer who had been accompanying us volunteered to deliver the letter to the embassy, which was located on one of the upper floors. A weatherworn Syrian flag hung from the façade, and everybody looked up at the windows. Then people began to drift away. But before they did, I thanked every one of them warmly.

One year before, on this very day, I had been in Tunisia, alone, not knowing what to think, unable even to imagine the tribulations that would be inflicted on our family. Today, in front of that dark, gloomy building I no longer felt alone: around me were people who believed in the same Canada I did, the democratic country of justice and equality where I had come to live twelve years earlier. A flush of optimism filled my chest. I was more determined than ever to keep up the struggle. Nothing, I vowed, was going to stop me.

— 8 —

HOME AT LAST

*I held him by the hand; his face was pale, there was distress
in his eyes, and he looked at me like a sad-faced puppy . . .*

LATE SEPTEMBER 2003. I hadn't forgotten the look of concern
and the sense of determination I'd seen on the faces of the MPs
when I'd spoken to the House of Commons Standing Committee on
Foreign Affairs. For the first time since Maher's arrest, I'd met with a
true and sincere response from politicians of all political parties. And
when I sat there among them, I had the feeling that his case was no
longer an issue that only the NDP wanted to talk about or that a
handful of Liberal backbenchers were prepared to support. Instead, it
was an affair that concerned all Canadians. Now MPs from the Bloc
Québécois, the Conservative Party, and even the Canadian Alliance
were asking questions and promising that this would not be swept
under the rug.

Although I'd been terrified of speaking before all these people,
I had done it and I realized it had given me a boost of courage. Now I
was ready to forge ahead.

"You know what I'm going to do," I told Kerry. "I've made up my mind to visit all the MPs in their parliamentary offices . . ."

"What a great idea! I love it! You can give them a copy of the time-line and ask them to put pressure on the government," she said.

"I'll start with the MPs I saw when I testified before the committee, but little by little, I'll knock on all their doors."

"More than three hundred MPs, that's a big order. But if you ask me, it's worth it."

She promised to help me; the two of us were as happy as school-girls who'd just learned a new game. I began right away by calling the offices of the MPs and making appointments with them. The first reactions were encouraging and filled me with enthusiasm and hope. I wanted my mother-in-law to join me on this new round of meetings with the honourable members. Our message, coming from the prisoner's wife and mother, would be even stronger than if I were going alone. We agreed that she would come to our apartment on Sunday, October 5, and that starting the next day we would begin visiting MPs who'd agreed to meet us.

No sooner said than done. I called the office of Conservative MP Bill Casey. As a member of the Foreign Affairs Committee, he was first on my list. My plan was to explain Maher's case and ask for his help. I didn't know him; I was concerned that he might just ignore me. I had no idea what influence political principles had on MPs' interests. So when we met, I was pleasantly surprised. His attitude was attentive, concerned; he was interested in finding out more about Maher's case; he would interrupt to question me about details. I handed him a copy of the chronology and asked him to help me in my efforts by putting questions in the House of Commons, by following up on the case in the Foreign Affairs Committee, and simply by keeping an eye on the file. He seemed quite open and gave me the distinct impression that my words were not falling on deaf ears. I didn't know what Bill Casey might do, but I was confident that I'd gained a strong ally in my ongoing battle.

⁂

Slowly, autumn was settling in. The trees were changing colour; the once-green leaves that had soothed our eyes all summer were giving way to masses of red, yellow, orange, and brown. No sooner had the leaves drifted gently to the ground and formed little heaps than they were carried off by a wind that quickly picked up and grew stronger. The weather was fine and warm. Not far from our apartment was a recreation centre with an indoor pool where I took Barâa for her swimming lessons. She'd learned a lot since she'd begun. She didn't flail about and bob up and down any longer, but moved with steady, rhythmic movements. One day while I was waiting for the lesson to end, I saw that there would be regular free swim sessions for women only.

"I'll go for sure," I promised myself. For me, it would be an ideal way to forget what an abnormal life I was living, and to dive into another world that would remind me of the sun-filled days I used to spend on the beaches of Tunis. My father had taught me to float on my back. "There's no better way to learn to swim," he'd drummed into my head. Later, I learned how to get around in the water on my own by watching the swimming competitions broadcast on television, and attempting to copy the champions. Of course, my efforts were modest ones, but over time and with hard work I learned to swim better and better. It had become one of my favourite sports. Now I was anxious for the sessions to begin, so I could rediscover the feeling of water and forget my daily cares.

⁂

OCTOBER 4, 2003. I was in the kitchen preparing dinner. I wasn't working that day, and I wanted to give my mother a rest. Even though she never complained, and enjoyed cooking, I knew her health was not that good and that she needed some rest. With the start of the new school year, she had decided to register for the English courses for immigrants in our neighbourhood. Our apartment was only a few minutes by foot from the school; it was easy for her to get there. She'd begun learning English last year, but when Maher had been arrested and then imprisoned in Syria, she'd dropped everything to help me. Houd was still a baby then and we were a good deal farther away from the school. But now Houd had grown; he was easier to handle, our apartment was nearby, and I could arrange to stay with him while she attended her two hours of class every day. I did all I could to encourage her; it was a way for her to be exposed to new ideas, new people, and to learn a new language. Even though my mother spoke French, she felt ill at ease not knowing English. She dreamed of learning enough words and sentence structures to get by on her own in her daily life.

The phone rang: it was Marlene Catterall. We hadn't spoken since the meeting of the House Foreign Affairs Committee. There was something strange about her tone of voice; I couldn't tell whether it was likely to be good news or bad. She told me that an announcement was expected soon, and to be ready.

"What does that mean?" I asked.

"I have no idea," she said in the same tone of voice. "All I know is that there's going to be an announcement about Maher's case, and it's going to be soon."

For me, her words were worse than some kind of guessing game. They'd awakened my curiosity and at the same time thrown me back into uncertainty. I hung up and sat there for a moment, lost in thought. The Supreme State Security Court is probably about to hear the case; soon they'll be judging Maher, I thought. Maybe Marlene is trying to warn me that things are about to take a new turn; but why didn't she tell me everything? But then again, maybe that's all she knows, maybe she didn't want to give me any false hopes; you never can tell what the Syrians are likely to do at the last minute.

Houd came toddling into the kitchen, pulling a little plastic dog along behind him. When the dog walked its tail wagged, which made it look almost real. Houd loved this toy; he would take it with him into every room in the apartment. I snapped out of my daydreaming, forgot Marlene's cryptic words, and stood there watching Houd and his noisy little toy with a smile on my face.

A bit later I called Kerry and brought her up to date.

"Funny! Whatever could be happening? What aren't they telling us?" she wondered aloud.

We were both convinced that the announcement had to do with the opening of the trial in Syria, and that Marlene had wanted to send a signal without causing undue alarm. Was the government afraid of the media attention that the trial would bring? Maybe they were worried that I would stir up a row in the press, knowing perfectly well that the trial would be held in the absence of the Canadian ambassador to Syria, and without the presence of James Lockyer, the legal observer whose visa application for Syria still seemed to be pending. Maybe they were trying, in a roundabout way, to calm my fears and leave me to stew in uncertainty. There were no answers and my teeth were on edge.

OCTOBER 5, 2003. Sunday morning. The children were bored; they were wandering aimlessly around the apartment. My mother was watching television, and I was slicing vegetables in the kitchen. That day I'd planned to go swimming. The phone rang: it was Marlene. I felt my stomach tighten. What did she want now? I wondered.

"Mr. Bill Graham, the minister, would like to talk to you personally, by telephone."

"I'm free. Will he be calling right away?" I asked Marlene.

"In a few minutes," she answered.

I could feel my throat muscles growing taut; I could sense the seriousness of the situation, but I wanted to use those few minutes to prepare myself for the worst and to find the proper words. Marlene had said nothing more and hung up.

The minister was not long in calling. I recognized his voice over the telephone. He insisted that I understand that he was calling from Italy, and that he was personally committed to keeping me advised about Maher's case. My hands were shaking, but no words came to my rescue. My mother was not watching the television any longer but bustling about in the kitchen.

"Madame Mazigh," he continued, "Mr. Arar has just been released by the Syrians. We are impatiently waiting for him to leave Syrian soil by plane in the company of the Canadian consul in Syria before we make the news public. Only a few individuals at the department are aware of the news. We are counting on you to keep it secret and wait until he's left Syria for good."

I listened in silence, not wanting to lose a word of what the minister was saying. I didn't jump for joy as I'd imagined so many times in my dreams. I didn't cry. I became calm, as if nothing had happened, as if suddenly amnesia had swept over me, wiping away all my misfortunes. I muttered a few words of thanks to the minister. My mother was giving me worried looks, as if to say, "Now what?" I hung up the telephone and turned to her.

"Maher is free. He'll be leaving Syria in a few hours."

I smiled and took my mother in my arms. She didn't believe me.

"You can't be serious," she said, her eyes filling with tears. One look at my face told her I was telling the truth.

"Yes, I swear it. The minister just told me that Maher is coming back to Canada, and by the grace of God he'll be here with us."

Barâa was listening to the conversation wide-eyed; she wasn't sure what was going on around her.

"Baba will soon be home, they've let him out of prison," I told her, smiling. But I could tell she was still a bit confused; she didn't know how to communicate her joy. Houd was looking at us with curiosity; he still couldn't talk, but our smiles told him all he needed to know.

But I didn't know just how to take the news. I didn't doubt that Maher had been set free, but I hadn't expected such an abrupt end. For so many months I'd learned to expect the worst, not to dream, and, most of all, to accept the idea that Maher would not be back for many years to come. Over those months I'd learned to control my emotions and to repeat, every day, that my life would be nothing but a succession of disappointments, all the while preparing myself to face new challenges. I'd been convinced that even Minister Graham's telephone call was to inform me that Maher's trial had taken place. In recent weeks I'd been getting used to the idea that Maher would be brought before the Supreme State Security Court. But now, this latest call told me exactly the opposite. It told me that my efforts were over, that my sadness had disappeared, that instantly I should be happy and clap my hands. My mind was telling me I should be delighted, but my heart didn't follow. Inside, I was too deeply hurt.

I called no one, stuffed my swimming things into a sports bag, and left for my swim. I needed to be alone; swimming would give me that. When I got to the pool, a few women, some of them with their children, were already swimming. I stepped into the pool, the cool water revived me, and I began to swim lengths, paying no heed to the time. As I swam, I was thinking that in one day Maher would at last be back with us. I tried to imagine how I could forget that year and begin a new life; my thoughts were muddled, I was torn between a new, still-elusive happiness that I was discovering and a sadness that I'd become accustomed to, that seemed too hard for me to break away from so suddenly. Back and forth I swam, through the cool water.

When I got back to the apartment, I called my brother Mourad in Tunisia to give him the news. He couldn't believe his ears; then the two of us broke into tears. Words failed us.

"Don't say a word to anybody," I finally managed to say. "I'm waiting for the Foreign Affairs minister to confirm that Maher has left Syria before he makes a public announcement."

"Of course; let me know as soon as you get the news," he said.

Then I called my mother-in-law, but she was not at home. The day before, she'd told me she would be coming this evening for our meeting with the MPs, and that her grandson would drive her to Ottawa. I wanted her to hear the news first, before I told Maher's brothers and sister. I rang Kerry at home. There was no way I couldn't tell her the news; she'd helped me every step of the way. It was unthinkable that she find out from anyone else. She answered the phone, a bit out of breath; she'd been working in her garden.

"Is everything okay?" she asked.

I spoke calmly, chit-chatting about this and that. Then I let it drop: "You know, they've released Maher. He's coming back to Canada."

Silence. Then I heard: "Oh my God, it's unbelievable!" Kerry couldn't believe her ears.

"I swear it's true," I repeated again and again.

Now she was laughing.

"You're as cool as a cucumber, letting it drop in the middle of our conversation. How did you find out?"

I told her about the calls from Marlene and Bill Graham, and what they had said.

"I'll be right over! I still can't believe what I'm hearing," she exclaimed.

Then I hurried out of the house. We needed groceries; I was out of milk, cheese, and bread. Plus I had no idea when Maher would be arriving. No one had given me any details. Foreign Affairs was supposed to let me know as soon as Maher had left Syrian soil. In my discussion with Mr. Graham, I'd understood that Maher and Leo Martel, the Canadian consul in Damascus, would be on the plane, but I still didn't know exactly where things stood. As soon as I'd picked up the items I needed, I hurried back home. Kerry hadn't arrived yet; the children were playing.

"Someone called," my mother told me.

"Who was it?"

"An Arabic-speaking gentleman. He said he'd heard from the Syrian Embassy that Maher had been released and wanted to congratulate us."

That startled me. I'd never talked with the Syrian Embassy. Why would they ask someone to call me? Who could it have been? I'd heard in the past that certain individuals of Syrian or Arab origin were attempting to exert influence on the Syrian ambassador, but I had no idea what effect they'd had. I'd always assumed they'd got nowhere.

This latest call upset me: the Canadian minister of Foreign Affairs was telling me that only a few people had been informed of the news and now an unidentified gentleman calls me at home pretending to have heard the news from the Syrian Embassy here in Ottawa. It didn't take me long to figure out that both Canada and Syria wanted to announce the news and take credit in the eyes of the public. At the same time, it struck me that this very gentleman might well be phoning the media and other people in Ottawa to tell them that Syria had released Maher Arar.

Meanwhile, Kerry arrived. We were both delighted; it was as if we hadn't seen each other for years. It was a special meeting, our first since Maher's return had been confirmed. Last October, a single telephone call had turned my life upside down; today, another telephone call should have put my mind at ease and put my life back on an even keel, but still I felt like my life was in turmoil.

I told Kerry about the man who'd spoken with my mother.

"We've got to talk to the minister immediately. He'll have to make the announcement before the story is leaked to the media," she said with a note of urgency in her voice.

I had the cellphone number of Robert Fry, Mr. Graham's assistant, and called him right away. Mr. Fry assured me that he would inform the minister and that a press conference would be held as soon as possible, in Italy, for Canadian journalists. Once more I rang my mother-in-law, but she was not at home, nor was her grandson.

✑

Kerry, the children, and I went to the park while my mother stayed at home. I knew that as soon as the news was released in Canada, I'd be snowed under with interview requests from the media, and I hadn't yet got used to the idea. Sitting on a wooden bench, Kerry and I watched Houd and Barâa at play as we tried to imagine what would happen when Maher returned. Kerry was certain there would be a lot of interest in his return and promised she would deal with the journalists. Through all the months that Maher was in prison in Syria, I had wished that journalists would call me and ask about him, hoping that they would write even a small article about him. Wasted wishes. No one paid much attention.

Now it would be different, I knew. Maher's unexpected return would cause a lot of curiosity and interest. Within a few hours, everything had changed. I no longer needed to meet the MPs. I would soon be meeting Maher after a whole year; it was a moment I was very nervous about. Who was the man I was going to meet after so long? What would he look like; how would he behave? How would the children rebuild their relationship with a father who had vanished for a year, and who was coming back into their lives with a new face? Houd, especially, didn't remember him at all; he knew only my face and my mother's. Kerry did her best to calm my worries, hoping that everything would go smoothly, telling me that at least the real flesh-and-blood Maher would be back in Canada, that he could tell us what he had been through. Her allusion to the sufferings that Maher may well have endured gave me goose bumps. Up until then, I'd kept the question of suffering and torture buried deep inside. I didn't want to think about it for fear of falling into despair and depression, and simply giving up the fight to save him. Now, the fact that Maher would be back with us, that he would be telling us about all he'd gone through in that year, touched off a new fear in me, one I'd never known before: the fear of confronting the painful past.

The telephone at home was ringing off the hook. Kerry was sitting in the children's room answering calls from the media and jotting down notes. The story had broken in Canada; Bill Graham had made the announcement from Italy. No reasons had been given for Maher's release. All the accusations of terrorism, plotting, being a dangerous person . . . all the whispered rumours, all the solemn assertions by anonymous persons, had miraculously evaporated. The Syrian promise to try him for membership in the Muslim Brotherhood or the al-Qaeda network came to nothing, I don't know why. For the moment, I could only think of one thing: when was I going to talk to Maher? Kerry kept talking on the telephone; journalists wanted interviews, comments, reactions. She asked Alex for help and he hurried over to lend a hand and answer questions from the media.

Meanwhile, the Department of Foreign Affairs alerted us that Maher would be stopping over in Paris, that he would be calling from there between midnight and one o'clock in the morning Ottawa time. It was the call I'd been waiting for for more than a year. The call I'd been waiting for that night in Tunis as I sat on the edge of my bed. I didn't know what to expect. What would we talk about? Outside, night had fallen and journalists had begun to arrive with their cameras, microphones, and television crews. It was the best way for me to speak to them, to avoid too many telephone interviews. The apartment began to look more and more like a studio in constant upheaval. The children's room had become an office where Kerry and Alex were answering the telephone; the living room was crowded with journalists, some sitting on the sofa, others standing, photographers and TV cameramen cruising about for the best angle. The children wandered in and out of my room and into the living room, looking for a quiet corner where they could play or a toy they'd left behind in their room.

The interviews followed one after the other in rapid succession; the questions were all the same. "How did I feel?" they wanted to know. Of course I was happy; I was smiling, my face was bright, my answers were upbeat: Maher would be arriving in Montreal the following day; the coming days would surely help us rebuild our family. I said not a word about my worries, my nagging doubts; those things were for me. As I was giving an interview, I saw my mother-in-law walk in the door. She was with her grandson who'd driven her from Montreal. His telephone had been switched off. Not having the faintest idea what was going on, she didn't know what to make of what she was seeing. I went over to her and told her that Maher had been set free, that he would be coming back to Canada tomorrow. She'd come to Ottawa to meet the MPs and ask for their help; she'd stopped off at her daughter's place and her grandson had driven her here. She hadn't suspected a thing. She couldn't believe her ears at first, then it began to sink in; she began to figure out what had happened; she wiped her tears and sat down with my mother at the kitchen table.

Things calmed down around eleven o'clock. The children were sleeping in my room, Kerry and Alex had gone home, my mother and mother-in-law were asleep in the living room. I'd stretched out on Barâa's bed, with the cordless phone beside me. There was no way I could sleep; Maher would be calling in an hour or two. My mind was racing. No matter how hard I tried, I couldn't sleep. Questions flashed through my brain, but the only answer was silence. There I lay in the dark, the minutes ticked by, but the telephone did not ring. I drifted off into a troubled sleep; it was impossible to tell dreams from reality. Suddenly the ringing of the phone made me jump. It was an official of the Department of Foreign Affairs on the line: in a few seconds I was to be connected with Paris. There was a moment of silence, then I heard the voice of a man I didn't know, speaking French. It was Leo

Martel, the Canadian consul in Syria, who was travelling with Maher. We talked for a few moments, then he said, "Here's Maher. He's right beside me."

There I was, waiting in the darkness. It must have been two or three o'clock in the morning, my heart was pounding. Then I heard Maher's voice greeting me. It was a faint and distant voice; I could hardly recognize it.

"How are you? How are Barâa and Houd?" he asked.

"We're all fine . . . we can't wait to see you," I answered, not really knowing what to say, the words not coming. Then he went on in a weak voice: "Monia, you know, everything you did for me, I'll never forget it as long as I live . . ."

There was a lump in my throat. Those were not the kind of words you used among family, I'd done no favour that I should be thanked for. Why does his voice sound as if he's given up? I wondered.

"Don't say that," I said. "I did what had to be done, that's all."

We said nothing more, just a quick goodbye and the call was over.

I hung up and closed my eyes. Maher's words echoed in my head. I tossed and turned; everything inside told me that a page in my life had turned and that a new one was about to begin. Maher would soon be back; the goal I'd set myself one year earlier had been reached. But what lay in wait for me afterwards? How would we continue along our path together, what would our life be like? The picture in my mind was clouded; nothing was clear.

OCTOBER 6, 2003. The Department of Foreign Affairs called; they would drive us to Montreal in an eight-place van. Along with me there would be Barâa, Houd, my mother and my mother-in-law, Kerry, Myra, and Marlene Catterall. Maher's flight from Paris would arrive at Dorval at about three o'clock. I would have to leave the apartment and drive to Kerry's place downtown, where the van would be waiting. Early that morning a CTV truck had parked in front of our building.

The journalists wanted an interview, and surely they wanted to film before we left for the airport. This time I didn't want any photos. I'd spent the entire evening in the apartment with dozens of journalists coming and going to take pictures and record interviews. I'd only slept a few hours. Now, this morning, I was mainly concerned with preparing myself for my first meeting with my husband in more than a year. Yesterday his voice over the telephone had sounded so far away, I'd been frightened: Was he still the same person? What will he be like today when we meet? These were the questions that were running through my mind; I really didn't want to worry about ducking the CTV cameras.

Houd understood none of what was going on around him. I kept telling him his Baba was coming; I was talking to him nonstop, but he seemed to be a bit short on words despite his twenty months. He'd never really been able to master the sound of "b." I was worried about him but didn't want to make anything of it. Still, I'd resolved to raise the matter with his pediatrician at our next appointment. At eleven o'clock everything was ready. My mother had made up a batch of mbatten, tiny balls of fried cooked cauliflower with parsley and eggs. The kids loved them. It would be something to munch on en route. We left the apartment by the back door. Barâa was delighted with the thought that the CTV truck would be waiting in front of our building while we'd left through the back. She was also looking different today. She was happy at the thought of seeing her father again, but there was a shadow of worry in her innocent eyes. I prayed to God that all would go well.

Kerry was waiting for us at her house. We were all ready to go.

The van was parked on the street; Marlene pulled up with Sarkis Assadourian in a car with other civil servants I didn't recognize. They would be driving to Montreal by car, while Myra and Marlene would be travelling with us in the van. Alex and Riad would join us later at the airport.

Kerry didn't think it a good idea for everybody to join Maher and me in our apartment.

"Your life will be like a circus for the next few days. Reporters will want to talk to you. You'll want to remove yourselves from the public eye for a while."

I knew she was right, but it was a message I didn't want to hear. Her words gave me the impression that we were important persons. As far as I was concerned, I hated the idea of behaving like that. I didn't want to become what I was not. We weren't a family of pop singers or famous actors. Still, going by the number of interview requests and media interest, it was becoming clearer to me that we were being treated as if we were.

"I can help you find somewhere else to live for a while, until things calm down a bit," Kerry assured me.

I offered no resistance. Like a boxer after a long bout, I needed some peace and quiet; I wanted to reconnect with my family. Strategy was the last thing on my mind.

Everybody took a seat in the van: the children, my mother, my mother-in-law, Kerry, Myra, Marlene, and me. A government driver was behind the wheel. Each of us seemed off in our own worlds. Barâa and Houd stared out the window; the two mothers chatted; Myra said nothing; Marlene and Kerry were checking messages on their cellphones. As I watched the landscape rushing by, I thought back to the last two days, how Maher's release had changed my life, my thinking, my hopes and my fears. Before, my only hope was to see Maher again; now I hoped that our lives would be peaceful. The day before yesterday, I was afraid I would never see him again. Now I was afraid of what our reunion might bring, the consequences of the torture, the suffering, the isolation. How strange that our desires, hopes, and fears can so totally change in a matter of hours.

The van finally pulled up in front of the terminal building at Dorval. We piled out like children from a schoolbus. What a relief to be able to walk, to move our arms and legs after being bent double for more than two hours. Myra, who was in direct communication with people from the department, led us to a special airport waiting room. Alex and Riad were already there. Only a few minutes to go until Maher's plane landed. I felt as though I was being operated by remote control: everybody was giving me instructions, everybody wanted what was best for me, wanted to help me – but I felt lost and alone; all I wanted was to get it over with as fast as I could.

There were dozens of journalists waiting in the airport, Kerry told me. There I was, waiting with the children, when a uniformed female officer from the airport authority advised me that I and Maher's mother were authorized to accompany her beyond the security barrier right up to the passenger gate to meet Maher. She handed me two passes, one for me, the other for my mother-in-law.

The plane had arrived. My hands were damp. It wouldn't be long until we met. I left the children with my mother in the waiting room and we moved off toward the gate. The airport officer led us down what seemed kilometres of corridors, up escalators, and then along the concourse until we reached the gate, where a handful of passengers had just begun to leave the aircraft. Maher's mother looked tired waiting there beside me, almost disbelief on her face.

Then I spotted Maher. His hair was neat and his beard had been trimmed. He was wearing a blue sweater I'd never seen on him before, his shoulders seemed a little bent, he was thin, his expression sad and frightened. I thought I saw a glimmer of hope flash through his eyes when he saw us standing there waiting for him, but the look of pain and humiliation remained. He kissed us both in a surprisingly cold and mechanical way, then together we retraced our steps back to the waiting room where everyone else was expecting us. I took his hand, and he leaned over and whispered, "I'm really scared. Are you sure it's all over and they won't put me in prison again?"

"Of course you're free," I assured him calmly. "Don't be afraid, you're in Canada."

We'd hardly spoken, but the way he moved, the musculature of his hand, his voice, the look in his eyes told me that this was not the same man I'd married nine years ago. His smile was gone, his optimism, his sense of ambition . . .

Finally we reached the waiting room. Maher's brother Bassam and his sister had arrived. Everyone rushed forward to kiss him, embrace him, touch him, hold him close. There stood Barâa in front of him; he took her in his arms and kissed her, but I could sense her hesitation, as if she didn't know what to do. Houd didn't like all the commotion. Maher turned to him to hug him, but he broke away and came running over to me. I took him in my arms; he calmed down. There we were in the waiting room: Maher seemed lost; now and then he tried to smile, but the result was not convincing. Barâa stood there beside him, a happy grin on her face, a bit nonplussed. Maher didn't know Kerry or Alex; he knew Riad only vaguely. They chatted with him, congratulated him, but from the look of bewilderment on his face I realized that he didn't know whom he could trust; he kept looking around, trying to catch my eye, as if asking for support, confirmation, a kind of assurance.

There was one question I had to ask Maher, but I didn't want anyone around us to hear me. I turned to him and whispered in his ear: "Did they beat you in prison?"

He looked at me, surprised, as if he couldn't possibly understand how anyone could spend a year in a Syrian prison and be treated well, then answered me with a simple yes.

The blood froze in my veins, tears flooded my eyes; I didn't know what to do. The SHRC's letter had been right all along; my worst fears were true. How I wanted to think of something else, but I couldn't. Why had they made him suffer? Why had they left him in prison?

Fortunately, Kerry extracted me from my nightmare. The media were gathered outside the door; they wanted some comment. I explained to Maher that interest in his case had been high, and that public opinion had played a critical role in demanding that he be returned to Canada. He seemed to understand. It wasn't long before he began to prepare a brief statement for the journalists outside. We were with him, I said; we would help him find the right words to thank everyone who had helped. One thing was certain: he couldn't speak for long, he tired easily. When he was ready, I took him by the hand and we moved forward, with Alex and Riad beside us. Kerry was walking in front. When the doors swung open, there in front of us was what looked like a horde of journalists, a forest of microphones, outstretched arms. I could see Kerry struggling with all her might to push them aside. Finally, airport security guards rescued her. They cleared a path and we took our places at a table that had been specially set up. The journalists sorted themselves out, facing us, some standing with their cameras, some sitting on the floor with laptop computers on their knees. I recognized many of them. Meanwhile, there was a steady barrage of flashing.

Maher spoke in a gentle voice, thanking all the Canadians who had helped him to be reunited with his family, and to find his freedom. Now and then he would pause, as if searching for the right word; but he said what he wanted to say and then fell silent. It had not been long, a few minutes at best, but I realized how painfully slowly time was passing. Then it was my turn; I had to say something. We'd all been concentrating so much on what Maher would say that I'd forgotten to prepare something. But the words came, filled my mouth, and I spoke. I thanked everyone who had helped us and mentioned that we intended to withdraw and rest for a few days.

Overcome with emotion, I couldn't leave it at that. Thinking of the physical and moral suffering that Maher had endured, of the man sitting beside me, frail and exhausted, suddenly I raised my index finger and my tone of voice changed.

"Maher's liberation is only a beginning of justice . . . ," I said.

It was impossible to turn away from him, that was clear; I was determined to do everything I could to support him.

Finally, it was over. Marlene, Sarkis Assadourian, Leo Martel, Myra, and the other civil servants had been waiting in an adjacent room, to give us a degree of intimacy with our friends and family. We'd made up our minds to spend the night in Montreal, at my mother-in-law's; the van that had brought us from Ottawa was waiting to drive us there. The Department of Foreign Affairs people would be returning to Ottawa. Marlene, Kerry, and Alex joined us, while Riad headed back as well. At last we reached St. Leonard, where my mother-in-law lived. It wasn't long before her little house was full of people.

My brothers-in-law, my sister-in-law and her children, they'd all come to see their brother and uncle. No one said a word of surprise at the sight of Maher, but shock and sadness was written all over their faces. As his mother had not had time to prepare supper, one of his brothers called out for pizza. Marlene, Kerry, and Alex wanted to head back to Ottawa, but my mother-in-law insisted they eat with us before they left.

The pizzas arrived. There wasn't enough room for everyone at the table so we found seats wherever we could. I watched Maher; he wasn't eating. My mother-in-law brewed Turkish coffee for her unexpected guests. Maher still had that look about him, the look of a man who didn't know where he was.

He would sit down and chat with one of the guests, then suddenly get to his feet, as if he were about to cry. I watched him in silence, not knowing what to do. When everyone had finally gone, I felt almost relieved. It was dark outside and we were all exhausted after a long day of emotion and surprises. Before leaving, Kerry told me: "Thanks to Riad, I've found a place where you can stay for a few days to avoid the media. Let's talk tomorrow and I'll tell you more."

As I thanked Kerry, I found myself wondering what kind of life I would have, living somewhere else than in my own home for several days. Houd's crying brought me back to reality. I caught Kerry's eye, then rushed off. Houd needed sleep; he hadn't had a wink since early that morning and now he was exhausted. Maher wanted to help calm him, but Houd wasn't happy about this new face he'd forgotten all about, perhaps buried deep in his subconscious; now all he could do was whimper. I laid him down on a mattress on the floor and changed him into his pyjamas; he quickly calmed down and in a minute or two was fast asleep. Barâa wasn't far behind. But before she drifted off, she wrapped her tiny arms around her father. He hugged her in return, and the two of them sat there for a moment, embracing. When I came back to turn out the light, both children were stretched out on the big bed; Maher was asleep on the small mattress on the floor. I closed the door and tiptoed into the other room.

⌒⁓⁓⁓⁓

The next day we spent the morning at Maher's mother's. Maher picked at his food in silence, but I had a feeling he wanted to talk. Finally he stood up, his face tense, and began to talk about what he'd seen in prison. He told of people packed into cells with no hope of ever seeing the light of day again. Then, suddenly, he broke into tears. I felt embarrassed in front of the children, my mother, my mother-in-law. Then my mother exclaimed, "Cry, cry, don't worry; it's the only way you'll find relief. Cry, you'll feel better . . ."

And so it went for the rest of day: words, memories, emotions punctuated by tears or sobbing, then silence. I felt that Maher wasn't telling us everything; I felt he was keeping the worst for later. His eyes told me more than I wanted to know about how much he'd suffered. Perhaps he felt embarrassed in front of the children, in front of his mother, and that made him hold back; perhaps it was the fear of telling his story, or being reminded of it that left him looking so distraught, so lost. I didn't want to be prying, so I left him alone.

A friend of Kerry's had driven down to Montreal with our car; he would be driving us back to Ottawa. The trip was long and gloomy. I was counting the minutes, but everything seemed to be happening in slow motion. At last we pulled up outside Kerry's house. She was happy to see us; she would be coming back to our apartment with us, then helping to take us to our new house. We had to collect our belongings, bring the clothing we'd need, Barâa's school bag, and whatever other important items we'd need for a week away from the apartment – which Maher had never seen. I'd rented it while he was still in prison. When he stepped through the door, he closed his eyes and said, "While I was dying in an underground grave, you were doing everything you could, day and night, to survive along with the children."

Then he shook his head and tears filled his eyes. I just stood there, helpless. Across the room, the little red light on the answering machine was blinking steadily. I walked over to the device and pressed the button: "You have twenty-one messages," it said in its mechanical voice. With an abrupt movement I pressed another button, this one to stop playing the messages. I didn't want to know who'd called. Now was the time to put a few things together and get out. Houd wanted to bring along almost all his toys. Barâa wanted to show her father all her new clothes. And there I was in the middle, trying to sort it all out as best I could, trying to cajole the one and convince the other. After several attempts, our things were in order and our family was ready to go off to spend a few days in hiding, far from curious eyes and persistent journalists.

The house we would be living in temporarily was an attractive one. The owners, a couple we knew, had gone to stay with their parents for the duration. I wasn't sure that it was necessary to move, but I was convinced of one thing: there would be plenty of telephone calls back at the apartment, and all that new pressure would not be helpful to our family in its search for peace and quiet. Maher hadn't yet told me the details of his ordeal; most of what he said were flashbacks, snapshots. I asked him nothing, leaving him free to talk about his experience when he felt ready to do so. I knew it would be coming, and I was afraid of listening to his story; even the thought of it gave me the chills. We were sitting in the living room while the children played in the next room. Two days had gone by since Maher had returned, two days that seemed to weigh on us like two long years. He looked at me long and hard and said, "You know, for ten months I lived in a grave, an underground cell. It was dark, narrow, and damp."

It was the second time he'd used the word *grave*. Then he began to describe the place in detail; my heart was pounding.

"After every interrogation session, they'd take me back to my cell," he said. "I was always thinking about you and the children. I was buried in my misery, but the thought of you helped me forget. At the start, I didn't know where you were, I was afraid maybe they'd thrown you in prison in Tunisia; I was so worried about you. When I was still in the United States, I begged the FBI agents to let me call you, but they refused. They kept telling me I would soon be on the plane for Montreal and my family. The first day I thought I would go mad; I walked up and down in my cell, I couldn't even think about sitting down on the metal bench. I kept telling the American agents, 'Let me take a plane to Canada, I want to go home,' but they wouldn't answer me. Every instant I dreamed I'd be set free, that it was only a nightmare, but things got more and more complicated. When they woke me up early in the morning in the New York jail and put me on a plane, I realized I'd never see you again. You know that little suitcase of mine, the American Tourister with my shoes, a light jacket, and the tea glasses we bought together? They took them away from me; I never saw them again."

Maher was gasping for breath, jumping from one story to another, as if he wanted to say everything all at once and couldn't manage to get anything out. He wanted to talk about the pain he'd suffered. He needed to be heard; I was caught up in this whirlwind of emotion.

"I bought some chocolate in Zurich, for my mother and for you, when I'd come back to Tunis. I put them in my little handbag, along with a pair of pants and some underwear. Well, they let me keep it. It was my pillow in my cell in Syria. When I got to Jordan, I still hoped they'd send me back to Canada. But after several hours of detention, they put me in a car. I was kept blindfolded and head down for the entire trip. I couldn't see a thing, and anytime I said a word someone would hit me on the neck, curse me, or threaten me. I had no idea where they were taking me. I thought my arms would come loose from my body I hurt so much. Then, many hours later they shoved me out of the car. The guards took me to a place where I could hear people speaking in loud voices, then they led me into a room and took off my blindfold. I lifted my head and saw an old photograph of the former president, Hafez al-Assad, and I understood I was in Syria. Then, all of a sudden, a police agent came into the room. He bared his yellow teeth and said, 'I heard you're from Canada, so what goodies do you have for us?' I realized he wanted cigarettes or money. I looked around me; there was my little travelling bag. I opened it and handed him the bar of Swiss chocolate. What an idiot I was, thinking I could get out of there with a piece of chocolate. The agent took the chocolate and left, then another one came and it was the same story; in a few minutes a whole lineup of agents trooped in demanding chocolate. They took all of it and vanished.

"But the worst was still to come. They took me down a staircase. The stench of urine, mould, and filth turned my stomach. When my eyes got used to the darkness I saw I was in a kind of cave. I would live there for ten months before they transferred me to Sednaya Prison. My cell was around two metres long, one metre wide, and two metres high. It was very dark, with no light except a little coming through a small hole in the ceiling with iron bars. The door was metal. It had a tiny opening where they gave me my food. There was a dirty sheet, two plastic bottles, and two plates on the floor. I often had to pee into one of those bottles."

I stared at Maher. He was ashamed to be saying such things about himself. I tried to react calmly, but deep inside I was shaking.

"Every time I told the truth they would beat me," he said. "George, the officer in charge of my file, kept calling me a liar. He'd say, 'You'll see what we'll do to you, you . . . ' and he'd slap me across the face. He had a sort of electric cable that he'd wave at me threateningly, and I don't know how, I'd feel the cable hitting my hands, it was like being cut by a razor. One day the session lasted for several hours, I was terrified. George threatened to send me to the torture chamber; I urinated in my clothes.

"They only let us take one shower a week, with cold water. The weather was hot at first so that wasn't bad, but when winter came I was shivering all the time; all my body shook when cold water touched my skin. George kept on telling me I was a member of al-Qaeda, that I was a terrorist, that I'd never get out of there alive. He'd beat me with his cable and would only let me go back to my cell if I told him what he wanted to hear . . ."

I closed my eyes. I didn't want to hear those words, I didn't want to hear of my husband being humiliated one more time. Maher told me about the days he spent in that prison, about his solitude, about how he constantly wanted to scream and, worst of all, about the cries of others who were being tortured.

"After each interrogation session, they'd throw me into a room where I could hear the screams of other inmates, their moaning and weeping. I couldn't see a thing, but I was terrified. I wanted to rip my ears off, their screams were so piercing . . ."

He told me the despair he felt, then suddenly the consular visits began and he believed he would soon be set free and returned to Canada.

"I couldn't say a word about my conditions to Leo Martel," Maher went on. "The guards made that clear to me before the meetings, but sometimes I tried to signal to him with my eyebrows that what I was saying wasn't the truth. I don't know if he understood me.

I couldn't see the sun. The food was disgusting. I hated the gluey rice and the dry bread we had to eat. Often, I thought I was going mad. It must have been a few months before they gave me a copy of the Qur'an and I could find comfort in its words. Your letters were like beams of light for me; I read them and reread them hundreds of times over. They kept me company. I didn't know exactly what you were doing in Canada, but I was certain you wouldn't let me rot in that hole."

Maher had been talking for more than an hour now. The children were watching television, so we weren't interrupted. I was feeling more and more ill at ease; Maher's words were echoing in my mind. He continued:

"When the consul's visits stopped, I was sure I was going to be buried alive in that prison for years. I hadn't heard anything from you, the pain was more than I could bear. I'd been there for months, I knew, I'd counted the days in my cell. Then one day the guard took me upstairs and I realized I had a visitor. Then I saw Leo Martel, the consul, and I was overjoyed. But it was a special visit. We were in the office of Hassan Khalil, the general in charge of military intelligence. The general himself was there. It was my last chance. I had to talk about the hell I was living through, about the torture and the abuse. I was taking a huge risk, but I knew I had to speak out, even if they killed me after."

Maher's face suddenly lit up as if he were proud to have rediscovered the courage that had been broken under so many months of torture.

"I spoke openly of the beatings, what I had to endure, the way I was being treated, and I demanded justice. General Hassan Khalil sat there like stone. Leo Martel glanced at him nervously. I demanded to be treated humanely. I demanded to see a lawyer. My little speech was over in a minute. I was sure they would beat me to death after what I'd said. But a few days later they transferred me to Sednaya Prison. No matter how bad the conditions were there, it was like paradise compared to the underground cell I'd lived in for ten months. I could see other prisoners, talk to them. I began to hope again . . ."

We were still sitting there, talking, when Houd came running in, climbed up onto Maher's lap, and for the first time said, "Ba-ba, Ba-ba." At last he was pronouncing the word for daddy, and yet for months he'd only been able to babble. Was he imitating his sister or had the sight of his father made Houd speak, made him say "Baba" to his father? I didn't know what to think, I was so moved by Maher's story, and by Houd's first articulate words.

⁓

Living in our borrowed house was like living in a hotel. We had all the comforts of home, but I was homesick for my apartment. Maher didn't really much feel like going out. He was afraid of being recognized. On his first Friday back in Canada, three days after his return, he didn't even go to the mosque for the Friday congregational prayer, an obligation for all Muslim men.

Instead, Riad and a friend came to our house and we prayed together. It was a good idea to keep away from crowds and large gatherings. Later we found out that journalists and cameras had been on hand that day at the main Ottawa mosque to get reactions from Muslims about Maher's liberation.

Maher had lost a lot of weight and was so weak he couldn't make any physical effort. He figured he'd lost twenty kilograms by the time he left the underground cell, he told me. In Sednaya Prison, he ate better. Some prisoners even had the right to cook their own meals and share their food; he'd been able to put on some weight. He could also see daylight. But he'd brought a profound mistrust of humans back to Canada. He was no longer the natural, spontaneous person I'd known for all the years we'd lived together. He'd become suspicious, touchy, and would worry constantly that we were being followed. At first I thought those were reflexes he'd picked up in prison; I was sure he'd soon revert to the good-natured, natural man I knew. But every passing day drove home to me that this year of suffering would haunt us for many years to come.

— 9 —

DOUBTS AND HOPES

this is only a beginning of justice . . .

After a little more than a week at our friends' house, we went back to our apartment. Our financial situation was the same as before. I was working part-time and receiving social assistance. With Maher's return, we were drawing an additional one hundred dollars. For him, work was out of the question: his mental and physical health were fragile, he needed rest – and besides, who was likely to hire someone suspected of terrorism, who was written about almost daily in the press? True, when he did go out, many people made a point of coming over to greet him and shake his hand. People recognized him, and that recognition was tinged much more with sympathy than mistrust. Still, between sympathy and a job offer lay a yawning chasm, and no one seemed ready to bridge it.

His state of forced idleness was not helping us in our daily lives. With every passing day, I could see Maher's self-confidence draining away, and there was nothing I could do to help. I was anxious to find another job myself, but all my applications remained unanswered. We were surviving on the flimsy hope that our situation would improve, that at least one of us would find a good job that matched our qualifications. But the truth was that our precarious financial situation created an invisible, creeping kind of pressure that we tried to overlook every day, doing our best to focus on our new life and finding the most pleasant ways to pass the time.

OCTOBER 23, 2003. Only a few days were left before the start of Ramadan, the month when Muslims abstain from food and drink from sunup to sundown. Maher was with us once again, but imprisonment and distance had done their job: each day I appreciated just how difficult the task would be. How was I to live with a broken man, how could I live with a personality that had been transformed, how could I reconcile it with my new role of mother, wife, and activist? In the morning I worked at the language school; in the afternoon I looked after the children; I went with Maher to his appointments with the psychiatrist where he could speak of his pain, to Amnesty International to speak of his life in prison, to the lawyer's office to ask questions and get advice. I was everywhere, an active presence in each of those aspects of his life. And each needed me in its own way.

I could hardly wait for Ramadan to begin, hoping that the month of fasting would give me some of the peace I'd been seeking for months now, and that I'd hoped to rediscover with Maher's liberation. But it was like a mirage: just when you think you've reached it, you realize that it was all an illusion, a betrayal of your senses. I remembered when I was still a little girl how I would go strolling in the souks of the medina, the centuries-old city that formed the historical heart of Tunis. It was as if I found there a sense of safety and serenity that permeated its narrow lanes and dark dead ends, sometimes lit by a few stray sunbeams that found their way through the high ceilings through a skylight. The strident cries of merchants inviting passersby to sample their honey-drenched pastries or of the perfume sellers dabbing the backs of hands with essence of musk or ambergris brought back the hard, cruel reality of a place that for centuries had been a symbol of social, economic, and religious organization, and today, in our time, had become a place deserted by the elite, a place overcome with poverty and decay. All that was left of its serenity was the impression enveloping me, which was quickly dissipated by the stench of rotting garbage and the vulgar shouts of boys playing ball. Still, in spite of the often hard reality, I continued to hope that one day our lives might return to a semblance of normalcy.

Marlene Catterall asked to meet us. She came that evening. We were all at home: Maher, my mother, and me. The children were already sound asleep. She seemed nervous. I watched her take one last puff on her cigarette in front of our building, then furtively deposit the butt in the little metal box next to the main entrance. I opened the door, greeted her, and led her into our apartment. The events of the last days had left us shaken. Maher especially was bearing the brunt. He read everything written about him, watched all the television programs. For me it was different; after I'd given an interview, I didn't want to see or hear of it again. It was as if I'd had enough of myself. How ridiculous I thought I looked; my first reflex was to switch off the television set. But it wasn't like that for him. The media's words entered his mind there to stay; for him, it was like another form of torture.

Only a few days after his return from Syria, "leaks" began to appear in the press. The source was always the same: Canadian government officials speaking on condition of anonymity. According to them, Maher had made many trips to Afghanistan. When he'd been arrested in the United States, the American authorities had decided, without informing their Canadian counterparts, to deport him to Syria since the Canadians had refused to charge him. He had spent ten days in Jordan, they said. The Syrians did not want to accept him. Finally, on the insistence of the Americans, Syria had finally agreed to imprison him ("U.S. Urged Canada to Hold Arar," Graham Fraser, *Toronto Star,* October 9, 2003).

But the leaks didn't end there. Now the aim was to undermine the idea that Maher had ever been tortured. Instead, he had simply been mistreated ("Arar Was Not Tortured Officials Say," Jeff Sallot, *Globe and Mail,* October 10, 2003). The image being created was that of a vicious terrorist who had spent his time in al-Qaeda training camps. What harm could possibly be done by roughing him up a little? The anonymous sources kept on flowing, and people in high places kept on talking: it was a hemorrhage. Maher had no idea how to react, how to behave. He had not addressed the Canadian public since his return from Syria; his mental state was still fragile. He wept easily. He woke up at night with a start, which gave me a terrible fright. It was impossible for me to get him back to sleep. He spent his days pacing back and forth in the little apartment like a caged animal. I'd never known him to be that way before; it was a habit he'd picked up from the many hours he'd spent walking from one end of his tiny cell to the other, but it only added to my nervousness. But of all the leaks, the one that appeared on CTV was by far the worst.

Alex called us with a trembling voice. CTV had asked him to respond to the latest allegations against Maher. Journalist Joy Malbon had reported on the nightly news that high-ranking officials in several departments (neither the individuals nor the departments were identified) had revealed to her that Maher, during interrogation in Syria, had given the names of other Ottawa residents suspected of being part of an al-Qaeda cell. Alex was shaken. True, he believed in our story and trusted us. But with the rumours flying thick and fast, doubt had begun to creep in and gnaw away at the bit of confidence that Maher had attempted to restore since his return.

It was a bombshell, and the consequences were disastrous for our family and the so-called "suspects." The following day, Daniel Leblanc, a journalist with the *Globe and Mail,* took up the same leaks, quoting high-ranking Canadian officials who claimed that Maher had given detailed information on other individuals suspected of terrorist links ("Officials Allege Arar Gave Data on al-Qaeda," Daniel Leblanc, *Globe and Mail,* October 24, 2003). The allegations were false and we knew it. Maher had never been a member of any terrorist cell. He'd never known anyone linked to al-Qaeda. We didn't know who was behind those leaks, or where the "information" came from, but the consequences of the allegations became increasingly clear to us. First of all, if they had been true, Maher would be made out to be a "traitor" in the eyes of the other suspects and would become a possible target. Secondly, if they were false, it was still likely that people would believe the rumours, and that would only reinforce their doubts about Maher, which might well lead to physical attacks against him, now identified as a presumed terrorist.

The media strategy of the people behind the leaks was a good one. Maher couldn't win. I hadn't realized how serious the situation was until Marlene's sudden arrival drove home to me that we were in danger. Marlene told us that she'd called the Ottawa police and suggested that we should ask for special protection. But her suggestion made Maher even more agitated. Now he was convinced he was the target of a smear campaign. But were we ready to go into battle against a masked adversary? Wouldn't it just be simpler to go into hiding, to keep away from the media, and let public opinion forget all about us? Our family had already gone through enough hardship and I wanted to put it all behind me, wanted to turn the page, to vanish into the anonymity of daily life.

A deep weariness swept over me. When Maher returned, I was sure the nightmare was over, but here we were, plunged once more into turmoil. Then I heard a faint voice inside me, and it sounded like my own voice: "So, you've already forgotten the lessons of the past? Why do you want to run and hide? You were never criminals as far as I know; you've always fought for justice to be done, and now, when Maher is there beside you, you want to give up the fight, you want to get out? What's the matter with you? Are you trying to fool yourself?"

The little voice would leave me no peace; it popped up in the midst of my thoughts, argued with me, begged me to stand up straight, look myself in the eye. Marlene left, promising to talk with some of her Liberal Party colleagues, to convince them to investigate the source of the leaks.

But we were not convinced that such an investigation would ever happen. The damage had been done, and we had become more and more determined that only a public inquiry could throw full light on all that had taken place, from Maher's arrest up to the present.

For the last few weeks, I'd been driving Maher to Alex's office for meetings with him and Kerry. No one else knew what Maher had been through since his arrest in New York, his flight to Jordan, and his imprisonment in Syria. Maher had to tell his own story. We had full confidence in Alex and Kerry. Riad, too, joined us for some of those meetings. We were certain that since they had both kept close track of the case for months, they were the best placed to listen and to write his account. Those were hard meetings for me to attend; it was as if I was watching the same horror movie for a second time. Once more I listened to Maher's story, and I felt shamed by his pain, suffocated by the torture he'd gone through. He would talk on and on, but when he finally stopped I knew that he'd reached the point where he couldn't hold himself back any longer, that he was going to explode, and everybody looked away, as if ashamed of ourselves as human beings.

Those were painful moments for all four of us, but they were most painful of all for Maher. As he told his story, Alex or Kerry would break in with questions. They wanted clarifications, explanations, and details for everything. Maher's job was not easy: not only did he have to speak but he had to answer questions as well. It was an interrogation all over again, but this time Maher could trust the people asking the questions; he wasn't afraid of them. Directly after those sessions we would go to pick up Barâa from school. Just the sight of her made me forget everything. No sooner had she got into the car and climbed into her seat than she started to chatter nonstop about her day, her teacher, her friends, her silliness, and the homework she had to do. From a sad, dark world I was transported into the innocent world of childhood, a world I didn't want to leave. Hungrily I listened to my daughter, giving her the fullest opportunity to tell us everything about her day. And when we got home, Houd was waiting for us with another story: he wanted to go play in the park. Maher couldn't resist; together the two of them hurried off.

OCTOBER 29, 2003. Since Maher's release, with the exception of Marlene Catterall, we hadn't spoken to any Canadian politicians or government officials. We'd spent most of our spare time looking for lawyers to defend Maher and working on the document that would describe everything that had happened to him. Both were immense tasks. Michael Edelson had been the first lawyer Maher consulted when RCMP agents had visited us in Ottawa. Now other names had been suggested. But lawyers specializing in terrorism were few and far between; there was a certain reluctance in the profession to take up a terrorism-related case, or perhaps a lack of courage. But the underlying question was: of course we needed a lawyer, but to do what? Maher had never been accused of any criminal or terrorist act, not in Canada, not in the United States, and not in Syria. So why should he even need a lawyer in the first place?

It was Maher's way of feeling safe and secure. It was a fragile sense of security to be sure, but at least it was something he could grasp. The lawyer he'd been denied or refused access to during the long months of his nightmare would, for Maher, be the person who could defend him against all the allegations, who could speak in his name when he could not. These were the reasons that led us to select Lorne Waldman and James Lockyer as Maher's lawyers. One was a specialist in immigration law, the other in criminal law.

Mr. Lockyer suggested that Maher should visit Bill Graham, the minister of Foreign Affairs, to relate what he had undergone before going public. It was agreed that the meeting would take place in the minister's office, and that its contents would remain confidential. James Lockyer accompanied us that day, along with Kerry and Alex. We met him at Alex's office before proceeding to the minister's office. He asked Maher to tell the minister everything he'd been through: "Don't hold back. Tell him what they did to you, now's the time to do it . . ."

Of the five of us, only Maher and I would be meeting the minister, who was accompanied by his assistant, Robert Fry. Mr. Graham weighed Maher's words carefully, communicating a mixture of sympathy and caution. He listened attentively while Maher described his arrest in New York, his torture in the Syrian prison, the inhuman conditions under which he was detained, and the visit by Leo Martel on August 14 when he'd told about being beaten in front of General Khalil. When he pronounced those words, Mr. Fry's face seemed to cloud over. He knew that Mr. Graham, in a press conference in Toronto the next day, August 15, had denied that Maher had been tortured. It was a sharp blow to the minister's prestige. Had the information been hidden from him, had he been misled; what had really happened? The minister betrayed no emotion, but he did promise us that he would have his staff carry out a little investigation to find out who said what, when. The meeting was over; we got up to leave.

From there, we were led into a large meeting room, where James Lockyer, Alex, and Kerry were waiting for us, along with a dozen Foreign Affairs officials. Mr. Sigurdson, the new head of Consular Affairs, was there, but I'd never seen the other faces before. The presence of so many officials caught us off guard. Maher and I cast questioning glances at Kerry and Alex, but I quickly recognized the same puzzlement in their eyes. For what seemed like hours we sat there, not knowing what to say. The atmosphere was oppressive. Then Maher broke the silence, describing his imprisonment. He didn't repeat exactly what he had told the minister, but he sketched out the broad outlines of what had been done to him. Some of the department officials were taking notes. Meanwhile, I was getting more and more uneasy; I wanted to get out of there fast. It was a relief when the meeting ended and we found ourselves outside.

In my opinion, the meeting with the minister had gone well, but the session with the officials, with their bored and tired expressions, had ruined everything. Imagine our surprise when we read in the newspapers that Maher's meeting with the minister had been made public, and that he had spoken of torture. Mr. Graham's office had given us repeated assurances that the meeting would be private. Now we no longer knew who to trust. Our lives had suddenly become an open book.

NOVEMBER 4, 2003. Maher and I were putting the finishing touches to his first public appearance. It would be a press conference, to be held at the Parliamentary Press Gallery in downtown Ottawa.

Speaking out in public after being imprisoned for more than a year, after losing confidence in people, after being accused of terrorism, wasn't going to be easy. But we were determined to go ahead: it would be a crucial step for us, and for others. For us, it would be both a matter of justice and a kind of therapy. It was as if the only avenue left to us in seeking justice was to speak of the injustice we'd suffered and demand that the government get to the bottom of the affair. We were also convinced we had a debt to repay to the Canadian public. We knew that all the people who'd supported us with their letters and their prayers, or simply with a kind look or a thought, were expecting some kind of a sign from us, they were waiting for us to tell them that we wouldn't remain silent in our little apartment, that we wouldn't draw the curtains and cut ourselves off from the rest of the world. We didn't want to respond to secrecy with secrecy; we wanted to confront it head on.

Kerry had drafted Maher's speech, based on the notes she'd taken when he'd given his account at the Department of Foreign Affairs. I put the finishing touches to my own remarks. Maher read and reread the speech, made a few changes, then sent it off to Alex, Kerry, and the lawyers for a last check. I wasn't sure how he would deal with all the pressure; I prayed constantly for everything to go well.

The month that had gone by since Maher's return from Syria had been eventful. At first, it was a time of strong emotions and of stories to be shared. Each of us had told the other of how our life had been while we were apart, with our sufferings and disappointments. Then Maher had begun to read the articles that had been written about him during his absence. He began to be familiar with the names of journalists, politicians, and human rights organizations; he was learning about his own past but also about a world he was going to be part of but had never known before his imprisonment.

Before making our way to the Parliamentary Press Gallery, we met at Kerry's office, which was not far away. I kept close to Maher. His speech was ready. We estimated that it would take a little more than a half-hour for him to read, but I was afraid he might crack in front of so many people.

Alex and Riad were waiting for us, along with Lorne Waldman, one of Maher's lawyers, who was on hand to deal with the legal and technical aspects of the case. We all felt emotional and nervous. It was a chilly day, but not cold enough for snow. We made our way through the streets of Ottawa, joking now and then to ease the tension. The Press Gallery was located in a building on Wellington Street, just across from the West Block of Parliament. When we reached the corner of Wellington and O'Connor, photographers appeared. Maher and I were walking a few steps ahead of our friends; we were dazzled by the constant flashing of cameras. We had to keep calm but my heart was pounding. The moment of truth was near.

It was a day that would remain engraved in my memory. When I think back, I see myself sitting beside Maher. Lorne, Alex, and Riad were at the same table. In front of me, the room was full of journalists. Then, suddenly, I spotted the politicians. There was Alexa McDonough, Marlene Catterall, and Irwin Cotler; other MPs came in and sat down. I caught sight of Bill Graham's assistant, Robert Fry. I felt my heart swell with joy – and with apprehension. Joy to witness at last the day when Maher would speak freely of his ordeal and relate exactly what he had lived through to the politicians, those who had helped us and those who had opposed us, to the intelligence agents and to the police. But I was afraid of the unknown. I had no idea how they would react; I didn't know whether our press conference would convince people and force the Canadian government to respond to our call for a public inquiry – or whether the government would turn on us and prolong the state of isolation and distress that our daily lives had become.

Maher began his statement by saying who he really was: an innocent man, a husband and father. He rejected all the allegations of terrorism made against him. Everything that had been said against him was false, he insisted; or lies extracted under torture. He spoke of the conditions he'd endured in prison in Syria, of his suffering, and of the disaster that had befallen him. He read his text slowly, stopping at times in an effort to hold back his tears, then continuing in a calm voice. I held his hand to comfort him and to give him the courage to keep going. It was almost more than we could bear.

As he enumerated the grisly details in front of the cameras, and as I listened to it once again, it was all I could do not to break down. When Maher had finished, the journalists erupted with questions. Luckily for us, a journalist sitting at our table was acting as moderator, but the questions kept coming. They seemed hypnotized by his story. At no time did I feel they were trying to intimidate him or corner him. But I could sense that Maher was getting tired; his eyes started to flutter nervously. I was afraid he would just stand up and walk out, but he held on. It was an extremely important moment for him, the moment for him to give his version of the facts, to tell his own story.

The press conference finally ended. We stayed on for a few moments to talk with Lorne Waldman, Kerry, Alex, and Riad. All of them were upbeat, and agreed that it had gone well. We felt reassured. Maher had done his best; he had passed the first test. He had been himself: natural and straightforward. We were satisfied, but we were waiting to hear what the press would say, how people would react. For the first time since his deportation, I had the feeling that media interest was focused on him, on his story and his way of telling it; my face represented the loving wife who had supported her husband. Slowly, inexorably, I was stepping aside, taking my place behind Maher. I was relieved to be rid of the heavy burden I'd been carrying – but I knew there was much more to be done before I'd be at peace again.

On our way home, Maher turned on the radio. We heard the announcer describing the press conference, and then Maher's voice echoing over the air. All the way back to the apartment, we listened in silence to his voice relating his story. I was driving and listening to him attentively. It was as if I was hearing everything for the first time. I was so moved I blinked my eyes and sighed.

My mother welcomed us with a barrage of questions: "How did it go? Were people interested? Did the government agree to a public inquiry?"

"I think Maher spoke very well; he did his best. Now we have to wait and see how the media react," I answered.

I couldn't suppress a smile. The fact that my mother was so interested in those questions meant that it was no longer a matter of concern only to Maher and me but to the whole family. Each of us, in his or her way, had been affected by this change in our lives, and each of us hoped to bring it to an end.

Our decision to go public led to a series of media interviews. For the journalists, the period of respite we'd enjoyed, far from the prying eyes of the press, was officially over. Now everyone wanted to meet Maher and ask him questions. He was encouraged by reactions to the press conference. There had been strong sympathy for his story but a lot of questions. The website was flooded with messages from the public. They provided us with our strongest support and most enthusiastic encouragement. Requests for interviews came thick and fast. There was no question of accepting or refusing any request but of fitting them all in without too much delay.

Our life had taken another turn: now it was a steady stream of radio, television, and press interviews. Once again our apartment was transformed into a studio, and we were constantly interrupted by photo opportunities. Time and time again before going to sleep, I found myself wondering: Did we make the right choice? Why didn't we just keep quiet? Why get mixed up with these interminable interviews and lose what's left of our private life?

Those questions remained unanswered. I was too tired to think. But deep down, a voice told me that despite our problems, we had made the right choice.

NOVEMBER 7, 2003. Kerry called us at home. She sounded worried and wanted to speak to us both. A journalist named Juliet O'Neill of the *Ottawa Citizen* was preparing an article on Maher and his story. She had obtained information that had never been published. I'd never heard of her and couldn't remember having spoken to her about Maher's case. I didn't know her motives and wasn't too worried. But Kerry was concerned that the article would harm Maher's reputation.

"Well, there's not much left of his reputation after all those anonymous sources they've been quoting since he came back," I exclaimed.

"I agree, but each new article seems to do a little more damage than the last," Kerry answered.

Maher, on another phone, listened carefully to what Kerry had to say, and we all agreed that we couldn't stop the reporter or change her mind. Still, all three of us had an uneasy feeling. Both Maher and I had believed that things would change after the press conference, that the articles speaking ill of him would stop, and our repeated calls for a public inquiry would be heeded. Kerry's phone call raised new questions, new doubts. Who was behind these media "leaks" and what were the real motives for publishing them? Why were we being harassed?

NOVEMBER 8, 2003. Tomorrow would be Saturday; I wouldn't be teaching, Barâa wouldn't be in school, there wouldn't be any of the usual "morning rush" when everything had to be ready by eight o'clock if we were to be on time. It was Ramadan; my mother began preparing dinner in midafternoon. Our household routine was different, everything moved more slowly. Maher said he was going to the barbershop at the shopping centre. But before he left, we remembered the article by Juliet O'Neill.

"Let me see if it's on the *Ottawa Citizen* website," said Maher as he turned on the computer. He quickly located the article. As he was reading, I sat down beside him. The article described Maher as a terrorist who had been trained to handle weapons, as someone who was recruiting other terrorists in Canada. The reporter wrote about a training camp in Afghanistan, about the sale of computers and suspicious electronic materials, about police knocking on our door and neighbours who said we'd moved. In it were all the ingredients to turn Maher into a dangerous terrorist and our family into people with much to hide and who were trying to elude the police ("Canada's Dossier on Maher Arar: The existence of a group of Ottawa men with alleged ties to al-Qaeda is at the root of why the government opposes an inquiry into the case," Juliet O'Neill, *Ottawa Citizen,* November 8, 2003). The earlier CTV report had made Maher out to be a terrorist traitor who "informed on" his accomplices; this latest article presented him as a threat, a man with links to al-Qaeda.

The article made it clear that these were the reasons behind the government's refusal to set up a public inquiry. But it said not a word about how the information had been obtained; the reporter asked no questions about its truth. In fact, she treated this information as if it were beyond suspicion, and justification for the actions of certain elements in the police. Maher was speechless; his face had turned white.

"Don't let it worry you. The day will come when you'll be able to defend yourself. For the time being, it seems to me we're going to have to take some lumps," I said to distract Maher and bolster his morale. But privately I could tell how deeply he was hurt.

"What do they want with me, these people operating out of their secret offices, well protected from justice? One whole year they did everything they could to destroy me. Now they're trying to put me in a mental prison, trying to destroy what's left of my humanity."

"It won't be easy for us to win justice. We'll have to be patient. Don't imagine that all you have to do is tell your story and nobody will challenge it, nobody will try to undermine you. Try to forget; time heals all wounds."

"I can never forget. It's too much. It's my life they're trying to destroy." He got to his feet and began to pace back and forth. Then he remembered his haircut and left the house.

I couldn't get the article out of my mind; it kept coming back to haunt me. When Maher came back from the barbershop his hair was shorter; he looked younger, but there was still that sad expression on his face.

"There in the barbershop I looked at the people sitting around me. I tried to look into their eyes, to see if they still believed me. I wanted so much to tell them loud and clear that the article was a lie, that I'm not the terrorist people are talking about."

I listened to him in silence with a lump in my throat.

MID-NOVEMBER 2003. It was the calm after the storm. Juliet O'Neill's article had dashed our fragile dreams. All that Maher had gained by his press conference, whatever confidence and sympathy he'd been able to establish, had been swept away by an article that relied on anonymous sources, that had not even taken the trouble to verify the facts, an article that used a confession obtained under torture. For Maher, it was like twisting a knife in a raw wound. For me, it felt like talons ripping our newborn hope to shreds, and I was afraid that turmoil was once again taking over our lives.

But slowly, surely, we were recovering; we began to understand that our decision to speak out, to call for an accounting, and to ask embarrassing questions would have consequences, that Maher's credibility would be attacked, and that our whole family would pay the price.

Media interest didn't let up. We continued to give interviews and respond to accusations, insisting that a public hearing be held to determine if elements of the Canadian government apparatus participated in, encouraged, or closed their eyes to Maher's deportation to Syria. We wanted to find out who was behind the media leaks. From every tribune, in the newspapers, before the most diverse audiences, we called for a public inquiry: it had become our overriding objective. But the Canadian government under Prime Minister Jean Chrétien categorically rejected our demand. Public opinion was our sole ally. We'd taken an important step; there was no going back. Day after day, the media were knocking at our door.

When Maher returned from Syria, I'd dreamed of starting a new life with our children, of turning the page. But the longer we lived together, the more I realized just how much Maher had changed – and how much I had changed as well. We were no longer the same couple; we no longer had the comfortable middle-class dreams we once had. Both of us had known suffering, but differently. Maher had undergone the horrors of mental and physical pain. He'd lost his faith in humankind; he'd lost confidence in himself. Time and again he'd concluded he would never see us again. Then suddenly he'd been delivered: the shock of the outside world, people around him, the smell of freedom, children running around in the house, interviews, and, above all, this new feeling of his own humanity that he'd lost in the underground prison in Damascus, that abruptly he was rediscovering.

And what had happened to me? A woman most of my fellow citizens now recognized in the street, a symbol, a model wife who had saved her husband, a kind of modern-day feminine version of Robin Hood. But I'd never seen myself in that light. What I'd become weighed heavily on me. I wanted to be recognized for what I was: a woman, a mother, and a citizen; I wanted none of the high-flown imagery. It wasn't a matter of modesty; it was just that the superficial perception was at odds with who I really was. The changes that had taken place had attacked us as a couple both from outside and inside; I wanted to preserve what was still left of us.

LATE NOVEMBER 2003. For the last few days, Maher had been working with Lorne Waldman to prepare a lawsuit accusing Syria and Jordan of torture in the Canadian court system. Syria's role was clear and well documented, but Jordan had benefited from a kind of amnesia that allowed an impression that nothing serious had happened there. And yet, the American aircraft that carried Maher had landed in Jordan. The Jordanian authorities had never admitted that Maher had spent hours in one of their prisons before being transferred to torture in Syria. What could possibly explain their underhand complicity, their mockery of human rights?

However, the fact that the Canadian State Immunity Act does not allow citizens of Canada to sue other countries in Canadian courts didn't help our cause. Maher and I had thought long and hard before embarking on this risky path. We knew that this law, designed to protect diplomatic relations between countries, would not be easy to change. But we'd come to the conclusion that torture could not be ignored; torture destroys both body and spirit; it destroys all that is human in us. The case would be of prime importance for Maher, but it would also give hope to other torture victims that they might obtain justice, and see their tormentors brought to trial. Far from revenge, or an attempt to win financial compensation, it would give a message to all countries that use torture that this is unacceptable, and that they will be called to account for it. To do nothing would be to forget all those killed under torture, and those who still languish in prison, beaten by their jailers, their fundamental rights stolen from them.

I could see that our life was moving in a new direction. We were no longer focused solely on our own misfortune; we had begun to understand that we must act on behalf of others, those who are afraid to speak or cannot speak for themselves. Who would have believed that one day Maher would be suing Syria, the country where he was born. But his forced return to Syria, his imprisonment and torture in its underground prisons had taught him one thing: that violence and injustice only grow when no one speaks out against them. On November 23, 2003, the lawsuit against Syria and Jordan was filed in Federal Court. But later, our fears were confirmed; the court rejected the case, invoking the State Immunity Act.

❦

Finally, after a month of fasting, the feast of Eid had come. The children were happy, looking forward to receiving gifts and dressing up in new clothes. This year Eid had special significance for us. Maher was a free man again; this year my joy was two-fold, to be celebrating the end of Ramadan and having my family reunited. These yearly celebrations can take on new meaning for us and remain engraved in our memories. That was certainly the case with this Eid. Houd had finally got to know his father; he loved to climb onto his back and tour the apartment perched on Maher's shoulders, delighted to be the tallest one in the house. Barâa had also become used to his presence; she was no longer awkward with him as she had been at first, not knowing quite what to make of him.

Nazira invited us to a festive lunch at an Indian restaurant not far from our apartment. It was one of the rare times we'd gone out as a family since Maher's liberation. The upheaval we'd experienced just after his return, the leaks in the press, and the constant interviews had exhausted us. All we could think about was finding some quiet time together. Nazira's invitation was the perfect opportunity to change the atmosphere, to celebrate Eid, and to behave like a normal family. The restaurant was decorated in the Indian style, with carved wood dividers separating groups of tables. The air was thick with the fragrances of anis, fenugreek, and curry. There were about thirty guests, including Marlene Catterall. We took a seat at her table. Barâa, dressed in red plaid, was sizing up the guests; sometimes she would whisper in my ear, asking if I knew this person or that. Houd was wearing a green sweater and green trousers. He was fascinated by the table setting, and began tapping the side of his glass with his spoon, proud of all the noise he could make. The food was delicious, a real culinary discovery.

Many of the guests came over to greet us and ask after us. For me, that human contact, the warmth of so many smiles and greetings were like balm for all the hurts we'd suffered. At the end of the meal, Nazira brought garlands of artificial flowers, placing one around Maher's neck and one around mine, like the garlands of real flowers they drape around tourists' necks in exotic travel destinations.

I felt a bit ridiculous there in the midst of the crowd and the applause. Then, in turn, Maher and I thanked Nazira, Marlene, and all the guests. The two women made short speeches, and then the guests began to leave; the celebration was over. A few minutes later, in the car, Barâa was clamouring to put one of the garlands around her neck.

"Smell it, Mama," she piped up. "How sweet the flowers smell!"

I took the garland and brought it to my nose. There was a faint scent of jasmine mixed with another that reminded me of musk.

"You're right," I told her. "I don't know where the smell comes from."

"Maybe the flowers are real," Barâa said, and we all burst out laughing.

*

I was talking to Alexa McDonough on the phone. The last time we'd seen each other was when Maher spoke at the Parliamentary Press Gallery. Our relationship had developed into a kind of friendship. For me, Alexa had become a teacher and guide, a tenacious woman in politics who had overcome obstacles to reach the pinnacle of her party, without ever losing her humanity or her openness. We were talking about this, that, and the other thing, children, the public inquiry, when she surprised me by saying: "Did you ever think of going into politics?"

The question hit me like a hammer blow. Even though I'd grown up surrounded by political analysis, the idea had never occurred to me. My father was always discussing politics with his friends and with me; he read local and foreign newspapers, and was always well informed about current or historical events – but he'd never belonged to a political party. He wanted to be free to think as he wished, which caused him problems but also made him proud to speak out and to criticize what was going on around him. I'd grown up with the notion that politics was a game of intelligence and strategy. All I'd done was to think things through and speak my piece, but I'd never dared support a political party, let alone play an active role. Alexa's question troubled me. I didn't know what to say.

"I've never thought of getting into politics," I answered.

She'd had the idea, Alexa said, and she wanted to share it with me. I could think it over, of course, but she would be very happy if I would agree to become a candidate for her party in the upcoming federal elections. Her words made me feel proud; she was one of the few people who understood my potential and my abilities; she took me as

I was, without trying to change or criticize me. She wasn't ashamed to talk to me because I was the wife of an alleged terrorist; she knew our family situation was difficult, but she treated me like a normal person. Alexa's proposal restored my self-confidence – but it also made me stop and think. I didn't know whether it was a good idea to get involved in politics at this point in my life, or if I should keep on trying to find a university position, even though two years of my career had evaporated as I struggled to free my husband and put our family life on an even keel.

EARLY DECEMBER 2003. More and more voices were calling for a public inquiry. Seemingly each day the name of a political figure or a human rights organization was added to the list. My own feelings were mixed. If the inquiry took place, Maher would have an opportunity to ask questions about what happened to him and hope to clear his name of accusations of terrorism. Yet I had the feeling that the inquiry would never take place, that our demands would never be heard, that uncertainty would continue to rule our lives. Jean Chrétien's government could not easily retract its decision, but everyone knew that Paul Martin was the prime-minister-in-waiting. Our job was to convince him and the people around him. Just how we would go about it was not clear, but we kept our hopes up. Meanwhile, we went ahead with our letter-writing campaign to the Prime Minister's Office.

It was becoming clear to me how much the nature of my work had changed. Before, when Maher had been in prison, I worked day and night to bring him back to Canada, so that he would be treated with dignity and justice. Back then, people around me had no difficulty in understanding what was at stake, and in giving all the support they could. But with his liberation and return, it became harder to explain why it was important to question the government, to know the role Canada had played in his arrest, deportation, torture, and imprisonment. The whole issue had become highly sensitive, it was slippery ground. Who would dare question such highly regarded and power-ful agencies as the RCMP and CSIS? Who would dare call them to account without worrying about repercussions, short- or long-term?

Yes, Canada is certainly a democratic country and not a police state. But it seemed some people were reluctant to embarrass the police when no one knew for sure whether Maher was innocent. In the meantime, leaks published or discussed in the press and on television had done their work. People had begun to wonder about Maher Arar; maybe he really was a terrorist hiding behind a mask of innocence. Nothing was clear. Many politicians were choosing to remain silent and not to join the chorus calling for a public inquiry so as to avoid any fallout from eventual revelations. There were political risks in taking a stand for or against a public inquiry. As the days went by, I felt more and more certain that the idea had become a political issue. If that were the case, then we would have to lobby to build support. It was hardly the kind of job I was familiar with, a job in which human suffering no longer mattered. All that counted were political gains and points scored.

DECEMBER 12, 2003. Paul Martin officially became the new prime minister of Canada. The same party was still in power, but I saw the change as a positive sign for our campaign. Even though the same MPs were still sitting in the House of Commons, we knew that the incoming prime minister would want to distinguish himself from his predecessor, Jean Chrétien.

Still, we weren't naive enough to believe that Paul Martin would break completely with the previous government and the morning after his victory proclaim that he would accept all the demands that the out-going government had rejected, including our call for an inquiry. But I was pleasantly surprised when I found out that Irwin Cotler had been appointed minister of Justice.

"What luck!" I said to myself when I heard the news. Mr. Cotler had been acting since the previous June as Maher's lawyer. We could hardly have hoped for better. He had supported the idea of a public inquiry, but it was not clear that as Justice minister he would be able to speak freely without being accused of conflict of interest. I rang up Cotler's office and spoke with his assistant:

"Congratulations on Mr. Cotler's appointment," I said. "I just heard the news."

The assistant seemed cold and distant. I immediately regretted having called; instead of getting carried away, I should have kept quiet. One month later I understood the assistant's reaction when I learned that Irwin Cotler had withdrawn from Maher's case. It was not a big surprise. I knew that as Justice minister, he didn't want to be accused of bias. His position was logical, but deep down I felt hurt, even abandoned.

JANUARY 21, 2004. I was not working today. As usual, I'd driven Barâa to school and straightened up the children's room. Houd was following me around. Maher was sitting in front of the computer reading the news. The phone rang. It was Kerry:

"Something serious has happened!"

Now what? I thought.

"The police have raided Juliet O'Neill's house. They're looking for the documents she based her article on. The journalists are all hot on the case. My phone is ringing like crazy."

I couldn't believe my ears. "What are the police up to, trying to scare journalists or what?"

Stunned, I stood in front of the window and watched the cars go by.

"I don't have any idea," Kerry said. "We'll soon see. For the moment, everybody's waiting to see what will happen next. Everybody wants to know if they'll raid other journalists."

It was to be a day of excitement. It was the top story on radio and television news. Journalists were outraged at the humiliation of a colleague; protection of sources once again became the object of controversy, but the heavy-handed police raid also showed Canada to be a country in which journalists were vulnerable. Maher's name was mentioned time and time again. Once more the media were after us, while we continued to demand a public inquiry.

Our position was a difficult one to sum up. Juliet O'Neill's article had depicted Maher as a dangerous terrorist. It had caused us grief; it had reminded Maher of his jailers and given anonymous sources a platform for attacking his reputation. But I didn't understand why there had been such a spectacular police raid, or why someone's house had to be searched.

It would have been so much more effective to have raided the police and intelligence headquarters to find out who had leaked the information. We'd never wanted to settle scores, find guilty parties, and punish them. We were looking for a civilized, equitable, and trans-parent process in which each party could present facts and proof, and would be questioned by a judge – which, I was certain, would allow Maher to effectively refute the allegations against him. This police raid had taken us by surprise. I couldn't figure out exactly what it meant and what impact it might have on our demands for an inquiry.

JANUARY 28, 2004. I hadn't yet replied to Alexa's proposal that I become a candidate in the upcoming federal elections. It was a hard decision to make. I didn't want to lose my freedom of thought, and I didn't want to get involved in partisan politics. At the same time, I found many of the social principles I believed in and could defend in the New Democratic Party. But from there to becoming a candidate, promoting a program, and lining up behind a common electoral plat-form was not something I felt comfortable with. In primary school, and later in secondary school, I'd always asked questions and raised doubts. I still remembered how much I'd enjoyed completing my essays or my dissertations on new subjects. I was always proud to find new aspects of the situation that were just as important as the subject I'd been asked to write about. To me, becoming a candidate would mean repeating political slogans; I found the idea rather stifling.

But I hadn't entirely ruled out the thought of a political career. Over the course of the past year, I'd learned to speak in public. I'd been able to convince people around me to act on my husband's behalf. I was sure I could bring the same qualities of perseverance and hard work to bear for the benefit of my fellow citizens. It would be an excellent opportunity to learn from my personal experience, to focus all that energy, all that desire for change, but this time over issues such as health, labour, the environment, and peace. The idea of a political career was tempting because it would allow me to do something else with my life, to get out of a vicious circle.

Life was becoming more and more difficult. At home, all we talked about was Maher's case, about our calls for a public inquiry, about our campaign to convince politicians and organizations how important it was. It had become our favourite subject of discussion, an objective to be attained, almost our *raison d'être*. The pressure was so intense that I sometimes worried about my own sanity. For me, the idea of political involvement seemed like a way out, a safety valve for venting the daily pressure that was building up inside me. But I couldn't make up my mind.

Alexa and I met that morning at her Ottawa apartment. We were to have a nice calm discussion, and I was to ask her my questions. She had arranged for one of her assistants to be there to explain the technicalities of being a candidate. By the end of the meeting I was feeling more confused than at the start. I still didn't know whether I was ready to leap into the political arena. I would have to solve the problem on my own.

I was getting up to leave when the telephone rang. It was Anthony, Alexa's assistant. He told her to switch on the television; the minister of Public Security, Anne McLellan, was making an important announcement concerning Maher Arar. None of us knew what to think. We sat there watching the television screen, as if hypnotized.

As the minister spoke I immediately understood that the government had decided to hold a public inquiry into Maher's case. Alexa turned to me; both of us were in tears.

"What wonderful news," Alexa kept repeating.

I didn't know what to say. I thought of Maher; did he know? Right away I called home. The line was busy. He knew, I was sure of it. I hurried out of Alexa's house. I wanted to get home as fast as I could. I'd forgotten all about my career in politics, all my hesitations. The public inquiry had been announced; it was another giant step toward justice. The trip downstairs in the elevator seemed to last an eternity. The car was parked next to a huge, dirty grey snowbank. I got in and drove off. On the way home, my whole life seemed to be passing in front of my eyes, the moments of despair followed by moments of brightness where hope had emerged, flooding me with light. One year ago, on this same date, I didn't know if I would ever see Maher again. Today, Maher was here with me in Canada, and the government had just announced that a public inquiry would be set up to answer our questions, and to give Maher the chance to refute the allegations against him.

I wondered what the inquiry would be like, and what the results would be. We would have to be patient and wait for the proceedings to begin. When I walked in the door Maher was waiting for me; for the first time since his return to Canada I could see a gleam of hope and joy in his eyes.

The Commission of Inquiry into the Actions of Canadian Officials in Relation to Maher Arar was established on February 5, 2004, in order "to assess the actions of Canadian officials in dealing with the deportation and detention of Mr. Arar." The Honourable Dennis R. O'Connor, associate chief justice of Ontario, was appointed commissioner of the inquiry.

The story I wanted to tell you in this book – of my struggle to have my husband freed – ends here. For not only was he released from prison and brought home to his family, but the commission of inquiry that we had been asking for so urgently was now going to free him of the false allegations that were weighing against him.

EPILOGUE

Man's hope is his reason to live and to die . . .
— André Malraux

I have written this book for the same reasons I have given hundreds of interviews over recent years: to honour my husband, who has suffered unjustly; to make sense of the terrible and uncommon adventure we have had; and to wave a warning flag under the noses of all those who take human rights for granted. Human rights will always be fragile – this is demonstrated again and again, even in democratic societies. We cannot afford to let down our guard.

This book is not intended to be a report on "the Maher Arar affair." Still, for readers who are not aware of the aftermath of the story, in the *Report of the Commission of Inquiry into the Actions of Canadian Officials in Relation to Maher Arar,* the Commissioner, Judge Dennis O'Connor, examined a number of questions, from Maher's innocence to possible complicity in his arrest in the United States on the part of the RCMP and CSIS, and including "leaks" of information damaging to Maher made to the Canadian media before and after his return to Canada.

I shall quote from the Commission's summary of the main conclusions in its press release of September 18, 2006, when the *Report*
was submitted in three volumes. Excerpts from the *Report* itself are in
italics.

I had known from the start, of course, that my husband was innocent,
but in our unfortunate circumstances, it had to be proven.

In the *Report,* Mr. Justice O'Connor declared: "*I am able to say categorically that there is no evidence to indicate that Mr. Arar has committed any
offence or that his activities constitute a threat to the security of Canada.*"

How much it had cost us in tears, tenacity, disappointment, physical and mental separation, and above all, hope, before we could finally
read and reread that single sentence!

The Commissioner continued:

> *The public can be confident that Canadian investigators have thoroughly and
> exhaustively followed all information leads available to them in connection
> with Mr. Arar's activities and associations. [They made] extensive efforts to
> find any information that could implicate Mr. Arar in terrorist activities. . . .
> The results speak for themselves: they found none.*
>
> On the role of Canadian officials . . . the Commissioner
> found: *No evidence that Canadian officials participated or acquiesced in the
> American authorities' decision to detain and remove Mr. Arar to Syria . . .
> and there is no evidence that any Canadian authorities – Royal Canadian
> Mounted Police (RCMP), Canadian Security Intelligence Service (CSIS) or
> others – were complicit in those decisions.* However, the Commissioner
> also notes that: *It is very likely that, in making the decisions to detain
> and remove Mr. Arar to Syria, the U.S. authorities relied on information
> about Mr. Arar provided by the RCMP. Although I cannot be certain
> without evidence of the American authorities, the evidence strongly supports
> this conclusion.* CSIS did not share information with the Americans
> at this time.

The Commissioner also found that both before and after Mr. Arar's detention in the U.S., the RCMP provided American authorities with information about Mr. Arar which was inaccurate, portrayed him in an unfair fashion, and overstated his importance to the[ir] investigation. Also that some of this inaccurate information had the potential to create serious consequences for Mr. Arar in light of American attitudes and practices at the time.

[. . .]

While he was detained in Syria, the Commissioner found that Canadian agencies relied on information about Mr. Arar received about him from the Syrians which was likely the product of torture. No adequate reliability assessment was done to determine whether the information resulted from torture.

[. . . The Commissioner] observed a failure of communication between Canadian agencies involved in the Arar case. *There was also a lack of a single, coherent approach to efforts to obtain his release.*

Finally, the Commissioner found that both before and after Mr. Arar's return to Canada, Canadian officials leaked confidential and sometimes inaccurate information about the case to the media for the purpose of damaging Mr. Arar's reputation or protecting their self-interest or government interests.

This detail in the Conclusions has not, in my opinion, received the response it deserved. Unfortunately, there was no real debate in the journalistic community on the impact of material from anonymous sources on the individuals targeted. Few journalists undertook any examination of conscience whatsoever; the subject appears to remain taboo in journalistic circles, hidden behind a wall of secrecy.

The Commissioner was able to confirm Maher's statements about torture by appointing as Fact Finder Professor Stephen J. Toope, a former Dean of the McGill University Faculty of Law, to determine whether Maher had actually been tortured, and what the consequences had been. After several interviews with Maher, his physicians, other detainees from the same prison, independent physicians, psychologists, myself, and other individuals, Professor Toope concluded on October 14, 2005 that: "*Mr. Maher Arar was subjected to torture in Syria. The effects of that experience, and of consequent events and experiences in Canada, have been profoundly negative for Mr. Arar and his family. Although there have been few lasting physical effects, Mr. Arar's psychological state was seriously damaged and he remains fragile. His relationships with members of his immediate family have been significantly impaired. Economically, the family has been devastated.*"

Our lives will bear the scars forever. When I was a little girl, I didn't fully understand my mother's words when she told me, "Human beings don't know what's good for them."

Why is she telling me that? I wondered. Isn't it easy to find out what's good for us? Seeing things through my child's eyes, I accused adults of complicating things.

The years that the public inquiry lasted changed Maher. He came to exist for that alone; it was his full-time job, his favorite subject of discussion, the topic he was most at home with. I will always look back with a smile to the day when Houd answered someone who asked what his father did in life: "He works at the Commission of Inquiry," the little boy replied innocently. Hardly surprising, because every day he saw his father get ready and then leave the house to attend the public hearings being held in Ottawa, or heard him discussing the inquiry with his lawyers on the telephone.

Maher's imprisonment in Syria had broken him – morally and physically. The public inquiry held him hypnotized, transfixed; he became a man obsessed. The search for truth he'd dedicated himself to drove him on; tirelessly he read his way through document after document, always in the hope that the inquiry would give him the answers he'd been denied. His name had been destroyed, slandered, his reputation ruined, his career crushed. The public inquiry was the only way for him to break the infernal cycle he'd been thrown into that fateful September 26.

Before my husband was arrested and my whole life collapsed, I believed I'd got the better of my mother, and of all the adults of my childhood. I thought I'd found happiness with my husband, two children, and a relatively easy life in Canada. All of it vanished in the twinkling of an eye. Happiness would never again taste the same to me.

Now I see it in a different light. I try to go beyond appearances and impressions. Our lives are fragile things; happiness is almost impossible to grasp. What we make of our lives every day is what brings us a little closer to happiness. When my husband was arrested by the Americans then sent off to Syria, I could have chosen to remain silent, to hide, to see myself as a victim and lament my fate. But I chose not to; I took another path.

When my husband returned to Canada, changed forever, after a year of imprisonment and torture, once again I could have remained silent, fled the media, found a job and tried to be forgotten. Once again, I refused that option. I don't regret doing what I did. My husband, my children, and I have all suffered as a result. But I believe that the inquiry, despite its ups and downs, despite our doubts and dreams, has brought us much, both as individuals and as a society. Maher was finally able to clear his name, and the whole question of national security as opposed to human rights was re-examined.

In the aftermath of September 11, the dominant view was that security must override individual rights. That doctrine is no longer viable. The public inquiry proved that nothing can be more precious than a just balance between security and human rights. Leaning too far in one direction or the other can only lead us onto dangerous ground for either human rights or security.

On January 25, 2007, four months after the publication of Mr. Justice O'Connor's *Report,* the Government of Canada, now led by Stephen Harper, presented us with its official apologies. In a letter addressed to my husband, Maher Arar, which I have framed and hung over my desk, he writes: "On behalf of the Government of Canada, I wish to apologize to you, Monia Mazigh and your family, for any role Canadian officials may have played in the terrible ordeal that all of you experienced in 2002 and 2003." It was I who insisted that our lawyer obtain that letter, its words written black on white. I wanted Barâa and Houd to be able one day to read those words, and not live their lives in the shadows.

Words that can disappear into thin air are not enough, I had learned. They must be recorded.

Over the last six years, I have lost what many families try so hard to build: stability. I lived my life from day to day, not knowing when misfortune would strike again. My husband's name, those of my children, and even my own were linked to terrorism. We were spied upon, scrutinized, and examined minutely. Even though I have long lost my childhood enthusiasm, I have not lost my ability to look at the world like a child. I have kept my naivety and a kind of innocence that has many times saved me from falling into depression and pessimism. When I learned later, in the course of the public inquiry, that certain individuals in the government apparatus had done their utmost to block my husband's return, and to obstruct me in Canada, I thanked God with all my heart for protecting my faith, and the hope that better days would come.

My two children, Barâa and Houd, were my constant companions in this search for justice; they were a constant source of inspiration, the wellspring of hope from which every day I drew the courage I needed to pursue my path. In their simple desire to play, speak, and simply to grow, they helped me keep my feet firmly planted on the ground. When I looked into their eyes, I understood that life goes on above and beyond our misfortunes, and that there is always meaning to be found, even in our worst of trials.

. . . it may be that ye dislike a thing and Allah brings about through it a great deal of good. — THE QUR'AN, CHAPTER 4 — AN-NISA [WOMEN], VERSE 19

ACKNOWLEDGEMENTS

I would like to thank many people who helped me during the writing of this book:

Lucie Dumoulin for her patience and professionalism in reading and reviewing the French text with me. Pascal Assathiany, Jean Bernier, and the whole team at Boréal for their encouragement and support.

Doug Pepper, Susan Renouf, and Jenny Bradshaw at McClelland & Stewart for their help and guidance throughout this process.

Patricia Claxton and Fred A. Reed for their meticulous and rigorous translation.

Michael Levine for his advice, his enthusiasm, and his encouragement.

Our friend Richard Swain for his devotion, receptiveness, good humour, and helpfulness.

My father and mother for their encouragement and for giving me all the love and affection in the world.

Finally, my husband, Maher Arar, who since the beginning of this project has been a pillar of support with his encouragement, his advice, and his patience.

PATRICIA CLAXTON has received two Governor General's Awards for Translation and numerous award nominations. She has a master's degree in translation and taught in the field for eight years. Her translation *A Sunday at the Pool in Kigali* by Gil Courtemanche, published in ten editions worldwide, was long-listed for the International IMPAC Dublin Literary Award and nominated for two other prizes. Her most recent translation is Jacques Godbout's *Operation Rimbaud*. She lives in Montreal.

Born in California, and a Quebec resident since 1963, FRED A. REED worked in the labour movement before becoming a freelance journalist, contributing to *Le Devoir*, *La Presse*, CBC, and Radio-Canada. At the same time, he pursued a literary career, winning the Governor General's Award for translation three times, twice for his English versions of works by the late Thierry Hentsch, and, with David Homel, for Martine Desjardins' *Fairy Ring*, as well as writing books on Iran, Syria, Turkey, and the Balkans.